VOODOO

LOUISIANA STATE UNIVERSITY PRESS   BATON ROUGE

VOODOO

AN AFRICAN AMERICAN RELIGION

JEFFREY E. ANDERSON

Published with the assistance of the V. Ray Cardozier Fund

Published by Louisiana State University Press
lsupress.org

Manufactured in the United States of America
First printing

DESIGNER: Michelle A. Neustrom
TYPEFACES: Calluna, text; Bourbon Grotesque and Metropolis, display
PRINTER AND BINDER: Sheridan Books, Inc.

Unless otherwise noted, all photographs are from the author's personal collection.

LIBRARY OF CONGRESS CATALOGING-IN-PUBLICATION DATA

Names: Anderson, Jeffrey E., 1974– author.
Title: Voodoo : an African American religion / Jeffrey E. Anderson.
Description: Baton Rouge : Louisiana State University Press, [2024] |
  Includes bibliographical references and index.
Identifiers: LCCN 2023031581 (print) | LCCN 2023031582 (ebook) | ISBN
  978-0-8071-8132-4 (cloth) | ISBN 978-0-8071-8180-5 (pdf) | ISBN 978-0-8071-8179-9
  (epub)
Subjects: LCSH: Vodou—Mississippi River Valley. | Vodou—Mississippi River
  Valley—History. | Vodou—Louisiana—New Orleans. | African
  Americans—Religion.
Classification: LCC BL2490 .A653 2024 (print) | LCC BL2490 (ebook) | DDC
  299.6/750977—dc23/eng/20231026
LC record available at https://lccn.loc.gov/2023031581
LC ebook record available at https://lccn.loc.gov/2023031582

This book is dedicated to my wife, Lynn,
and my sons, Michael and David.

CONTENTS

ACKNOWLEDGMENTS

The number of individuals to whom I owe my thanks is vast. At the top of any list must be my wife, Lynn, and my children, Michael and David, who allowed me to pour endless hours into research, writing, and travel as I worked over several years to complete my writing. They all suffered through years of lectures from me about a subject that I am not at all certain they wanted to learn that much about. Plus, my wife's proofreading skills have helped me produce a manuscript that is at least somewhat comprehensible.

The University of Louisiana Monroe and its administration have also been highly supportive. Naming me the William R. Hammond Professor of Liberal Arts from 2014 to 2017 allowed me to visit Senegal, Benin, Togo, Republic of the Congo, Haiti, and Cuba so that I could gain some firsthand experience with Voodoo's closest living relatives. In particular, I am grateful to Ruth Smith, Director of the School of Humanities, and the former Dean of the College of Arts, Education, and Humanities, Sandra Lemoine. Both encouraged my research in every feasible way. Another colleague who deserves recognition is the late Mary Linn Wernet, former Head Archivist and University Records Officer at Northwestern State University of Louisiana. She and her staff provided invaluable research assistance and somehow managed to copy more than 6,000 pages for me in only two days. Similarly, I owe thanks to Fred Adams, Professor of French, for his help translating difficult passages.

While traveling for my research, several people played key roles. To begin, I would have made no headway without excellent interpreters, including Birame Ka of Senegal, Marc Idjigberou of Benin, Kongo Trepasse Aprederme of Republic of the Congo, Jony Louis of Haiti, and Alexis Alarcón and David Mourlot of Cuba. All went well beyond simple translation to help me adjust to different cultures, arrange travel, and avoid danger.

Along the same lines, I am grateful to Yvon Mabiala, Don and Jana Stelzer, Brock and Polly Vandever, Debbie Hawkins, Grete Viddal, Carolyn Morrow Long, Rick Love, Ousseynou Ndiaye, Abdou Diallo, Pape Gningue, Richard and Fran Kelly, Kirsten Atchley, Nazirou and Dado Thiello, Terry and Nancy Sullivan, the Yoakum family, Oumar Diallo, Dwuana Dukuly, Dominique Ntisibatala, Armand Ludovic Banguyssat, Dimina Nadineno Josué, Arsene Degla, Joseph Pierre Léonard, Jean Kumba, and Phyllis Van Es—all of whom helped me gain connections in the various places I visited.

I am also thankful to the vast number of people who took the time to speak with me about Voodoo, Vodou, Vodún, Vodun, Vodu, and other African and African diasporic faiths. Without help from the following people, this book would have been impossible to write: Sallie Ann Glassman; Brandi Kelley; Elliot Schwab; Miriam Chamani; Daouda Diallo; Demba Sow; Sileye Ba; Mariama Ba; Niane Ba; Kardiata, Aminata, Ayssata, Fatimata, and Amadou Ba; Samba Bah; Abou Ba; Thierno Ba; Ali Ka; Amadou Samba; Mounirou Dabo and Marie; Mady Kande; Thierno Mama Juldé Séydi; Jenabah Jallo; Lethiou Mané; Georges Mané; Salvador Mané; Amy Sow; Bacary Bodiang; Demba Balde; Moussa Balde; Roger Sambou; Ismail Aïdara; Ismail Cisse; Daouda Bodian; Fatou Mbengue; Thierno Diené; Samba Ka; Boydo Ka; Birahim Ndiaye; Balla Konate; Abourahmane Fall; Koffi Aza; Zannou Desire; Ganlonanisimael; Kpoffon Yehoun; Daagbo Hounon Houna II of Ouidah; Ginette Hounawanou; Meyè Lokossou; Laté Anagonou Ayolomi II; Dah Agassounon; Dah Midjonon; Dah Afodégonkou Gbenoukpo; Yehouenou Valdez; Bernard Akonpka; Pastor Akiti; Albertine Houenowkpa; Hounon Nïmantchee; Madame Agbogan; Kowouvi Treka; Djiwonou Kokou; Djanato Kodjo; Hounno SoFa Vodounou-Nossim yao FaFovi; Samuel Avisse; Habadadzi Antoine and his brother, Sanvi Komla Jacques; Djomakou Koami Agbé; Tohio Gabriel; Ashley Barkus; Martial Adoukonou; Ahanhanzo Glèlè Basile; Bocovo; Roger Atinssonou; Tholi Zakaria; Hounnon Klegbe; Obambi-in Lingala; Toukoula Mayi Armel; Robert Gomo-Debat; Ramses Bongolo; Fotseng Nzodgou; Nkodia Daniel; Miabeto Auguste; Mbemba Lubienga Armel; Nika Célestin; Kidzounou Olivier; Mafoua Nelson Clement; Mbadzi Christian; Roch Mampouya; Albert Nzahou; Mahoungou Martine; Maniangou Jean; Mavioga Medard; King Atouo Leandre;

Marcel Mbaloula; Amadou Cisse; Djissa Gabin; Dahsegnon; Sodewaye Sovessi; Bokossa Azonnakin; Tchekpo Dagnon Hounon; Aglossi Germain; Dohouga Azonwagbo; Klidjaha Emanssime; Lahoungbe Akogniwe; Hounon Fadekon; Guezo Edgard; Hyppolite; Hounongan Papa Djrado Blomankpon Blodedji Nan-Yeme Ahidazan Azansien Justin; Todjoclounon Gbèffa; King Segbedji Aholou Amagnihoun; Maistre Sam; Bocono Tchegnon; Hounnongan Hôssou Adankanlin; Balogoun Corneille Couchoro Hounnansin; Adagbazin Hinnoussi, Adagbazin Roger; Avlèketé Klounon Degbo Metokanji; Djissa Gabin, Todjiclounon Gbiffa; Euvonie Georges Auguste; Elza; Elien Isac (Samba 'L); Ati Joseph Fritzner Comas; Madame Leslie; Madame Serette; Oreste Crénio; Chenet Jean Pierre; Patrick Azema; Emil dit Hountor; Mambot Lorlotte; Eric Pierre; Ayida; Dupoux Marie Garlene; Jimmy Clermont; Jacky Pierre; Appolon Andy; Guerrier André; Rosiny Normil; Fenold and "Che Guevara"; Pablo Milanes; Odilia Solo Soyet; Ariel Lopez; Eriberto Antonio; Ernesto Antonio; Jean Antonio; Joachin Nelson; Derlice Bonhomme; and Marcelyn Oreste.

Finally, I thank the editors, scholars, and students who helped me along the way, including Rand Dotson, Catherine Wessinger, Brian Sivils, and Dovie Milstead.

VOODOO

INTRODUCTION

What Is in a Name?

The term *Voodoo* is well known to Americans. For most, it carries the weight of more than a century of denigration. To the general public, the term denotes malevolent magic. Mental images of pin-filled dolls encompass their comprehension of *Voodoo,* a misunderstanding aided in no small part by the New Orleans tourist trade. As many a scholar has noted, the image of malevolent Voodoo magic is misleading and masks a complex religion that was an important part of Mississippi River valley society between the eighteenth and twentieth centuries. Nevertheless, even among those who better understand the nature of the faith, considerable confusion surrounds just what the term *Voodoo* describes.

To begin with, there are numerous religions to which observers have assigned the label *Voodoo.* Three of these stand out more prominently than the rest. The first is the traditional religion of the Ewe, Fon, and related peoples from the Bight of Benin region of West Africa. As one might deduce, this religion was one of the major ancestors of other religions that have acquired its name. Scholars, seeking to reflect local practice as well as distinguish this faith from its New World relations and escape the negative connotations of *Voodoo,* often call it *Vodun* or *Vodu.* It must be noted, however, that *Vodun* can be a potential source of confusion as well because it has, at times, been preferred among anthropologists and other social scientists when speaking of the various descendants of the West African religion. Their reason for doing so was that they feared *Voodoo* was simply too freighted with negative stereotypes to have a place in scholarship.[1]

The second—and by far the best known—form of Voodoo is a Haitian folk religion. It was this faith that has historically been the focus of the negative stereotypes that grew up around Voodoo of all varieties.[2] As with West African Vodun, scholars have largely abandoned *Voodoo* as the term of choice. They have used a variety of words in its place, including *Vaudou, Vodoun,* and *Vodun.* Since 1986, when Haiti developed its first official Kreyòl orthography, these spellings have been gradually supplanted by *Vodou,* the term employed throughout this work.[3]

The final variety of Voodoo, and the subject of this work, was the religion associated with New Orleans, Louisiana, which developed during the eighteenth and early nineteenth centuries, flourished throughout the nineteenth century, and faded during the earlier twentieth century. As one might guess, this faith counted Vodun from the Bight of Benin among its ancestors. Notable among its other forebears were the traditional beliefs of West Central Africa and Senegambia. It was also heavily influenced by an influx of Haitian immigrants into South Louisiana during the years surrounding the turn of the nineteenth century, though the historical evidence suggests that the faith had begun to develop well before their arrival.[4]

The orthography of the North American variety of Voodoo has varied just as much as that of its African and Caribbean cousins. Carolyn Morrow Long, a pioneer in the recent study of the religion, refers to it as *Voudou,* reflecting her focus on the religion's New Orleans leadership. This spelling she prefers because it was the most common one during the nineteenth century, when Voodoo was at its height. Yvonne Chireau, who briefly addresses Voodoo in *Black Magic: Religion and the African American Conjuring Tradition,* uses both *Voodoo* and *Vodou,* reflecting her belief that Louisiana's Voodoo was imported from Haiti. In sources produced during the early twentieth century and before, authors' preferred terms included *Voodooism, Vou Dou, Vaudoo,* and *Voudoo.* Today's typical spelling of *Voodoo* began to frequently appear during the last two decades of the nineteenth century, and its place as the norm was fixed by the writings of Robert Tallant during the 1940s and 1950s.[5] One can make a compelling argument for the employment of any of the above spellings. *Voodoo: An African American Religion* shall employ *Voodoo,* however, for the simple fact that for today's scholars and popular readers alike, it is the most familiar. After all, though one of the alternate spellings might better represent usage prior to the late nineteenth century, even then there was no universally agreed-upon version. Though the predominance of *Voodoo* was fairly late in coming, it has become by far the most popular spelling. Using an alternative would unnecessarily force readers to translate the term while failing to escape the negative connotations that are tied to the belief system.

Like the spelling of *Voodoo,* the distinctions between hoodoo and Voodoo depend heavily on who explains them. At present, the consensus amongst knowledgeable laymen and scholars alike is that the words represent two distinct phenomena. Catherine Yronwode, a longtime student and practitioner of African American magical traditions, argues that the term *Voodoo* is best understood as representing a religion in Louisiana with West African roots that is distinct from hoodoo, a magical practice of West Central African origin. She further states that in most of the writings where *Voodoo* appears as an appellation for magical practices, it is an error on the part of white authors or an effort by their African American informants to use terminology with which someone from outside their culture would be familiar.[6] Scholars have generally adopted a similar approach to the topic. Carolyn Morrow Long, by far the most thorough recent scholar of the faith, describes Voodoo as an organized religion of the nineteenth century and earlier, but she describes hoodoo as a magical practice built around practitioner-client relationships.[7]

What may seem a clear distinction becomes blurry when one delves deeper into the sources. For instance, though scholar Yvonne Chireau distinguishes *Voodoo* and *hoodoo* in much the same manner as Yronwode and Long, she goes on to state that "in the African American vernacular, Voodoo was often applied . . . to describe any exercise of spiritual powers for malevolent purposes."[8] Zora Neale Hurston, one of the luminaries of the Harlem Renaissance, took a somewhat different stance, arguing that *Voodoo* was no more than a European name for magical practices that Blacks called *hoodoo.* To further complicate matters, Hurston's writings about hoodoo contradicted her contention that it was simply a magical practice. In addition to the spells and charms one might expect, she described initiation rituals and spiritual forces that constitute a religion rather than the utilitarian practices that scholars typically associate with magic.[9]

Nineteenth-century sources were equally conflicted as to the precise meaning of the terms. One early work to use the word *hoodoo* appeared in the *Memphis Appeal* during Reconstruction. According to the article, *hoodoo* and *Voodoo* were synonyms, a statement in keeping with the later writings of Hurston.[10] The same interpretation appeared in an 1870 article entitled "Negro Superstitions." The author, who never used the word *Voodoo,* instead employed *Hoodoo* to refer to "heathenish rites" that "exist in Louisiana even at the present day."[11] The fact that he tied hoodoo to communal ritual indicates that he intended to describe something more than magic alone. In 1886, famed Louisiana author George Washington Cable turned his hand to Voodoo in an article he entitled "Creole Slave Songs." Like his predecessors, he judged *hoodoo* a synonym for *Voodoo,* explaining that the latter was the correct term. *Hoodoo,* he believed, was an African American corruption of the original word. According to Cable, however, *Voodoo* properly described a supernatural being rather than the religion which honored it.[12]

So, what is one to make of the apparent disjuncture between modern distinctions regarding *hoodoo* and *Voodoo* and the historical tendency to equate them? Perhaps the best definition comes from the files of the Federal Writers' Project. In 1940, workers interviewed a New Orleans woman named Laure Hopkins—"Lala" for short. After watching Lala perform a spell designed to grant wishes, the workers asked, "Is this a form of voodoo?" She responded, "Voodoo means the worker, hoodoo the things they do."[13] In their notes, the two FWP workers used the *Century Dictionary* to dispute the definition, but Laure Hopkins' words reflected an insider's perspective—something very difficult to come by in the study of Voodoo. Nineteenth-century folklorist and author Mary Alicia Owen recorded a similar use of terminology in Missouri Voodoo, stating that she had only heard two practitioners speak of themselves as *Voodoos* but that their "humble admirers, however, often speak of them as 'Voodoos' and their deeds as 'Noodoos.'"[14]

As the sources make clear, *Voodoo*—by any spelling—does not accurately reflect historical usage. The word *hoodoo,* encompassing as it did religious and magical actions, came closer to describing the historical faith. Despite the historical nature of this study, however, the author will employ modern understandings of *Voodoo* and *hoodoo* throughout this work. The reason for this is simple. Unless one uses *Voodoo* in the modern, conventional sense, one must either use *hoodoo* in its place or invent another name for the religion. Considering the recent consensus that *hoodoo* describes magic, the first option would surely confuse most readers. Inventing a new term for the religion, on the other hand, would not only confound but would create a far greater distortion of the past than would adopting modern terminology. Using *hoo-*

doo in its modern sense misrepresents the past even less than does the use of *Voodoo*. After all, though once a broad term that embraced practices beyond those defined as magic by Western observers, it certainly also included the supernaturalism with which it is now associated.

Another problem is determining the boundaries of Voodoo. For one, what sets Voodoo apart from the hoodoo-like practices of conjure? The query is easy enough to answer. Conjure, by both modern and historical understandings, is magic. Moreover, it is an English term associated with areas initially settled by the British and their enslaved workers. Voodoo, in contrast, includes magic as but one element in a broader faith that honors a pantheon of gods, ancestors, and other spirits.[15]

Along the same lines, one could justly ask just how defined Voodoo's membership was. Mary Alicia Owen stated that practitioners who had undergone a period of fasting and other trials became members of a group called the Circle. The Circle, she explained, was a "society for the dissemination of knowledge" in which members met at night to discuss their doings and share news of Voodoos elsewhere.[16] A similar situation would be implied almost two generations later by Lala Hopkins, when she stated that she and those she called her "co-workers" would meet each Friday in a specific location where they would be approached by clients seeking protection and luck. On the other hand, it seems clear that not all practitioners were part of such bodies, a fact confirmed by one of Owen's informants, who stated that they could even be tolerably successful workers of magic without membership in any such society. He nevertheless disparaged such practitioners as "low down."[17]

Likewise, how does one determine which expressions of African American spirituality properly constitute Voodoo and which are aspects of a different creolized African tradition? Separating Voodoo from other creole religions depends heavily on historical context.[18] While locales across the United States saw aspects of African religion survive into the nineteenth century, only in the Mississippi River valley did these preserve a name, a priesthood, and a complex system of communal rituals decades beyond emancipation.[19] Moreover, though some of these factors existed elsewhere in colonial times and beyond, they show little direct overlap with Mississippi River valley Voodoo. Along the Atlantic Coast, for instance, African American John Canoe parades featured masked participants singing, dancing, and playing percussion instruments during the antebellum period. This festival was unknown in the Mississippi

River valley. The same can be said of festivities associated with New York's Pinkster, originally a Dutch celebration of Pentecost that became primarily an African American spring celebration. *Voodoo: An African American Religion* addresses only those expressions of African creole spirituality that demonstrate a clear historical connection with the variety of Voodoo best documented in Louisiana.[20] The range of North American Voodoo encompassed areas bordering the Mississippi River and its tributaries as well as a strip along the Gulf Coast on either side of the river's mouth.

Recently, Kodi Roberts has raised the question of whether one can justly describe Voodoo as an African American faith. According to his 2015 *Voodoo and Power: The Politics of Religion in New Orleans, 1881–1940,* the common understanding of Voodoo as a distinctly Black American faith rests upon "racialized perceptions of cultures that treat them as if they were insular or distinct."[21] Arguing against the perception that the religion was predominantly African or African American, he maintains that it was essentially a multicultural phenomenon that drew together people of different skin colors, sexes, and classes. The prevailing opinion, he asserts, grew out of identity politics that sought to portray the faith in a pejorative light by associating it with a population defined as inferior by the Jim Crow laws and pervasive racism of the late nineteenth and early twentieth centuries. *Voodoo: An African American Religion* will in many ways agree with Roberts, backing his claims that Voodoo was not a wholesale import from an imagined past and that its practitioners were indeed drawn from all segments of society. On the other hand, while numerous reports of Voodoo arrests during the nineteenth century record white participation, they were always described as being in the minority, making it difficult to describe the faith as a cross section of Mississippi River valley society.[22]

In short, several factors clouded the meaning of *Voodoo* in a Mississippi River valley context. Considering the numerous Old and New World faiths called by that name, popular and scholarly misconceptions of the tie between hoodoo and Voodoo, and difficulties nailing down the geographical range of the faith, it is no wonder historians have found it difficult to write on the subject. While explaining what was not Voodoo is fairly simple, describing what was is far more difficult. *Voodoo: An African American Religion,* however, attempts to do just that.

Chapter 1 is a brief overview of the Mississippi River valley and its inhabitants with an emphasis on the ways in which their diverse spiritual traditions contributed to the creation of Voodoo. While it is true that many of the elements that interacted to form the religion originated in Africa, they did not shape the faith in a vacuum. After all, the plantations on which enslaved Africans labored occupied land once claimed by countless generations of Native Americans, many of whose descendants still resided in the area. Neither can one discount the importance of the French and Spanish Catholics who founded those plantations and imported the unwilling laborers who toiled on them. Often overlooked was the relatively late arrival of settlers from the United States and emigrés from the newly established Haiti, both of which arrived in force during the years after 1800 and drastically changed the demographic composition of the Lower Mississippi River valley.

The second chapter, "African Spirits in the Mississippi River Valley," elaborates upon the African contributions to Voodoo by examining the highly fragmentary record of its gods. At the heart of this chapter is the conviction that examining the proper names for deities is the most direct route to following the interwoven strands of the religion's African heritage. Drawing upon nineteenth- and early twentieth-century primary sources, secondary texts from scholars of religion, as well as conversations with modern-day adherents of African and Afro-Caribbean faiths, it examines the two dozen or so named deities and numerous unnamed ones that authors and other investigators have claimed for the religion. In addition to identifying which gods were genuine or likely so, it discusses their places of origin and roles within the Mississippi River valley pantheon and examines why some African deities throve in the New World while others seem to have disappeared.

Chapter 3, "The Voodoos and Their Work," turns from the gods to those who served them. While the most visible ministerial title within the religion was *queen*, it was far from the only one. As with most religions of Africa and its diaspora, the priesthood was broader than a single office. On the other hand, unlike many of its Old and New World relations, Mississippi River valley Voodoo was characterized by its majority female leadership. These practitioners, while serving the deities as part of their religious duties, also earned livings from performing supernatural deeds for paying clients. Although these magical practices resembled the conjure found elsewhere in North America, they were nevertheless distinct, not least in the degree of Catholic beliefs and paraphernalia woven into their fabric. Like their counterparts outside of the Mississippi River valley, successful Voodoo clergy reaped temporal benefits, including status and sometimes wealth.

With the gods and their servants investigated, Chapter 4, entitled "Working with the Spirits," examines how the Voodoos interacted with the divine through sacred ritual. Sadly, no one saw fit to record much of what composed the ceremonial corpus of the faith, and those accounts that remain were recorded by outsiders who understood little about what they witnessed. Fortunately, a few descriptions of ritual spaces and weekly gatherings have survived, though they fail to provide a clear picture of the typical gatherings of the Voodoo faithful. Much more detailed are a handful of accounts describing the initiations into Louisiana Voodoo, called openings, that marked one's passage from casual participant in the religion to a spiritual adept. More plentiful, if less exact, are records of the annual St. John's Eve gatherings, later manifestations of which took place along the banks of Lake Pontchartrain. Voodoo in the Upper Mississippi River valley, meanwhile, was more systematically but even less thoroughly documented, and almost all of the extant detail survives in the writings of folklorist Mary Alicia Owen.

The final chapter, a slimmed-down version of which appeared in the May 2023 issue of *Nova Religio,* addresses the underlying assumption of the rest of the book that Voodoo is no longer a living tradition in the Mississippi River valley. Beginning with a consideration of the forces that worked to suppress the faith, it proceeds to ask, "Did the religion truly die?" The answer, it seems, depends less on evidence of continued existence than upon interpretation. Visitors to New Orleans, confronted by the city's many Voodoo shops and avowed practitioners, are apt to assume the historical religion is alive and well. Almost all lack the awareness that they represent a blend of supernatural entrepreneurship and genuine Haitian Vodou and that the driving force in their appearance in the Crescent City is not a living tradition, but New Orleans's reputation for exotic African diasporic magic, long fostered by popular authors, movies, television, and the city's tourist industry. Some scholars, though, have made well-reasoned arguments that Voodoo has survived in the form of Spiritual churches. While it is true that these congregations have absorbed a substantial quantity of orphaned Voodoo practices, their origins lie outside of the historical African diasporic tradition. Just as importantly, most members of Spiritual churches have vociferously denied any connection to Voodoo. Though the religion is best understood as a historical one without a direct living descendant, it has certainly left a legacy in the Mississippi River valley—not least through its vibrant hoodoo, which shows no signs of disappearing.

The end matter rounds out the volume and provides some primary sources for scholars who wish to dig more deeply into the history of the religion. A conclusion wades into the murky waters of cultural politics to tackle the question of just who, if anyone, has authority over the interpretation of Mississippi River valley Voodoo. Even though claims of ownership conflict and can result in widely different interpretations of just what Voodoo was or is, the discussions are beneficial in that they help to prevent the development of a consensus that could well reduce the religion to a caricature of its historical self. Next, an appendix records and translates all the Voodoo songs, chants, and prayers that I have been able to collect from sources with at least some claim to credibility. It is intended as an aid to future scholars of the religion and should save them the trouble of collecting these widely scattered sources.

Though much of Mississippi River valley Voodoo's history has been lost beyond recovery, *Voodoo: An African American Religion* attempts to systematize the surviving knowledge. To be sure, much remains to be investigated. For example, while no less than three scholarly biographies of Voodoo Queen Marie Laveau have appeared since the turn of the twenty-first century, nothing comparable has appeared on her slightly less well-known contemporaries Jean Montanée and Jim Alexander. Important New Orleans practitioners who postdated Marie Laveau, such as Marie Comptesse and Laure Hopkins, remain virtually unknown to scholars and the public. Likewise, comparative studies of Voodoo and its relatives in Haiti, Benin, Togo, Cuba, and elsewhere remain to be undertaken. My fervent hope is that *Voodoo: An African American Religion* will prove a useful aid those who undertake serious study of this once neglected and still much misunderstood religion.

THE PEOPLES OF THE MISSISSIPPI RIVER VALLEY

Voodoo, like so much of African American culture, is a combination of elements from a multitude of sources. Among the more prominent roots of the religion were the Mississippi River valley's indigenous inhabitants, French and Spanish settlers, waves of African immigrants, Anglo American settlers, and refugees fleeing the Haitian Revolution. The now-traditional tale of the faith's beginnings treats it as an import from Haiti during the late eighteenth and early nineteenth centuries. Haiti itself acquired its Vodou—so goes the story—because of early eighteenth-century French raids along the coast of the Bight of Benin. This single-source interpretation is untenable, though it continues to inform both popular and scholarly understandings. Interpreting Voodoo as a layered creole religion, molded by a succession of influences over more than a century, is far more productive.[1]

Having taken a multiple-origin approach as a starting point, choosing the proper method of comprehending the interplay of these sources is vital. Two competing models for understanding such faiths can be drawn from the literature that examines Caribbean manifestations of African Creole Religions. The first of these comes from the scholarship of Haitian Vodou. In a detailed study of the religion, folklorist Harold Courlander wrote that in the literal sense Vodou "consists of the rites, beliefs, and practices . . . built around the similar religious systems of the Dahomeans and the Nagos." He then went on to state, that in "a wider sense it applies to similar but distinct ritual activities of other cults."[2] It was with this latter viewpoint that Courlander and most other scholars have approached the Haitian faith. As understood by them, Haitian Vodou includes several groups of deities—referred to as nations or *nanchon*—based on their place of African origin. Devotees serve each group through distinctive rituals that can vary significantly depending on the *nanchon*. The fact that these spirits and rituals may differ from each other in both outward appearance and African origin does not, however, make them parts of different religions in the Haitian context. On the contrary, Vodou has developed as an umbrella faith that melded them into a single religion in which each believer accepts the existence of multiple nations and frequently honors deities from more than one of them.[3]

An alternative model for understanding Mississippi River valley Voodoo appears in the literature of Cuban Santería. Cuba, like Haiti, has strong African religious traditions. Scholars have treated them quite differently from Haitian Vodou, however. Rather than speaking of the non-Christian spiritual world of Cuba as a single faith, they tend to divide it into a variety of different religions. The most important of these are Santería, also known as Regla de Ocha or Lucumí, and Palo Mayombe, also known as Regla de Palo. The former represents a creole version of Yoruba traditional religion, while the latter derives primarily from the Kongo of West Central Africa. As in Haiti, these two divisions have their own deities and rituals, but also like Haitians, Cubans will sometimes serve more than one set of spirits. For example, many devotees of Santería occasionally turn to the spirits of Palo, particularly when they are in need of magical assistance. In short, despite the similar religious milieus of the two islands, scholars typically treat the traditional beliefs of Haiti as composing one religion, while dividing those of Cuba into two or more.[4]

Though it is quite possible that the Voodoo practitioners of the Mississippi River valley may have maintained some degree of segregation between beliefs originating in different regions of Africa, using the Cuban model to understand their beliefs is highly problematic. After all, the historical record is rather fragmentary, and many of the sources that address the religion express whites' aversion to it rather than meaningful details of its beliefs and practices. Nevertheless, there is little evidence that either whites or African Americans recognized more than one version of Voodoo or even the separate nations one finds in Haitian Vodou. At the same time, a series of cultural layers is evident within the faith. No one African people or group of similar peoples can be said to have contributed the bulk of Voodoo's beliefs. As a layered religion, the faith seamlessly combined gods, ceremonies, words, and ritual paraphernalia from a wide range of African societies as well as peoples encountered by enslaved African Americans.

THE PERSISTENT NATIVE AMERICAN PRESENCE

Though African faiths were central to the ancestry of Voodoo, the religion was clearly a creole one, demonstrating a New World development that drew its spiritual material from beyond the confines of the enslaved's former homelands. Long before the arrival of Europeans or Africans, the Mississippi River valley was the home of many Native American peoples. Found in the area of the modern state of Louisiana were the Natchez, Acolapissa, Houma, Chitimacha, Atakapa, Avoyel, Natchitoches, Caddo, and Choctaw. A host of other peoples lived along the more northerly reaches of the Mississippi. It was in American Indian soil that the Old World seeds of Voodoo would take root.

Native American beliefs, though far less evident in Voodoo than those of later settlers, nevertheless contributed to the formation of the African American faith. American Indians believed in a world peopled by spirits. The religions built around them varied greatly, however. For the Natchez, the last of the Mississippian culture's mound builders, religion was organized around divine leaders and devotion to the sun. Many others envisioned a spiritual world divided into three levels: the Upper World, This World, and the Under World. Humans lived in This World, while deities and lesser spirits lived in the other two. All believed that spirits dwelt in this world, despite their origins outside of it. Magic was one way to utilize their power. What modern Americans would call medicine was another.[5]

Unlike in areas settled by the English, Native Americans were not generally pushed to the frontier of settlement in the Mississippi River valley. On the contrary, they remained a vital part of society throughout the colonial period and through much of the nineteenth century. During the early years of the French era, local peoples provided refuge to the European settlers in times of hardship and served as key trading partners. The colonists' reliance on the

Indians as well as a severe shortage of French women, led to many sexual relationships between French men and Native American women. The Indian presence remained strong for much of the next two centuries. In 1834, John H. B. Latrobe mentioned seeing "many Choctaw Indians . . . prowling about New Orleans and Natchez."[6] Houmas and Chitimachas were also a common sight around New Orleans, where they traded with whites and African Americans.[7]

The close contact between those of African descent and Native Americans contributed to the rise of Voodoo. At the very least, Native American religions likely supported the survival of African belief systems because of their shared understandings of a world peopled with spirits. For instance, southeastern American Indians typically understood illness as a manifestation of the workings of ghosts, witches, or the spirits of animals. The herbal remedies used to treat ailments were themselves spiritual in nature, designed to drive out the evil influences within the sufferer. African Americans, like whites, would have encountered some aspects of these ideas through their frequent interaction with Native Americans in the streets and markets of New Orleans and elsewhere along the Mississippi. The interaction between the two races also explains the presence of Native American herbs, such as devil's shoestring and sassafras, in Louisiana hoodoo and herbalism.[8]

In other cases, the exchanges of knowledge likely went much deeper. African Americans in and about St. Joseph, Missouri—the northernmost known outpost of Voodoo—had considerable contact with Native Americans, and many were themselves of American Indian descent. Marie Laveau, the best known of New Orleans's Voodoo priestesses, reportedly had significant familiarity with Native Americans as well. One informant interviewed during the 1930s by workers employed by the Depression- and early World War II–era Federal Writers' Project recalled that Marie Laveau was friends with a man nicknamed "Indian Jim." According to FWP records, he earned this nickname because of his mixed African and Indian parentage. Some believed Laveau was herself of Native American ancestry.[9] Marie Dédé, during an interview with Federal Writers' Project workers during the 1930s, stated that Laveau "used to trade her business with the Indians for herbs."[10] Her relationship with them was so strong that they would often stay overnight in huts in Laveau's side yard. Native American religions' support for Voodoo—at least in the case of herbalism—was clear, albeit difficult to trace in full.[11]

THE FRENCH AND SPANISH

Small numbers of Europeans began moving into what had been the Native Americans' Lower Mississippi River valley during the late seventeenth century, hoping to find wealth and to develop a barrier to British expansion westward. Their method of exploration was to descend the Mississippi from Canada, a feat eventually accomplished in 1682 when René-Robert Cavelier, Sieur de La Salle, reached the Gulf of Mexico and thereby claimed for France all the land drained by the Mississippi and its tributaries. Soon there followed a series of outposts, culminating in the founding of New Orleans in 1718. By the 1720s, several thousand settlers had provided a tangible, albeit sparse, French presence.[12]

Louisiana's economy was precarious at best under French rule. During those early decades, money was a scarce commodity along the Mississippi. Much of the income available came by way of the fur trade, piracy, and commerce, legal and illegal. A small plantation sector had developed early in the colony's history, though its crops of rice, indigo, and cotton were only marginally profitable.[13]

Despite their tenuous existence, those early planters provided the basis of the society necessary for the appearance of Voodoo. Agriculture required laborers. The French government strove mightily to convince its citizens to migrate into the Mississippi River valley but met with only limited success, mostly in the form of nearly 2,500 indentured servants. There was little to draw anyone into a poor frontier society that was easily cut off from the mother country in times of war, experienced periodic famine and epidemic disease, and continued to rely on Native American peoples for protection and often, the basic necessities of life. France responded by deporting criminals and other undesirables, who proved ill-suited to hard labor. The first calls for slaves began in 1706. Thirteen years later, 450 enslaved Africans arrived in Louisiana aboard two ships, having embarked at Ouidah, a city in modern Benin.[14]

Louisiana remained a French possession until a disastrous war with its archrival Great Britain that ended in 1763. Though they stripped it of most of its possessions, the British allowed France to keep the portion of poverty-stricken Louisiana to the west of the Mississippi and New Orleans on the eastern side. Seeing the writing on the wall and realizing that the colony had failed in its purpose of preventing British expansion, the French had already secretly negotiated the transfer of Louisiana to their ally, Spain. Within a few years of the end of the war, New Orleans and the portion of Louisiana west of the Mississippi became the newest additions to the Spanish Empire.[15]

Under Spain, the region's economy drastically improved. France had valued Louisiana far less than its wealthy, plantation-driven Caribbean colonies. Spain, in contrast, saw the former French land's potential to become a wealthy plantation society itself and went so far as to fund the development of Louisiana with wealth generated from its more prosperous colonies to the south. By granting trade monopolies to its new colony, encouraging immigration of Spanish-speaking Canary Islanders, welcoming French-speaking Acadians, and encouraging the growth of the neglected plantations, Spain brought a measure of prosperity to Louisiana. The free population of the Lower Mississippi River valley and its environs soared from 3,654 white inhabitants to nearly 20,000 between 1763 and 1800. With economic growth came a need for increased labor, which Spain readily provided in the form of slaves. Between 1763 and 1800, the number of slaves in southern Louisiana jumped from just under 4,600 to 24, 264.[16]

Though Voodoo was not itself an import of primarily European origin, French and Spanish slave importation indirectly molded the religion by determining just which Africans would contribute to its formation. Initially, the French favored slaves embarked from the city of Ouidah, once an independent kingdom on the Bight of Benin until its conquest by Dahomey in 1727. Between 1719 and 1728, the French imported 1,748 slaves from this port. Even by 1720, however, slaves were arriving from other portions of Africa, most notably from the extreme western tip of the continent, known to scholars as Senegambia. By the second half of the 1720s, the Senegambians had supplanted slaves from Ouidah as the most numerous people, with approximately 3,909 ultimately disembarked in Louisiana by 1743. Slaves from other portions of Africa were few and far between, with the only notable exception being a single shipload of under 300 that arrived from Cabinda, a port in what is now Angola, in 1721.[17]

Whatever their place of origin, Louisiana slaves encountered Catholicism in Louisiana. The priesthoods of both France and Spain were strongly interested in missions. Their desire to Christianize bondspersons persuaded the French government to require Christian instruction for all slaves in the 1724 Code Noir, the body of laws that defined the rights and duties of slaves and their masters. Though priests in Louisiana often complained that the religious stipulations of the code were inadequately enforced, they at least defined the process by which African religions could begin to take on Catholic features.[18]

Catholicism had a profound effect on the religion of the Mississippi River valley's African American inhabitants. The surviving evidence indicates that Voodoo adherents frequently practiced Catholicism as well. Marie Laveau's obituary described her as having been married in St. Louis Cathedral, for instance. Zora Neale Hurston reported that of the six practitioners she encountered in New Orleans, three were Catholic, two Protestant, and one without religious affiliation. Rather than interacting with them as two distinct faiths, Voodoo believers drew no sharp distinctions between them, allowing them to operate in what one scholar of Haitian Vodou has described as symbiosis. During the process of creolization, through which African religions adapted to the society of the Mississippi River valley, Voodoo took on many aspects of Catholicism, including physical items like candles, rituals such as prayers, and theological concepts, including the veneration of the saints. Perhaps the most pronounced instance of this symbiotic relationship was the rise of saint-deity correspondences, in which believers in Voodoo linked each of their deities to a particular Catholic saint, a development paralleled in many other African creole religions.[19]

In addition to helping to contribute a Catholic presence to the Mississippi River valley, Spanish policies created a large population of free African Americans. Unlike the French, the Spanish did not accept Native American slavery, allowing some slaves to successfully sue for their freedom on the grounds that they were of Indian blood. Others bought their freedom through *coartacíon,* the practice of allowing enslaved people to purchase their freedom whether their masters were willing or not. Perhaps even more important, while the French Code Noir required anyone wishing to free a slave to seek permission from the government, the Spanish Código Negro did not, allowing willing masters free reign to liberate bondspersons as they saw fit. Alongside the liberalized provisions for emancipation, the culture of the colony was also changing. As time passed, white fathers became increasingly willing to openly acknowledge their children of mixed race and, when possible, free them. The practice of acknowledging children accelerated the development of the Lower Mississippi's hierarchical racial classification, which conferred higher status on racially mixed people. They eventually developed into people neither Black nor white—Creoles of Color—who were freed from an assumed equivalence with slaves. These free people of color would provide much of Voodoo's leadership.[20]

AFRICAN IMPORTS

The Bight of Benin

While Europeans would provide the conditions that allowed Voodoo to develop, it was the enslaved themselves who began the process of shaping the creole religion. Slaves from the Bight of Benin region were the founders of the Lower Mississippi's Black society. Though quickly surpassed in numbers by peoples of Senegambian origin, they remained a persistent presence in the area throughout the French and Spanish periods. Among the major peoples of the area were the Fon and Ewe of modern Benin, Togo, and surrounding areas as well as the Yoruba, who are today concentrated primarily in Nigeria. As the founding generation, their traditional beliefs would prove important to the creation of Voodoo.[21]

Much like the Native Americans whom they would largely supplant, Africans of the Bight of Benin dwelt in a world filled with spirits. Though specifics of the traditional religions varied from people to people, there were some commonalities throughout the region. For instance, believers typically accepted that there was a supreme being, who was the ultimate source of all things. To the Fon and Ewe, the name of this feminine deity was Mawu, while to the Yoruba, he was the masculine Olodumare. The peoples the Bight of Benin generally understand the supreme being as all-powerful and ever-present but separated from humankind. Thus, temples and ceremonies in this god's honor were rare and remain so today.[22]

The spirits below the supreme being most commonly received the devotion of their followers. A variety of powerful spirits or lesser gods were one focus of worship. These beings, called *edro* or *vodu* by the Fon and Ewe and *orishas* by the Yoruba, generally possessed specific functions and were called upon by their followers with these in mind. Ancestral spirits were also revered by many Africans from the region, to the extent that some scholars rank them as more important than the lesser gods. In addition, most peoples also believed in spiritual inhabitants of plants, animals, and features of the landscape as well as other beings, which often aided magical specialists or inhabited their charms.[23]

The various spiritual forces were honored in many ways, depending on which people group was involved. For instance, deities had their priests. Magic was also worked by specialists who knew the spiritual properties of the materials necessary for charms. Some specialized in doing good while others focused on evil. Many peoples recognized a distinct class of witches, who worked harm simply by thinking it—without the aid of magical materials. Divination was also a prestigious occupation, especially among the Yoruba. Those without in-depth knowledge of a specific deity or class of spirits could join a so-called secret society, which often combined religious, governmental, and social functions. Even chiefs, kings, and doctors performed spiritual roles. The very complexity of these practices and beliefs on which they were based could fill several volumes without completely describing the faiths of the Bight of Benin region.[24]

Senegambia

Africans from the western tip of Africa, called Senegambia by scholars, were also important to the early shaping of the Mississippi River valley's spiritual world. Though the first of them arrived slightly later than those from the Bight of Benin, they nevertheless proved numerically dominant during the French colonial period. As was true of the Bight of Benin region, the inhabitants of Senegambia were from a variety of people groups, though a few of the more prominent were speakers of Mande dialects, notably the Bamana (also known as Bambara) and Mandinka, as well as Wolof, Fulbe, and a host of others.[25]

Unlike in the Bight of Benin region, there was a sharp religious divide in Senegambia between expanding Islam and the traditional religions it sought to supplant. European observers during the era of slave trading frequently remarked that the Mandinkas were devout Muslims. Though they continued to cling to some traditional beliefs, including a strong attachment to magical amulets, they had adopted so much Islamic culture that they even wrote their language in Arabic characters. Many Wolofs and Fulbes were also Muslims. In addition to marking the inhabitants of Senegambia as distinct from their Bight of Benin counterparts, Islamic jihads against traditional religionists also helped support the slave trade. Both sides profited from the enslavement and sale of captured soldiers.[26]

Traditional belief systems remained strong in Senegambia, despite the presence of expansionist Islam. Their traditional beliefs resembled those of the peoples who lived along the Bight of Benin. The Bamana of the Kingdom of Segu—chief foe of the Mandinkas—believed in a supreme being known as Bemba. Below Bemba were his children, two deities known as Faro and Pemba, who between them created the world, and a variety of lesser deities and spirits. The Bamana believed that at death, humans both became ancestral spirits and were reincarnated among the living. Like their Muslim neighbors, they also held to a firm belief in magical amulets.[27]

West Central Africa

West Central Africans went from composing slightly less than 5 percent of the total slave imports during the French period to becoming the largest ethnicity brought into the colony under Spanish rule. In fact, Africans from the Kongo nation of West Central Africa outnumbered any other single ethnicity in Louisiana and accounted for almost 34 percent of those sold in Louisiana between 1719 and 1820. Only their minimal presence during the early colonial period explains why their culture did not emerge as the dominant force in the development of Voodoo. As they entered a region with an established creole faith, they added a new layer to the existing religion rather than supplanting it or developing a distinct belief system.[28]

As was true of those from the Bight of Benin and Senegambia, the peoples of West Central Africa believed in an elaborate spiritual world. Like other African groups, they generally understood their world as created by a supreme being, called Nzambi a Mpungu by the Kongo people. They likewise believed in a variety of lesser gods and spirits as well as the potency of magic and witchcraft. Scholars tend to argue that the most evident difference between the traditional faith of this region as compared to others was a heightened emphasis on the spirits of the dead. Some modern authors maintain that all deities began as human spirits, having outgrown the status of ancestors as the date of their death receded into the ever-more-distant past. Some even argue that Nzambi a Mpungu was himself once an ancestral spirit.[29]

Unlike their more northerly fellows, many West Central Africans had encountered Catholic Christianity by the late fifteenth century. In 1491, the Kingdom of Kongo began the process of becoming a Christian nation when its king converted to Catholicism, which had been introduced into the region by the Portuguese. By the sixteenth century, the monarchs and short-handed priesthood were sponsoring missionary work, and one king, Afonso I, thought of his wars of conquest as religious crusades. According to scholar John K. Thornton, by the early seventeenth century, most of the kingdom's subjects professed the faith of their monarch. The traditional religion of the area did not simply disappear, however. Instead, the prominent place held by the dead simply entered into the folk Catholicism of the region. It found expression in reinterpretations of Christian holidays, such as All Souls Day (November 2), as festivals in honor of the spirits of the dead as well as in embrace of the Catholic saints as the Christian equivalent of traditional Kongo ancestor veneration. To some extent, the faith of some West Central Africans had already become a layered religion many generations before they became unwilling laborers in the Mississippi River valley.[30]

Layers

Describing precisely what aspects of Voodoo came from each region of Africa is far from simple, but many broad aspects of the layered faith can be accurately described. For example, the deities appear to have come primarily from the Bight of Benin region. Monsieur Danny or Blanc Dani, one of the major deities, originated in the city-state of Ouidah, later conquered by the Fon. The Fon called this spirit Dan. The equally prominent Liba or Papa Lébat had come to the New World with the same peoples, among whom he had been called Legba. A deity known as Assonquer may have come from the Yoruba, where he had been known as Osanyin. Other deities whose names have survived in the documentary record had no obvious prototypes in the Bight of Benin, but the three mentioned above were the most commonly mentioned of Voodoo's lesser deities. Moreover, the name for the religion itself derives from the Fon and Ewe word *vodu,* meaning "spirit" or "divinity."[31]

The spirit world was not peopled entirely by deities from the Bight of Benin. Voodoo placed significance upon the spirits of the dead, for instance, a likely marker of West Central African influence.[32] Two Federal Writers' Project workers learned something of the importance of ancestors firsthand while interviewing an elderly practitioner named Robinson but calling herself "Grandma" and "Madame Ducoyielle." In addition to passing along some information about lesser spirits and the saints, Ducoyielle took the workers to the St. Louis cemeteries (No. 1, No. 2, and No. 3). There, she showed them how to call on the spirits of the dead in order to harm enemies, gain money, win luck, and obtain other benefits. She also stressed the importance of giving the dead offerings in order to win favor. Significantly, many of the spirits with whom Ducoyielle interacted were either her own relatives or had been known by her during their lifetimes, a clear link to African traditions of ancestor veneration. Louisianans' historical use of *zombi* to mean "ghost" or "spirit" and sometimes "wizard" likewise indicates West Central African influence. In Kikongo, the language of the Kongo people, *nzambi* refers to the spirit of a dead person and *zumbi* describes an animated corpse, meanings very similar to that of *zombi* in Louisiana.[33]

The magical side of Voodoo—hoodoo to today's scholars—was itself obviously layered. The first mentions of what would one day be called *hoodoo* appeared during the eighteenth century. During the colonial era and the early nineteenth century, *gris-gris* and variations thereof were the names most commonly applied to African American magic. In 1758, Antoine-Simon Le Page Du Pratz wrote a history of Louisiana in which he briefly discussed slaves' attachment to "little toys which they call *gris, gris.*"[34] His subsequent discussion of the power these items held for the enslaved makes it clear that they possessed spiritual importance. In 1773, magic appeared in a prominent court case involving a group of slaves who attempted to kill a man named Augustin, an overseer for Don Francisco Bellile. Their tool was a spiritual poison, composed of the gall and heart of an alligator, which they referred to as *gri-gri.*[35]

The word *gris-gris* reflects the foundational influence of West Africa on Voodoo. Identifying a single people group or region of origin is problematic. Today, both the Bight of Benin and Senegambia employ terms resembling *gris-gris* to describe much the same thing as the eighteenth-century Black inhabitants of the Mississippi River valley. The Ewe use *gris-gris* as a general term for magic, for instance. During the eighteenth century, slave trader Nicholas Owens attested to what he called "gregory bags" on Sherbro Island off Sierra Leone and drew a picture of a "witch or gregory" as used by the Mandinkas.[36]

In addition to the widespread use of terms resembling *gris-gris* in West Africa, Mississippi River valley sources give evidence of multiple origins for the word. In the 1773 *gris-gris* case, the man engaged to prepare the death charm spoke only what the sources style "Mandringa," an apparent reference to the language of the Mandinkas. Moreover, he appears to have been the first of the accused to use the word *gris-gris.* Nearly a century later, an article from the *Memphis Appeal* described hoodoo doctors of African origin making items called *grigats* for their clients. Though the article described the practitioners as "Congoes," other details from the article make it clear that the author believed them to have arrived in the country aboard the *Clotilda*, the last known slave ship to enter the United States. If the writer was correct in his belief about their arrival in the country, then they had been purchased in Ouidah, part of the Fon Kingdom of Dahomey by then.[37] Few of the *Clotilda's* cargo were themselves Fon, however. The hoodoo doctors spoken of in the *Memphis Appeal* were most likely Yoruba. Both *gris-gris* and the practices it defined must be described as originating from peoples from both Senegambia and the Bight of Benin, though it is safe to assume that the numerically superior Senegambians had a proportionate impact on the early magical practices of the region.[38]

The word *hoodoo* is of even more indeterminate origin. The author of the *Memphis Appeal* article that referred to former slaves from the *Clotilda* used *hoodoo* as a synonym for *Voodoo*, pointing toward a likely origin along the Bight of Benin. What is more certain is that newspaper articles mentioning hoodoo had begun appearing in places far from the Mississippi River valley within two decades of the Civil War. In 1870, the *Georgia Weekly Telegraph* reported that African Americans in Jones County used "hoodood" to mean they had been swindled, cheated, or otherwise deceived. Within a few years, the same newspaper had begun to use *hoodoo* in reference to harmful magic. By 1879, at least two West Virginia newspapers were using the word to describe political organizations in the state, some of them secretive, a fact that hints at knowledge of hoodoo's religious connections. In 1881, Arizona's *Tombstone Epitaph* spoke of the arrest of a Native American medicine man, whom it described as a "hoodoo operator."[39]

Clearly, *hoodoo* had become a well-known word by the 1880s, but that fact alone does not say much about its origin. In addition, accounts linking hoodoo to Voodoo were rare outside of areas bordering the Mississippi and its tributaries. Moreover, when the word appeared outside the Mississippi River valley in such a way as to indicate religious connotations—as was the case in the West Virginia papers—those whites who wrote about it demonstrated little understanding of the term. Arizonans, moreover, seemed not to have even linked *hoodoo* with African Americans. Even in Georgia, where African Americans appeared to have sometimes used the word to describe magic, it was uncommon enough that the 1870 *Telegraph* article had to explain it to readers, surely unnecessary had it been in widespread use for a significant time period.[40]

The possibility that *hoodoo* was a rare term outside the Mississippi River valley was supported by African Americans interviewed by folklorist Harry Middleton Hyatt during the 1930s and early 1940s. One informant stated that *hoodoo* was "hardly ever" used in South Carolina and seemed to agree with Hyatt's statement that hoodoo "seems to be over in New Orleans mostly."[41] Another interviewee who had grown up in South Carolina stated that he had never heard *hoodoo* as a child. A former slave from Florida similarly claimed that *hoodoo* was a new word that had entered the state following emancipation. Significantly, the time frame given by the Floridian informant roughly corresponds to hoodoo's appearance in the popular press. If newspapers introduced the word outside of the Mississippi River valley, this development would do much to explain the varied meanings of the term in areas far from the great river.[42]

Hoodoo's link with the Mississippi River valley and Voodoo help explain the lack of understanding outside of the region. The term gained currency in the media only after the Civil War, with an early use of the word in reference to African American supernaturalism appearing in the *Cairo Democrat* of Illinois in late 1865. The same *Memphis Appeal* article that discussed the making of grigats also gave early evidence for its use in the Mississippi River valley. The article, like many works before and since, treated *hoodoo* as synonymous with *Voodoo* and defined both as simply magical practices. At the very least, it clearly demonstrates that *hoodoo* was in use in the Mississippi River valley at an early date.[43]

Other nineteenth-century writings likewise emphasize a special connection between hoodoo and the Mississippi River valley. For example, the first publication with a national audience to mention the term *hoodoo* was *Lippincott's Magazine,* which in 1870 carried a story describing its practice in New Orleans. Its author, Thaddeus Norris, wrote about what his contemporaries commonly called *Voodoo,* but that he termed "the rites of the 'Hoodoo.'"[44] He went on to vaguely describe hoodoo as a "heathenish" ceremony involving singing and dancing. Moreover, the already well-known *Voodoo* appears nowhere in the article. When referring to magical practices outside the New Orleans area, the author eschewed *hoodoo* in favor of "conjurer" and "conjuring." Works from later in the nineteenth century likewise identify hoodoo as from the Mississippi River valley. Mary Alicia Owen, for instance, used *hoodoo* as the term to describe the magic associated with the Voodoo practices in Missouri.[45]

Moreover, works from the region show much greater recognition of hoodoo's religious features than elsewhere. For instance, a short piece picked up from Tennessee's *Memphis Avalanche* by the *Huntsville Times* described a "hoodoo priestess" named Margaret Jones. Kentucky's *Louisville Courier-Journal* made reference to a "Hoo-Doo Queen" in an 1872 article, terminology in keeping with a New Orleans practice of calling female Voodoo practitioners "queens." Outside the Mississippi River valley, journalists never defined practitioners of hoodoo or other magical systems as ministers.[46]

The link between hoodoo and the Mississippi River valley renders it quite possible that the word was an import from one of the three regions of Africa that contributed the most to the region: Senegambia, the Bight of Benin, or West Central Africa. The evidence suggests that the Bight of Benin is the best candidate. For example, if the author of the *Memphis Appeal* article was correct in his identification of the former slaves as being cargo on the *Clotilda,* then the port of Ouidah in the Kingdom of Dahomey was their point of embarkation. Similarly, Mary Alicia Owen identified the practice of Missouri hoodoo with those possessing Guinean ancestry. In a North American context, Guinea was a vague term encompassing a vast swath of territory extending from the Bight of Biafra to Senegambia that included the Bight of Benin. If Owen was using the term in the typical fashion, then she was, at least, excluding West Central Africa from consideration.[47]

The strongest evidence for the origin of *hoodoo* is in the word itself. Its similarity to *Voodoo,* a word of established Bight of Benin provenance, is a strong indicator of origin. The fact that in historical usage, a Voodoo was someone who practiced hoodoo makes the case for the Bight of Benin all the stronger. According to Judy Rosenthal, a scholar of West African Vodu, there are two likely originals for *hoodoo.* The first, *hu do,* is a combination of two Ewe words that together can mean "spirit work" among other things. A second possibility is the Ewe *hu du,* which literally translates "eating blood" but figuratively means "eating spirit" or "eating vodu." The latter specifically describes the Ewe religious practice of eating sauces made from sacrificial animals and of eating kola nuts dipped in the blood of sacrifices. Both interpretations fit the Mississippi River valley context of hoodoo as well as its relationship to Voodoo. In light of the scant documentary record and philological investigation, the Bight of Benin seems the most likely place of origin for *hoodoo.*[48]

Other terms used in the magic of the Mississippi River valley show clearer-cut origins. *Zinzin,* a word occasionally encountered in reference to positive charms, comes from the language of the Bamana of Senegambia. *Wanga,* a word used for harmful charms, most likely arrived with enslaved West Central Africans. Priests and magic workers in the area were commonly known as *oganga* or *nganga* in the region, words strongly resembling the term used for the Mississippi River valley charm. Significantly, there are no records of the word *wanga* in use during the early colonial period, reflecting the fact that West Central Africans were relative latecomers.[49]

There was, of course, much more to Voodoo than words. Hoodoo, for instance, included a multitude of ritual items, movements, and spiritual concepts drawn from an array of African and sometimes European and Native American sources. Likewise, initiation ceremonies were an important feature of Voodoo as well as a practice common in sub-Saharan Africa. In the Old World context, these rituals typically allowed one entrance into so-called secret societies, such as the Gorovodu Society found in portions of the Bight of Benin and in Ghana. These societies were numerous and remain prominent features of African and African creole cultures throughout the Atlantic World. Communal festivals, large and small, and the spiritual leaders who presided over them were vital aspects of Voodoo as well. As with magic and initiation, these were features found throughout the religions of the African Diaspora.[50]

AMERICANS AND HAITIANS

The inhabitants of the Mississippi River valley—never a stable or homogenous population—were to witness additional massive changes in the years around the turn of the nineteenth century. The first of these and ultimately the largest was a massive influx of Americans into the region, culminating in the United States' 1803 purchase of the western portion of the Mississippi River Basin from France. Following the U.S. acquisition, the native creole population—French, Spanish, and Afro-Latin alike—saw its population gradually swamped in a flood of Anglo-Americans from the Upper South, mid-Atlantic, and New England, who would eventually realize the commercial potential of the river system in ways that their predecessors never had. In those areas with a small Latin population, the new arrivals quickly became dominant. Near the mouth of the Mississippi, where the largest population of French and Spanish arrivals had settled, their number preserved their political power into the 1830s, but they were unable to significantly slow the growth of the Anglo population, whose slaves also began to supplant those whose ancestors had been imported by the French and Spanish.[51]

The English-speaking newcomers had little experience with Voodoo. Their lack of familiarity with the beliefs of their new home in no way implied unfamiliarity with African creole spirituality, however. Arrivals from New York would have been somewhat familiar with the African American Pinkster celebrations, while those from the Atlantic coast were likely to have encountered the winter John Canoe festivities. Such experiences gave Anglo-Americans the background to understand and to sometimes participate in certain Voodoo ceremonies, such as the St. John's Eve gathering, which took place at night on June 23 and/or 24. Hoodoo-like magic, known as conjure, rootwork, mojo, or tricking, was also a common feature of life throughout the American South. Hoodoo easily interacted with these related magical systems. After all, these varieties of supernaturalism all focused on manipulating spiritual forces. In such a milieu, abstract concepts of cultural purity could be easily overcome by pragmatic desires to succeed, a process already demonstrated through the melding of magical words and concepts within the Mississippi River valley.[52]

In addition to adding population and a new corpus of magical thought to the Mississippi River valley, the arrival of Anglo-Americans and their slaves inaugurated a period of increased attention to Voodoo. Though colonial references to the religion exist, they were rare and usually brief. Immigrant whites, although familiar with African creole cultures, were not used to encountering full-fledged African religions complete with gods and priests. Some felt compelled to record their experiences with what they judged an exotic, primitive superstition. One consequence was the blossoming of interest in Voodoo, which found its most visible form in a surge of newspaper articles during the nineteenth and early twentieth century that addressed the religion. One far-from-complete compilation of these articles lists over 400 that appeared in New Orleans newspapers between 1820 and 1940. The newcomers' fascination with Voodoo was largely responsible for establishing New Orleans's reputation as one of the United States' major hubs of African American spirituality. The sensational nature of the portrayals, which sometimes bore titles such as

"Voudou Vagaries: The Spirit of Marie Lavau to be Propitiated by Midnight Orgi[e]s on the Bayou," both sold papers and guaranteed that the religion would have a none-too-favorable standing in the opinions of nonbelievers.[53]

A second influx of outsiders was to occur only a few years after the US acquisition of Louisiana. In the short run, these arrivals arguably had as great an impact on what is now southern Louisiana as the Americans. For example, in 1799, census takers recorded New Orleans's population as just over 8,000. By 1810, the population had more than doubled. Doubtless, some of the increase came in the form of white settlers from the city's new owners. Childbirth certainly accounted for additional growth. During this period, however, the largest single source of increase to the population of what is now Louisiana was the former French colony of Saint-Domingue, which had just gained its independence as Haiti. The migration into the Mississippi River valley lasted from the start of the slave-led revolution in 1791 until 1815, well after Haiti had established its independence, though it peaked in 1809–1810 in response to thousands of French colonials being expelled from Cuba, where they had temporarily settled following their exodus from Saint-Domingue. Though whites had the most reason to flee the wrath of slave rebels, many managed to bring bondspersons with them. Mixed race men and women—most free and some slaveholders themselves—doubled New Orleans's population of free people of color. All told, the arrivals added between 15,000 and 20,000 Francophone settlers to the Mississippi River valley, with perhaps as much as 90 percent settling in New Orleans and its vicinity.[54]

Haiti is itself home to Vodou, whose roots stretch back to a variety of African peoples, though those from the Bight of Benin and West Central Africa seem to have had the greatest influence on the religion. As with most Afro-Caribbean faiths, the process of creolization led to believers accepting many aspects of Catholicism into their beliefs, and Catholic prayers are commonly part of Vodou rituals. We know much about the religion's deities, called *lwas*, including that they are divided into a variety of nations based on their origin within Africa and that many correspond to specific Catholic saints. The gods are served by both male and female priests, known as *oungans* and *manbos*, respectively, who center their ritual activities around a temple or *ounfò*. Ceremonies typically involve offerings of foods to the gods, dancing, the making of ritual designs from corn meal or ashes known as *vèvès*, the waving of flags, and perhaps most importantly, the possession of the participants by the deities.

Though it is possible for anyone to follow the Vodou gods, a series of initiations are necessary to advance in spiritual knowledge and standing.[55]

The similarities between Vodou and Mississippi River valley Voodoo are striking, and it is understandable that some authors have simply treated the latter as a North American creolization of the former. Robert Tallant, for example, stated that it was the arrival of West Indian planters and slaves fleeing the revolution that "was to be the beginning of organized Voodoo in Louisiana."[56] His great critic, Zora Neale Hurston, wrote much the same, stating that the Saint-Domingue slaves "had retained far more of their West African background than the continental Blacks."[57] The massive influx of refugees doubtlessly reinforced the creole religion, especially as practiced in Louisiana, and almost certainly influenced its development and longevity.

On the other hand, the assumption that the introduction of Vodou was the foundation of Voodoo is unwarranted. For one, Du Pratz, who first recorded the use of the term *gris-gris* in Louisiana also mentioned gatherings of slaves to dance the Calinda, a dance that George Washington Cable later associated with Voodoo. Du Pratz himself stated that slaves made their gatherings into what he called a "Sabbath." Plus, many of the features of Haitian Vodou ceremonies were either rare or unknown in Voodoo. There are no mentions of the common Haitian religious ground drawings known as *vèvès,* for example, in Mississippi River valley sources. In addition, while many of the deities of Haiti were present in the Mississippi River valley, many others were not. Moreover, some gods recorded in Louisiana have no parallels in Haiti. Similarly, notable figures associated with Voodoo have little or no connection to Saint-Domingue. Famous practitioner Jean Montanée, or Dr. John as he was known to whites, was reportedly a native of Senegal. Marie Laveau was born in 1801, prior to the arrival of large numbers of refugees, and had no known ancestors from Saint-Domingue. Finally, while the idea that Voodoo originated in Haiti might be persuasive in the context of Louisiana, where so many Saint-Domingue refugees settled, it is less so when one considers manifestations of Voodoo in places further afield, such as Missouri.[58]

Clearly, Voodoo was no Haitian import. Similarities in dances, spirit possession, adoptions from Catholicism, and the like can be explained in part by later influences from the Saint-Domingue refugees and by the fact that both Voodoo and Vodou developed out of African roots within a French Catholic colonial context. Voodoo—despite its affinities with Haitian Vodou as well as other African creole faiths—is best understood as unique to the Mississippi River valley.

Though the Mississippi River valley, especially Louisiana, would retain some of its distinctiveness, it had firmly integrated into the United States by the 1840s. Antagonism between Creoles and Americans would continue, even while individual members of each population cooperated to build New Orleans into the second-largest city in the country by the time of the Civil War. Large numbers of Irish and German immigrants would further swell the region's population, much as they did elsewhere in the country. By 1862, the Lower Mississippi would become arguably the most important battleground of the Civil War, with South Louisiana occupied by Union troops for approximately three years.[59]

Throughout this period and beyond, Voodoo survived, with its existence emerging into the national consciousness as the nineteenth century progressed. The religion that caught the public's attention during the decades prior to 1900 had not been a static set of beliefs and rituals. Instead, it bore the imprint of the peoples who had shaped the environment in which it developed. At the same time, the racial outlook that had led to the importation of slaves to the region and the inadvertent development of Voodoo also motivated whites to despise the religion. Voodoo, by any measure, was both a regionally distinctive religion and a profoundly American faith.

2

AFRICAN SPIRITS
IN THE MISSISSIPPI
RIVER VALLEY

Throughout its history, the record of Voodoo has been fragmentary. For this reason, describing fine points of its theology, the precise roles of different leaders in the faith, the import of distinct ceremonies, and the full personalities and purviews of its deities is impossible. Nevertheless, during the period from the Civil War through World War II, the documentary record was better than before or after, with newspapers, magazines, archival manuscripts, and even novels preserving information on many aspects of the religion. For that reason, it is possible to construct something of a snapshot—albeit a blurry one—of Voodoo during that era, beginning with a sketch of the creole spiritual cosmos shaped by Africans and their descendants in the Mississippi River valley into an African diasporic religion unique to the region.

THE GODS

At the heart of what made the religion distinct from that of both the Christian majority and its historical antecedents were its deities. Disinterest and racism, sadly, has meant that there has never been a systematic listing of the divinities, much less an in-depth study. Moreover, one consequence of the death of Voodoo as an intact, living religion is that producing a complete catalog of the spirit world is no longer possible. Fortunately, enough fragmentary evidence exists to examine the gods whose names have survived in light of the much more plentiful information on their likely African forebears and Caribbean relatives.

The First Recorded Deities

References to specific Voodoo spirits began with an 1820 article in the *Louisiana Gazette*. The brief account described an illegal nighttime gathering of slaves, free Blacks, and one white that was broken up by local authorities. Among the sparse details included in the work are statements that the meeting took place in the Tremé suburb and that the attendees had been worshipping "an African deity called Vaudoo." Among the items seized by authorities was an image that the article described as "a woman, whose lower extremities resembled a snake."[1] While it is possible that the term *Vaudoo* or *Voodoo* was being used in reference to a specific deity, the witnesses or journalist most likely mistook a general term meaning "deity" or "spirit" as a proper name, a usage which is more in keeping with what one finds in connection with West African Vodun.[2]

More important to identifying a specific deity is the reference to the image of the woman whose legs appeared snakelike. One possibility is that it may have represented a local manifestation of an aquatic spirit known in much of Africa as Mami Wata and with a Haitian parallel in the *lwa*, called Lasirenn. In different parts of Africa, she is, among other things, a protector of those washing or bathing, a danger to travelers on rivers, and a source of other spirit beings. Believers commonly consider her to resemble a mermaid in that her lower body resembles that of a fish. Many depictions of Mami Wata include the presence of snakes, and some give her double tails, which can appear quite serpentine in their own right. Though less common than the half-fish, half-woman representations, Mami Wata sometimes appears as a woman with snake tails in the place of legs. Haiti's Lasirenn—likewise a mermaid—is a protector of fishermen and rescues victims of shipwreck. At the same time, she has a reputation for kidnapping young boys in order to bring them to her underwater realm. A second, less likely alternative is that the image was a version of a common representation of the Virgin Mary crushing a serpent under her heel. Archaeologist Kenneth Brown has argued that one such depiction of Mary, discovered during a dig at the Magnolia Plantation quarters near

Left, an image of Mami Wata with a serpent photographed in the fetish market in Abomey, Benin.

Right, a Haitian image of Lasirenn, a possible source or parallel for an image seized from a Voodoo ceremony in 1820, that appears in Lakou Letan Liben of Jérémie, Haiti.

Natchitoches, Louisiana, was connected with Voodoo. In the eyes of enslaved workers, the small metal pendant depicting the Virgin trampling a serpent underfoot while standing atop the globe may well have been associated with the Haitian *lwa* Ezili Freda, a spirit of love and beauty who originated in what is now Benin.[3]

Additional early mentions of deities come from two 1850 news articles that refer to an image or images called the "Voudou Virgin." The earlier of the two appeared on July 3, 1850, and described Marie Laveau's attempt to reclaim from city officials what the article referred to as "a statue of a virgin," which she claimed they had obtained through fraud. The author of the brief notice contemptuously described the image as a "bad looking rag-baby."[4] Near the end of the following month, a second article appeared. It reported on the seizure of Voodoo paraphernalia by police during a raid that had happened sometime prior. Among the items was a carved wooden "relic of reverence and veneration" that the author called the "Voudou Virgin." He described it rather unhelpfully as "something between a Centaur and an Egyptian Mummy."[5] Despite the conflicting descriptions, the chronological proximity of the two articles and the similar circumstances described in them makes it likely that both referenced the same image. If it had a connection to the Virgin Mary of Catholic belief, as its name suggests, then it may have represented a spirit described nearly a century later as Mama You or a deity whose name was never recorded.[6]

Monsieur Danny and Dambarra

Among the most commonly mentioned deities in the Louisiana variety of Voodoo was a spirit known variously as Monsieur Danny, Daniel Blanc, or Blanc Dani. The first work to reference him by name was George Washington Cable's novel, *The Grandissimes,* which appeared in 1880. Its brief reference to the Voodoo god merely described him as "the head imp of discord" and suggested the superstitious might credit him with some unpleasant weather described at that point in the book.[7] Five years later, famed journalist Lafcadio Hearn recorded a song, which he described as one that "used to be sung by Louisiana field hands," that called upon the deity as follows:

Tout, tout, pays blanc—Danié qui commandé,
    Danié qui commandé ça!
    Danié qui commandé.

Hearn, who did not recognize this Danié as a Voodoo spirit, translated the first line of the song as "All, all the country white (white man's country)—Daniel has so commanded." The second and third lines can be translated as, "Daniel has so commanded that! Daniel has so commanded." The journalist went on to speculate that perhaps the song referred to the biblical Daniel.[8]

That Hearn's Danié was almost certainly not the prophet Daniel can be confirmed by a second record of the song that appeared in a 1904 novel by Helen Pitkin, called *An Angel by Brevet: A Story of Modern New Orleans.* Her version reads as follows:

Blanc Dani,
Dans tous pays blanc
L'a commandé
Blanc Dani, Dans tous pays blanc
L'a commandé.[9]

It can be translated as "White Dani, in all the whites' country, there you rule. White Dani, in all the whites' country, there you rule."[10] In this fictional account, which the author claimed was firmly rooted in fact, the song is part of a Voodoo ceremony. Shortly after the congregation sings the song, the presiding priestess becomes possessed by a deity, apparently Monsieur Danny, and responds to a young woman's request for help winning a man's affections. Participants describe the being as a "gret sperrit" and a "white man."[11]

The Python Temple in Ouidah, Benin. The deity honored there, called Dan, was the original of Haiti's Danbala Wèdo and New Orleans's Monsieur Danny.

Monsieur Danny is a creole version of the Fon and Ewe deity Dan or Da, most prominently associated with the city of Ouidah in modern-day Benin. The city was once the heart of a small coastal kingdom, which was conquered by the expansionist Kingdom of Dahomey in 1727. Dan, envisioned as a heavenly python, was the primary deity of Ouidah, and following its fall became a major god in Dahomey as well. According to Vodun belief, the deity is ancient, having assisted in the creation of the universe, the motion and stability of which he continues to maintain. In its relationship with humankind, Dan is benevolent and associated with wisdom. Today, it is also prominently connected to wealth and prosperity. Often, Dan is understood as androgynous, or as part of a pair with a second serpent associated with the sky, Ayido Hwedo, who is visible as the rainbow. The Haitian version of this god, Danbala Wèdo, maintains many of its African characteristics. New World believers frequently understood him as a serpent of both earth and sky and as the husband of the heavenly rainbow serpent, Ayida Wèdo. In both its original homeland and in Haiti, Dan/Danbala is particularly associated with the color white.[12]

As with many other Voodoo spirits, the precise role of Danny of Louisiana is only partially clear. The multiple references to him and the surviving song, which speaks of him commanding in the country of the whites, demonstrate that he was of considerable importance, like his African and Haitian counterparts. The seemingly odd statement that he was envisioned as a white man is in keeping with Haitian Vodou, in which believers depict many of the *lwa* as white in their religious art. Haitian Vodou practitioners, for instance, identify Danbala with St. Patrick while simultaneously considering him a serpent *lwa*. Moreover, Dan and Danbala's preexisting association with the color white provided a route to his interpretation as a white man. On the other hand, George Washington Cable's identification of him as a spirit of discord was likely an error or captured only an aspect of a broader role as mover of the atmosphere. If Cable indeed meant to imply that Danny had a role in the workings of the weather, then his description was not out of keeping with African antecedents.[13]

Curiously absent from direct references to Monsieur Danny are descriptions of him as a serpent. That believers did consider him in that light, however, is indicated indirectly by the prominence of snakes in Voodoo ritual. For example, an 1875 account of a ceremony that supposedly took place around 1825, describes a man assisting the presiding priestess holding aloft a huge red-and-black snake of an indeterminate species, speaking to it, and passing it over the heads and laying it around the necks of participants. With each pass, he repeated the name "Voudou Magnian."[14] Decades later, Charles Raphael told interviewers working for the Federal Writers' Project that Marie Laveau never used live snakes but called upon "the spirit of the snake" in her rituals. Though no observers noted a connection between this snake spirit and Danny, the historical background of the deity renders it probable that they were one and the same.[15]

Considering that Monsieur Danny was almost certainly a serpent deity, one might well ask why the print sources do not make the connection explicit. One plausible answer is that the few writers to speak of the deity by name simply knew little about him. In fact, concluding anything else from available evidence is quite difficult. At the same time, Afro-Creole informants might have intended for their white questioners to remain in the dark, fully understanding that Christian listeners would be quick to associate Monsieur Danny with what the biblical book of Revelation called "that old serpent, which is the Devil, and Satan."[16] Moreover, despite the fact that serpent deities have appeared in diverse cultures around the globe, even those whites with a scholarly leaning were apt to find their veneration bizarre. The anonymous author of the nineteenth-century work, *Ophiolatreia: An Account of the Rites and Mysteries Connected with the Origin, Rise and Development of Serpent Worship in Various Parts of the World,* began by calling devotion to them "one of the most remarkable, and, at first sight, unaccountable forms of religion the world has ever known."[17] Building upon such fascination, ethnologist Joseph J. Williams effectively defined both the West African and Caribbean forms of Vodun/Vodou as what he called a "serpent cult" in his 1932 *Voodoos and Obeahs: Phases of West Indian Witchcraft.*[18] In such a cultural context, withholding information on the role of snakes in Voodoo was a wise course of action. After all, sharing too much could discredit one of the faith's chief deities.

Helen Pitkin mentions another spirit, Dambarra Soutons, who may well have been connected to Monsieur Danny. Though she gives no information about its form or function, the appearance of its name in a chant immediately following the name of another spirit called Vert Agoussou suggests that the two might be linked. Regardless of its ties to other divinities, the spirit is likely the same as a Monsieur D'Embarras referenced in 1880 by George Washington Cable as an "imp of death."[19] The similarity between the names Dambarra and

Danny as well as the close similarity between the former and the name for Haiti's serpent *lwa*, Danbala, suggests that the two could be connected or perhaps even the same deity. When the author asked Hounon Houna II, claimant to the supreme chieftainship of Vodun in Benin, and his court for ideas about the origin of Dambarra, they agreed that it was the rainbow serpent, Ayido Hwedo. A Professor Ganlononisimael in attendance explained further that Dan Bada is a praise name for the snake deity, which he described as both male and female, but added that in Benin, Ayido Hwedo is not associated with death. On another occasion, Hounon Nïmantchee, the head of Togo's Vodu priesthood, likewise identified Dambarra as a deity he called Dan Blada. Haitian Vodou ministers also tend to identify Dambarra as one of the divine serpents. For example, Euvonie Georges Auguste, a prominent *manbo* from Port-au-Prince, stated that it is identical to Ayida Wèdo and should therefore be associated with life and creation, adding that the apparent connection of Dambarra with death likely arose from the Vodou concept that new life grows out of death. A Jacmel Vodou *manbo* known as Madame Leslie stated that it was a snake spirit that can be found in places with many trees.[20]

Voodoo Magnan (also Magnian or Maignan), mentioned occasionally in the documentary sources, may likewise be connected with Danny. Much like Danny, each time the spirit appeared, it was a key part of ceremonies, and observers often linked it to a live snake. Cable, discussing him in an 1886 article on slave dances, treats *Voodoo* as a name and *Magnan* as a solemn title, though just what the latter meant is hard to determine. The word does not appear in modern French dictionaries. An Old French word, *magnan,* meant "worker," and it may well be the sense intended in the context of Voodoo, considering that the deity's devotees were calling on it for aid. The words, *magnane,* Louisianan French for "brandy," or *magnanime,* meaning "magnanimous," are possible original words that were altered either by the speakers or those who recorded their words. Of course, the term need not be French at all and could well be of Africa derivation.[21]

Spirits called Monsieur Danny or by connected names are not found outside of Louisiana, but a Grandfather Rattlesnake held a prominent place in the folklore of nineteenth-century African American Missourians. According to folklorist Mary Alicia Owen, those who hoped to serve as Voodoo ministers began to learn about Grandfather Rattlesnake and a dance in his honor following their initiation and instruction in the workings of magic. In keeping with African and Haitian concepts of Dan and Danbala, Rattlesnake was ancient, having originated while a supreme being, called Old Sun by one of Owen's informants, was creating animals from pieces of clay. Unlike every other being, Rattlesnake originated from a piece of Old Sun's body that the latter had torn from himself and thrown into nearby weeds. Rattlesnake was known for his wisdom and at one time had a female counterpart—a sister in this case—whom her brother later transformed into snakeweed after she repeatedly healed those he poisoned with his bite. In Owen's day, believers considered him the founder of Voodoo and performed a dance in his honor—reportedly circling around a living rattlesnake—in order to gain intelligence and cunning. Though it is possible that this local spirit may have originated independently, it seems unlikely in light of its similarities to Monsieur Danny, his African predecessor, and his Haitian parallel.[22]

Grand Zombi

Another Louisiana Voodoo deity strongly associated with serpents was Grand Zombi, but as with Monsieur Danny, this spirit's precise characteristics are hard to come by in the documentary record. An 1890 article in New Orleans's *Daily Picayune* described it as "the mysterious power which guards and over-shadows" followers of Voodoo. The anonymous author went on to portray it as particularly associated with the city's Congo Square, the making of gris-gris, and death. Two years later, the fictional short story "Clopin Clopant," also published in the *Daily Picayune,* spoke of it as a vengeful spirit from the former colony of Saint-Domingue that brought misfortune and death with it when it arrived in New Orleans alongside refugees who had fled the Haitian Revolution. An 1894 news article from the same paper linked him to the making of magical items and claimed that Black New Orleanians called upon him to help end a drought. Live snakes figured prominently in apparent connection with the Grand Zombi in an accompanying description of a St. John's Eve ceremony. Much later, an informant interviewed by a Federal Writers' Project worker stated that Zombi was the name of the snake that Marie Laveau kept to work magic of many sorts.[23]

The name *Grand Zombi* means something akin to "Great Spirit" in Louisiana French, indicating that it could well be a praise name or title for another spirit, potentially Monsieur Danny. The word *Zombi*, however, is probably of West Central African origin rather than from the Fon and Ewe languages from which *Danny* derived. Scholar of New Orleans Voodoo Carolyn Morrow Long connected the deity with Nzambi a Mpungu, supreme creator god of the West Central African Bakongo people. If that link is accurate, the historical similarity between the status and function of Nzambi a Mpungu and those of Dan would have provided potential grounds for merging in North America. On the other hand, among the Bakongo, the word *nzambi* can refer to a dead person when followed by that person's name, meaning that Grand Zombi could conceivably be a particularly important ancestral spirit.[24]

Alternatively, *Grand Zombi* could well derive from some other term, most likely one originating in the Kikongo language of the Bakongo or a related West Central African people. The prime candidate is the Kikongo *simbi,* a general term for water spirits. This interpretation is indirectly supported by a parallel situation in Haiti where a family of *lwa* known as Simbi survives. One of their number is known as Grand Simba and is the ancestor of the rest of the group. Moreover, while various members of the family are either associated with white and/or are envisioned as serpents, they are by no means identical with Danbala.[25]

This Grand Zombi-as-*simbi* interpretation may be embodied in the oldest surviving Voodoo song from the Mississippi River valley, written down during the Civil War, which went as follows:

> Simbé maman oun déré.
> Simbé! Simbé! Papa O
> Simbé! maman oun déré.
> puis: Assou Ladedan Lacatra,
> Assou Assou Ladedan.[26]

The song, which appeared in a pro-Union newspaper in 1863, was reportedly part of a ceremony during which participants called upon a spirit the journalist referred to as the "grand Simbé." The similarity in name and title meaning "great" suggests that it might well be a French form of the name later anglicized as Grand Zombi. Alexis Alarcón, an expert on both Haitian Vodou and Cuban Vodú, suggested that the song was a petition for aid to one of the spirits known in both Haiti and Cuba as Simbi.[27] In contrast, a group of scholars from the Centre International de Recherche-Education sur la Civilisation Kongo (CIRECK), led by Miabeto Auguste and Mbemba Lubienga Armel of the Republic of the Congo, suggested that the song derived from a Kikongo original that is traditionally sung at the birth of twins for the purpose of keeping away the devil. The 1863 Voodoo song, they stated, should be translated as follows:

> Catch, mother, the whites.
> Catch! Catch! Father, oh,
> Catch! Mother, the whites.
> Assou follow to capture the genitals.
> Assou follow to capture.

In the context of the American Civil War, the CIRECK scholars suggest it was a call that was meant to protect the South from northerners and that it calls on spirits to stop the northern soldiers by grabbing them by their reproductive organs. In this translation, *simbé,* rather than being a deity, is a verb meaning "catch," "arrest," or "hold." Assou, meanwhile, is a Congolese name that may have referred to a person present at the ceremony. On the other hand, perhaps both interpretations of the song hold elements of truth. After all, it makes just as much sense if one treats *simbé* as a noun rather than a verb.[28]

Further complicating matters is the fact that a Jan Zonbi (or Jean Zombie) exists among the *lwa* of Haiti and *luá* of Cuba. This spirit reportedly began its existence as a historical figure during the days surrounding the Haitian Revolution, when he was said to have killed French settlers on the orders of Jean-Jacques Dessalines. It is highly likely that this man intentionally drew on a Bakongo term—most likely *nzambi* used in the context of spirits of the dead—for his surname. Later generations would deify him. In modern Haiti, Jan Zonbi is one of the Gede *lwa* who are associated with death, though he is not a particularly prominent member of the family. Descendants of Haitians living in Cuba, whose ancestors immigrated to the area surrounding Santiago during the first half of the twentieth century, accord considerably greater importance to the *Guedé luá* they know as Zombí. He is the owner of cemeteries and allows sorcerers to make zombies of the walking dead variety. As such, he is respected but avoided.[29]

A final possibility, suggested by Carolyn Morrow Long, is that Grand Zombi was a creation of journalists who had heard stories of zombies, Haitian or otherwise. This seems unlikely, however, considering the difference between Louisiana's deity and the walking dead of Haiti. Moreover, the word

A modern New Orleans Voodoo altar built in 2022 for a Fet Gede Ceremony at the New Orleans Healing Center, honoring the Haitian Gede Family of *lwa*. Courtesy of Catherine Wessinger.

zombie was part of Louisianans' vocabulary before the first reference to Grand Zombi. For instance, the word zombie appeared in Cable's *Grandissimes,* where it meant "spirit" in 1880. An author styling himself J.A. used it similarly in a French poem he published in New Orleans's *Time-Democrat* in 1886, translating it as "specter." It also appeared in an 1887 collection of Louisiana folktales by Alcée Fortier, though it meant "wizard" there.[30]

Nevertheless, it is just possible that the term could have been introduced into French during the late nineteenth century and quickly fashioned into an imagined Voodoo deity. Published stories in English-language newspapers, for instance, sometimes mentioned beings known as zombis. A story initially called "The Unknown Painter" and featuring a spirit called the zombi began to circulate in American newspapers beginning with its printing in an 1838 edition of the *Wilmington Advertiser.* Over the years, variations appeared in many other periodicals across the nation through the 1890s. Another fictional tale that referenced a being called Zombi appeared as "A Romance of Martinique" in a Pennsylvania newspaper in 1879. Several others across the nation reprinted it in short order. The timing of these references was such that the word *zombi* could have conceivably gained currency in the lower Mississippi River valley through fictional accounts of a spirit thus named. [31]

While each of these theories of the origin of Grand Zombi has something in its favor, none of them is demonstrably the best explanation. The evidence, such as it is, points toward one of two mixed interpretations. First, Grand Zombi may have begun its existence as what the 1863 article called the "grand Simbé." Authors writing in English, already familiar with the word *zombi,* may well have used it to express the spoken *Simbé.* In this sense, the name *Grand Zombi* may have been an unintentional creation of journalists that they applied to a similarly named spirit. On the other hand, it is entirely possible that Grand Zombi and Simbé—like Jan Zonbi and the various Simbi of Haiti—were completely distinct beings, each with its own origin in West Central Africa and/or Haiti.[32]

Lébat

Lébat or Liba was another divinity to see frequent mention in the sources. As was true of other deities, he was first mentioned by George Washington Cable in *The Grandissimes,* where he was called Papa Lébat. Cable's brief description stated merely that he "keeps the invisible keys of all the doors that admit suitors" and that he favored libations of beer sweetened with black molasses.[33] Helen Pitkin also mentioned him under the name of Liba. In *Angel by Brevet*, she describes the opening of a Voodoo ceremony as beginning with a Hail Mary followed by participants chanting the following:

> Bon jour Liba,
> Ouvert la porte,
> Bon jour mon cousin.[34]

In translation, the invocation reads:

> Good day, Liba,
> Open the door,
> Good day my, cousin.[35]

As always, fictional accounts are problematic as sources for historical fact, but in this case, the authors seem to have expressed genuine Voodoo knowledge. For instance, two ceremonies described by Federal Writers' Project workers that seem to have honored Lébat as a central figure, included offerings of beer, though there is no evidence of it having been sweetened with molasses. One of the rituals also featured a sweet soft drink and various sweet foods.[36] A version of the chant, meanwhile, was recorded much later by Federal Writers' Project worker Robert McKinney, an African American. The context was preparation for a 1936 visit to a graveyard by McKinney, a fellow FWP worker, and the elderly Voodoo priestess called Madame Ducoyielle. As the group prepared to leave, its members lit two candles, passing the match under each after lighting it. As they allowed the match to burn out while holding it, Robinson called out "Labat ouvre la port," meaning, "Labat open the door," and she followed the statement with "Go spirits, open the way for us. Pass before us!"[37] A similar chant was in use during the nineteenth century, according to another woman interviewed by McKinney. In Haiti, calls for the local equivalent of Lébat, known as Legba, to open the gate for the *lwa* typically appear in the opening stage of ceremonies. Songs for Legba to open doors for the singers are also well known there as the *lwa* stands between the world of humans and that of the spirits. Likewise, a deity known as Legba and similar names across the Bight of Benin is associated with entrances, where his im-

A shrine to Legba at the entrance to the Attitijon Shrines near Lomé, Togo. While images to Legba were likely never quite so visible in the Mississippi River valley, he remained an important spirit in at least the New Orleans area.

ages frequently appear, and is the primary source of communication between humans and the spirits, or *vodun* as they are known in Benin.[38]

Beyond opening the way to the spirit world, Lébat was particularly associated with the St. John's Eve ceremonies that took place on June 23. According to FWP information, Alexander Augustin, celebrants would make circles in the water of Lake Pontchartrain near Spanish Fort and throw food into the lake. The purpose, as he understood it, was to thank Papa Le Bas, whose name either Augustin or the FWP worker translated to mean "the Father below" and whom the informant interpreted as Satan.[39] Former slave Josephine McDuffy similarly linked Lébat with St. John's Eve when she spoke with a Writers' Project worker. According to her, she once wanted to attend a ceremony in order to see a spirit she knew as "Papa Limba." Unfortunately, she provided no further information on just how the spirit and the day were connected.[40]

The frequency with which his sobriquet was recorded indicates that, as along the Bight of Benin and in Haiti, Lébat was particularly important. For example, Marie Dédé, who had been friends with Marie Laveau's daughter reported that the Voodoo Queen called on him, along with other spirits, by knocking on the floor and asking who was there. At times, what the informant called "Papa Lela" would respond from the ground. So prominent was Lébat that a Voodoo healer who worked with Laveau supposedly adopted the name Da-pa Laba. Details about the man are hard to come by, however, and only a single reference has survived in the documentary record. The informant, who had seen the healer dancing at a Voodoo ceremony in New Orleans's Congo Square more than half a century before, may well have mistaken a man possessed by Papa Lébat as a man named Da-pa Laba.[41]

Assonquer

Assonquer, who appears several times in the documentary record, is more mysterious than Lébat, but sources indicate he was associated with love and luck. Like some of his fellows, he appeared first in *The Grandissimes,* which characterizes him as the god of good fortune and depicts one of the protagonists calling upon him as part of a love spell. The materials employed in the ritual consist of a green wax candle, pound cake, natural sugarcane syrup, and cordial, implying that these represent his preferences. In contrast to the foregoing, a Voodoo practitioner interviewed by Federal Writers' Project workers referred to one On Sa Tier as "a spirit for bad news," though just what she meant by her statement is unclear.[42]

That Assonquer was indeed called upon in matters of love was confirmed by the best-known Depression-era Voodoo priestess, Lala Hopkins. According to her instructions, one could keep a man or woman at home by performing a ritual that required burning three white candles, drawing blood from one's arm, mixing the blood with black ink, and using the ink to write the name of one's beloved nine times. Having completed these steps, the performer was required to promise to pay a spirit she called "Onzoncare." Once proof of the lover's fidelity had been secured, Onzoncare would accept recompense in the form of a sheep's head with a bottle of whiskey poured in its mouth. The payee, so Hopkins stated, must place it under a tree at midnight and wear a red cap and red clothes but no shoes while doing so. The head's placement should be accompanied by the indebted man or woman stating "Onzo[ncare] this is for you."[43] A few days after Hopkins' recital, the government workers asked who the spirit was. The Voodoo woman simply described it as a spirit from "Tete Albert's book." The book she referenced, *Le Petit Albert*, was grimoire popular in France and its former colonies, but neither Onzoncare nor Assonquer appear in its pages.[44]

More mysterious than his purpose is his origin. Hounon Houna II stated that it was the American version of a deity known in Benin as Azewe, from the family of the healing and earth vodun, Sakpata. New World ministers proposed additional possibilities. Several Vodou *manbos* and *oungans* suggested that he was likely the equivalent to the *lwa* Onzonfè or Konzonfè, described by prominent *oungan* Eric Pierre of La Gonâve as related to Ogou Feray, *lwa* of war and iron. Both are members of the Petwo *nanchon* or nation, a group of fiery, powerful spirits, second only to the cool, even-tempered Rada nation in popularity. Unlike his more famous kin with far-reaching power, Onzonfè is specifically the *lwa* of wire or metal in the ground. Another elderly *oungan,* who went by the nickname "Hountor," stated that he had heard of Assonquer as a *lwa* localized in Saint-Marc, Haiti. In contrast, a famed Cuban Vodú priest of Haitian ancestry, Pablo Milanes, reported that the spirit was probably Osun Cla, a kind of Legba, which he described as possessing a mass of keys that can open all doors. Some American *manbos,* meanwhile, have described another possible correspondence, a *lwa* known as Ossange or Osanj, judged by Vodou believers to be part of the Nago *nanchon.* Like Onzonfè, Ossange is of the Ogou family of *lwa,* but believers classify him primarily as an herbal healer. He is also understood as a retired warrior, a priest of Danbala, and a sailor who serves with Agwé Tawoyo, chief *lwa* of the sea and its islands. Curiously, the functions of none of these Caribbean deities meshes well with the few known characteristics of Assonquer.[45]

Considering the bemusing lack of functional similarities between the Assonquer of the documentary record and his proposed originals, name resemblance is perhaps the best route to identifying the African deity from which he most likely developed. Among the possibilities suggested to the author, Onzonfè and Ossange appear to have at least at one time been the same spirit, as indicated by their connection to Ogou and their similar names. Meanwhile, Haiti's Ossange and the Azewe mentioned by Hounon Houna II share a common link to healing. The most likely origin of all these deities is the Yoruba deity known as Osanyin, a god of medicine whose symbol is a bird perched atop an iron bar, a symbol still employed in the Cuban religion of Lucumí or Santería, which also preserves Osanyin as an important *orisha*. While our knowledge of the historical Assonquer does not fit the much better documented Osanyin or his Caribbean counterparts, a lack of extant information may be the culprit rather than genuine dissimilarity.[46]

Agoussou

Cable also linked a second deity that he called Miché Agoussou, meaning Mr. Agoussou, to love and indicated that the divinity favored the color red.[47] Helen Pitkin referred to the same spirit as Vert Agoussou, *vert* being French for "green." Beyond the reference to color, Pitkin supplied little detail other than that Agoussou was the patron deity of a wangateur, or magic worker, she described. The existence of this spirit was confirmed by a lone reference in a Federal Writers' Project document, stating that he responded to calls by Marie Laveau by answering from the ground.[48]

Agoussou's ancestry is easy to trace, however, because he more or less maintained his original African name of *Agasu*. According to tradition, he was the offspring of one Aligbonon, daughter of the King of Tado, and a spiritual leopard, and is considered the ancestor of the Fon people of what is now Benin. His ancestral home was the city of Allada in the southern portion of the country. The kings of that city as well as Porto Novo and Abomey trace their descent from him, and he remains a deity associated with those of royal lineage. In addition to being a prominent forebear, he has risen into the ranks of *vodun*. In Haiti, it is as a *lwa* that he is remembered under the name Agasou. There, believers associate him with water, and he reputedly takes the form of a crab, an animal that scholar Alfred Métraux describes as having once aided Agasu during his human life.[49] Though Agoussou appears to have diverged considerably from his Fon origins, his presence in Louisiana, as in Haiti, indicates that perhaps members of the royal family found themselves enslaved there.

Jean Macouloumba

Several deities appear only once or twice in the documentary record, and for that reason are difficult to verify as genuine presences in the Mississippi River valley. Among the more likely to have been an actual Voodoo spirit was a being known as Jean Macouloumba or Caloumba to Pitkin and Colombo in an 1896 article entitled "Dance of the Voodoos" that appeared in New Orleans's *Times-Democrat*. Pitkin gives no information on his function other than to bring up his name in connection with pleas for healing and in magical work to cause sickness and death. The anonymous author of the earlier article—a particularly sensationalist piece—provided no description, only referencing what appears to have been his name in a song he reportedly heard during a St. John's Eve dance. The song itself references a spirit alligator and a fiddler crab, though it is unclear what the relationship between the two and Jean Macouloumba might have been.[50]

The nature of the works mentioning Jean Macouloumba—one fiction and one dedicated to titillating racist imagery—render any conclusion on his existence problematic. On the other hand, several of the divinities mentioned by Pitkin can be verified by consulting the Writers' Project papers. Moreover, the fact that the divinity appears in two sources under slightly different names suggests independent sources of information for each author. To further complicate matters, there is no readily identifiable original for the spirit in West Africa or Haiti, but there are some indications that perhaps the spirit, if it existed, came from West Central Africa. This possibility was proposed by Togolese Vodu priest Habadadzi Antoine, and some informants from the Republic of the Congo backed up the suggestion.[51] Members of CIRECK stated that the word *makulumba* can mean "a traveler who does not stop, only travels."[52] As an alternative, they suggested that Macouloumba could be related to the Atlantic Ocean, known as *Kalunga*. The former proposal is more probably correct, considering that it is identical in pronunciation to the American spirit's surname. Jean, they posited, might have derived from *Nza,* a contraction of the Kikongo *Nzambi*.[53]

To support their contention, the CIRECK scholars proposed a translation of one of the Voodoo songs honoring Jean Macouloumba that appeared in *Angel by Brevet*.[54] The original reads as follows:

Jean Macouloumba, honhé! honhé! honhé!
Jean! Jean! Laisse qua houmna pi no pou' l'elle bé na!
Caloumba! Gou-doung! Gou-doung! Gou-doung!

The francophone spelling should be corrected to Kikongo, they suggested, as follows:

> Nza Makulumba, howe! Howe! Howe!
> Nza! Nza! Laisse kwahuma na pi na pu lele bena!
> Kulumba! Ngundu! Ngundu! Nugundu!

This, in turn, they translated to read:

> God who never rests, honor! Honor! Honor!
> God! God! Let nature be at rest. They are sleeping.
> Never resting! Ngundu! Ngundu! Ngundu!

This song, the scholars explained, would most likely be used to ask God to calm a storm. They stated that within this context, *ngundu,* would be a loud drumbeat representing the sound of the tempest. Pitkin's version of the chant is not explicitly connected with storms, though it is an appeal to the spirit world for healing, a situation that the lyrics could fit reasonably well. Pitkin also described drumbeats linked to the gou-doung/ngundu sounds, but stated the words themselves were voiced by "frenzied revelers." To be sure, a firm determination on Jean Macouloumba's place in Mississippi River valley Voodoo is impossible, though the sparse evidence and support from West Central African scholars argues in favor of him having been a genuine spirit.[55]

Vériquité and Charlo

Two deities, Vériquité and Charlo, appear only in Pitkin's novel, though both were likely historical spirits. The former appears as little more than a name in two portions of the book, with a rare descriptive feature being that a New Orleans priestess burned a votive candle to him.[56] Charlo, on the other hand, received a more thorough treatment, with participants in a ceremony described as stooping to welcome him as if he was a young child and "stroking his head." The spirit then received offerings of a type of gingerbread known as stage planks along with sugared water. One of the characters further explained that those who encountered the spirit should provide whatever Charlo desired when he visited their houses but that stage planks and sugar water should always be offered. Pitkin followed this account by depicting a Voodoo priest possessed by Charlo who drank from a bottle of anisette and distributed information about how to heal the ill and to harm.[57]

Tracing Vériquité's development is quite simple because its name remains very similar to those of its African forebear and Haitian cousin. In what is now Benin, one Avrikiti or Avlekete is a deity of the sea, understood as the one who provides fish for humanity. His temples are typically located near the ocean.[58] According to folklorist Harold Courlander, the African spirit survived in Haiti under the name Avélékété. He found it most commonly in the northern part of the country, where believers considered it part of the Kongo and Petwo *nanchons.* The latter fact is rather odd considering that *nanchons* typically represent the African origin of the deities that compose them, which is clearly not the case for Avélékété. Milo Rigaud, in contrast, stated that what he knew as Aizan Avélékéthé was a member of the Rada *nanchon,* a designation more in keeping with its historical origin. Benjamin Hebblethwaite has noted that the *lwa* descended from Benin's Avrikiti or Avelekete appears most commonly in Haiti as Ayizan Velekete, going on to clear up the apparently contradictory accounts of Courlander and Rigaud by explaining that it is served in the Kongo, Petwo, and Rada *nanchons.* The Haitian *lwa* has diverged considerably from the original Avrikiti, having gone from male in Africa to female in the Caribbean and having become primarily a divinity of entrances and public places, including Vodou temples and markets, rather than the ocean. The shift in function is a consequence of the merging of Avrikiti with what had originally been a separate deity, known as Aizan or Ayizan in Benin, who has roughly the same function as Haiti's Ayizan Velekete.[59]

Despite the greater extent of information available on Charlo, his origin is a bigger mystery than that of Vériquité. There is no clear West African predecessor, but a former traditional religionist, Maviola Medard of the Republic of the Congo, suggested a West Central African origin. He posited that Charlo might well be the same as what he knew as Kalo. He described Kalo as someone who is "big and grown" but who looks like a child because he had been born a witch. *Oungan* Appolon Andy of Jérémie, Haiti, proposed an alternative, stating that Charlo was the same as a little-known *lwa* called Charles Nago, who is also a child spirit. Cuban priest Pablo Milanes indirectly supported this suggestion when he identified Charlo with St. Charlo, whom he agreed was a child. If, indeed, Charlo and Charles Nago are connected by more than the similarity of their names, their origin may well be the Nago—more commonly known as Yoruba—people. While both possibilities are suggestive, either identification is far from conclusive.[60]

Joe Feraille

Equally mysterious, but for unique reasons, is one Joe Feraille. Readily identified by folklorist Harold Courlander as the Louisiana equivalent of the Haitian *lwa* Ogou Feray, he is problematic in that no source links him to Voodoo worship. He is, instead, known through a few Louisiana folksongs recorded during the first half of the twentieth century. If Courlander was correct in his determination, Joe Feraille was quite likely a deity of iron and war, like his counterpart in Haiti and his presumed ancestors, the deity known to the Yoruba as Ogun and to the Fon and Ewe as Gu. Though evidence supporting Joe Feraille's place in the Voodoo pantheon is sparse, scholar Joshua Clegg Caffery has noted that the folkloric Joe Feraille shares the characteristics of capriciousness, jealousy, and impatience with Ogou Feray and that songs about the former sometimes resemble Haiti chants honoring the latter.[61]

Divinities from Missouri and Elsewhere

A handful of deities have been recorded only outside of Louisiana. One of them, reportedly worshipped in a settlement called the Gulf, near Lenox, Massachusetts, supposedly originated in Louisiana. According to an 1884 article, originally from a Boston newspaper but reprinted in Palmyra, Missouri's *Marion County Herald,* Gabriel Hoose and his wife, Celestia, brought it north after Mrs. Hoose stole its image from her Voodoo priest father six months or more prior to the story's publication. What the anonymous journalist called an "idol" was of cast bronze or brass and resembled a woman with a round, almost featureless face, exceptionally long arms, and "ample drapery." Its possessors referred to it as Eomny. The reporter decried the presence of Voodoo in the land of Cotton Mather and Jonathan Edwards and stated her belief that the Hooses were engaged in a scam in which they pocketed the offering money from their approximately thirty-member congregation. Despite both the journalist and her informants' description of Eomny as a Voodoo divinity, a being of this name is otherwise unknown in the religion and its African and Caribbean relations.[62]

In addition to the lonely Massachusetts deity, a handful of spirits from

Missouri Voodoo have survived in the documentary record, all of them preserved in the writings of folklorist Mary Alicia Owen.[63] The aforementioned Grandfather Rattlesnake was joined by Samunga, Old Sun, Old Boy and his wife, and the Moon in the role of divinities. Of these, Owen uncovered the least information about Samunga, whom she knew only as a being called upon when one went to gather mud for ritual use by saying:

> Minnie, no, no Samunga,
> Angee see sa soh Samunga.[64]

She gives a bit more detail about the others. Old Sun created living creatures from clay, Owen explained, and accidentally destroyed all but the turtle and the separately formed Grandfather Rattlesnake by breathing fire upon them. He then recreated life and climbed into the heavens to protect his creation from a second fiery destruction and from whence he illuminates the world during his waking hours. Old Boy and his wife, sometimes also known as Old Master and Old Mistress, Owen linked to conjure. Old Boy she further described as "an old devil." His wife, meanwhile, was a conjurer and dispenser of venom to snakes, and according to one informant, was the sister of Grandfather Rattlesnake. The last of the gods described by Owen was the moon, which her informants understood as a female frog who had volunteered to light the world while Old Sun slept. To bring this about, Grandfather Rattlesnake and his followers skinned her and placed her in the sky. While similar beings exist in Africa, their English names make linking them to any specific heritage in Africa or elsewhere difficult, though Owen concluded that they were created from the interaction of African and Native American beliefs.[65]

Other Deities

Finally, some divinities survive only as names recorded in old documents, while others were probably no more than creations of imaginative authors. Mama You is one of the former, with her lone mention being a brief reference in a 1939 Federal Writers' Project oral history. The only details supplied by the document are that she was "the mother of the child Jesus" and that she would sometimes answer from the ground when called by Marie Laveau. The informant included Mama You's name among the epithets of other deities who can be independently verified, however, making it probable that she was a genuine spirit. West African and Haitian practitioners variously suggested that Mama You was not present in their countries; that she was the equivalent of their Grann Aloumba, Mama Brijit, or Mami Wata/Lasirenn; or that she was a deity confined to a specific locale but otherwise unknown. In light of the widely divergent responses, it seems more likely that the Writers' Project informant was mistaken about the name or that Mama You was unique to Louisiana.[66]

Among divinities of dubious authenticity is what may have been a spirit known as Héron, which was referenced in a chant published by George Washington Cable in his 1886 article, "Creole Slave Songs." The chant read as follows:

Hé-ron man-dé, Hé-ron man-dé, Ti-gui li pa-pa, Héron man-dé, Ti-gui li pa-pa, Hé-ron man-dé, Hé-ron man-dé, Hé-ron man-dé, Do sé dan go-do.[67]

Cable learned the chant from journalist Lafcadio Hearn but was unable to translate it. While Cable's rendering of the song seems to treat *Héron* as a name, it may well be something else entirely or may simply refer to the type of bird known in French as a héron and in English as a heron. That there is no African or Haitian deity of the name known to have been connected to the faiths that would later contribute to the shaping of Voodoo suggests that Héron should not be numbered among the Voodoo pantheon.[68]

Two well-known authors of the pre–World War II era introduced several deities of debatable authenticity into the lore of New Orleans Voodoo. Lyle Saxon was the first to do so in a 1927 article for the *New Republic,* entitled "Voodoo." It described the writer's recent attendance at a Voodoo gathering. During the ceremony, a priestess named Mamma Phemie reportedly credited a spirit called Pichotee for revealing to her that the author's life was in danger. No other author has identified a divinity of this name in the Mississippi River valley, Africa, or the Caribbean.[69]

Four years later, Zora Neale Hurston published "Hoodoo in America," in which she named five spirits: the Great One, Great Moccasin, Kangaroo, Jenipee, and Death. The last of these, described by Hurston as a being called upon to kill others, is impossible to either verify or discount as a Voodoo spirit because of the near-universal belief in spirits who function as bringers of death. Kangaroo and Jenipee, who stop one from worrying and hold sway over weddings, respectively, appear nowhere else in the literature of Voodoo and have no clear African or Caribbean antecedents. Moccasin was reportedly a source of power and a motivator of the other spirits. The Great One, who Hurston claimed became her patron through an initiation, spoke through storms and was reportedly honored with offerings that included among other items serpent-shaped bread and two bouquets of yellow, red, and white flowers. The serpent motifs and the connection of the Great One with storms suggest that they may have ties with Monsieur Danny or Grand Zombi.[70]

In light of the sparse evidence for deities introduced by Saxon and Hurston, it may well be that they were the creations of the authors. Though they were skilled writers, their Voodoo-related works tended toward the sensational. Moreover, both have reputations as being somewhat unreliable. Historian Lawrence N. Powell, for example, has described other of Saxon's writings as "more anecdotal reinvention than anything else."[71] Hurston is known to have misrepresented some of her sources and to have passed off fiction as folklore in "Hoodoo in America" and elsewhere.[72]

Of course, it is possible that the authors did not engage in deception. It may be that the spirits they described existed only in the Mississippi River valley and, like Mama You, just happened to have their names recorded very late in the history of Voodoo. On the other hand, it may have been the authors rather than their readers who were the first to receive false names. The practice of hiding the true names of deities from outsiders by substituting other sobriquets in their places exists in Haiti today. As *oungan* Oreste Crénio of Artibonite, Haiti, explained, true names are required to summon a divinity. Guarding such names prevents others from utilizing their power. While it may be that Saxon and Hurston's informants withheld divinities' true names, there is no evidence that they did so or that any other Louisiana Voodoo priest engaged in such substitution. It seems likely, but far from certain, that the names originated with the authors.[73]

Table 1. The Deities of Voodoo

Independent First Name	Characteristics	Source Recorded	Confirmation	Origin
Vaudoo or Voodoo Magnian	Powerful deity; sometimes depicted as chief of the deities	1820	Yes	Fon, Ewe
Unnamed female deity	Statue of a female with lower limbs resembling serpents; possibly linked with the worship of Vaudoo	1820	No	Insufficient information
Unnamed female deity	Statue of a female that resembled either a rag doll and/or a cross between an Egyptian mummy and a centaur	1850	Yes	Insufficient information
Simbé	Reportedly a Voodoo spirit called upon during the Civil War to aid the Confederacy	1863	Yes, if identical to Grand Zombi	Probably Bakongo; *simbé* may be a different word meaning "catch" or "hold," though Cuban scholar Alexis Alarcón believes it to be the same as the Cuban Vodú and Haitian Vodou deity Simbi
Miché Agoussou, Mon Agoussu, Vert Agoussou, or Yon Sue	Deity of love; represented by St. Anthony or St. Peter	1880	Yes	Fon
Assonquer, Onzoncare, or On Sa Tier	Deity of good fortune or bad news; represented by St. Paul	1880	Yes	Fon, Ewe, Yoruba
Monsieur Danny, Daniel Blanc, Danié, or Blanc Dani	Deity of discord; possibly also connected with storms; described by one source as being a white man; represented by St. Michael	1880	Yes	Fon, Ewe

Table 1. The Deities of Voodoo (*continued*)

Independent First Name	Characteristics	Source Recorded	Confirmation	Origin
Papa Lébat, Laba, Liba, Legba, Papa La Bo, Lela, or Limba	Keeper of entrances; opens communication with deities; represented by St. Peter or St. Anthony	1880	Yes	Fon, Ewe, Yoruba
Monsieur D'Embarras or Dambarra Soutons	Deity of death	1880	Yes	Likely Fon, Ewe
Grand Zombi	Important Voodoo spirit who may be the same as Voodoo Magnian, Monsieur Danny, and/or Simbé; associated with gris-gris, rain, and death	1880; or if Simbé, 1863	Yes, but primarily through the existence of the common noun "*zombie*"	Probably Bakongo
Zombis	Multiple spirits with unknown powers; possibly another name for the spirits of the dead or a general name for deities	1880	Yes	Multiple possibilities, though Bakongo seems most likely
Eomny	Represented in Massachusetts by a molded figure of a woman with very long arms, a rounded face, and "ample drapery"	1884	No	Claimed to be of Congo origin by its female owner and to have been brought from Louisiana to Massachusetts by her and her husband sometime between 1882 and 1884
Héron	Unknown, though context suggests it is possibly a name for a deity	1886	No	Insufficient information
Samunga	Called on by Missouri practitioners when gathering mud	1891	No	Probably West Central Africa based on similarities to modern names in the region

Table 1. The Deities of Voodoo (*continued*)

Independent First Name	Characteristics	Source Recorded	Confirmation	Origin
Grandfather Rattlesnake	Uncreated serpent spirit from dawn of creation	1893	Indirectly as Monsieur Danny	Probably Fon and Ewe influenced by Native American beliefs
Old Sun	Creator	1893	No	Probably mixed Christian and Bight of Benin ideas of creator deities
Old Boy and Wife	A devil and his wife, the latter of whom gives venom to snakes	1893	No	Probably mixed Christian and African ideas of tricksters
The Moon	Female divinity; understood as a skinned frog who volunteered to light the world; controls the growth of plants and movements of waters	1893	No	Unclear origin but possibly Native American (Cherokee folklore, for instance, associates the moon with water and a frog)
Colombo, Jean Macouloumba	Unknown	1896	Yes	Insufficient information but possibly Kongo
Vériquité	Depicted in source as being involved in a love spell; represented by St. Joseph	1904	No	Fon, Ewe
Charlo	Child spirit	1904	No	Possibly Yoruba or Kongo
Pichotee (of uncertain authenticity)	A spirit who reveals danger	1927	No	Insufficient information
Great One (perhaps identical to Blanc Dani)	Connected with storms and snakes	1931	No	Insufficient data but bears a resemblance to African snake deities

Table 1. The Deities of Voodoo (*continued*)

Independent First Name	Characteristics	Source Recorded	Confirmation	Origin
Great Moccasin (perhaps identical to Great One)	Gaining power	1931	No	Insufficient data but bears a resemblance to African snake deities
Kangaroo	Stops petitioners from worrying	1931	No	Insufficient data
Jenipee	Marriages	1931	No	Insufficient data
Death (probably identical to Monsieur D'Embarras)	Causes deaths for petitioners	1931	Yes, though by another name	Widespread in traditional religions
Joe Feraille	Mischievous character from Louisiana folk songs who may be connected with Voodoo	1934	Yes	Fon, Ewe, and Yoruba via Haiti
Mama You	Represented by St. Mary, mother of Jesus	1939	No	Insufficient data
Spirits of the dead	Aid or harm the living	Best attested in the early twentieth century	Yes	Widespread in traditional religions
Animistic spirits	Various roles	Attested through charms and in Missouri Voodoo tales, which treat them as important gods	Yes	Widespread in traditional religions

Sources: "Idolatry and Quakery," *Louisiana Gazette,* 16 August 1820, 2; "Curious Charge of Swindling," *Daily Picayune,* 3 July 1850, 2; "Obtaining a Statue Under False Pretenses," *Daily Delta,* 3 July 1850, 3; "The Virgin of the Voudous," *Daily Delta,* 10 August 1850, 2; "Tribulations des Voudous," *L'Union,* 1 August 1863, 1; "Voudooism," *Daily Picayune,* 22 June 1890, 10; Marie Louise Points, "Clopin-Clopant: A Christmas Fragment of Early Creole Days," *Daily Picayune,* 25 December 1892, 22; "Popular Superstitions and the Long Drought," *Daily Picayune,* 18 October 1894, 3; George Washington Cable, "Creole Slave Songs," *Century Magazine* 31 (1886): 815–817, 820; Mary Washington, interview by Robert McKinney, transcript, Northwestern State University of Louisiana, Watson Memorial Library, Cammie G. Henry Research Center, Federal Writers' Project, folder 25, 8; "Marie Leveaux," transcript, Northwestern State University of Louisiana, Watson Memorial Library, Cammie G. Henry Research Center, Federal Writers' Project, folder 25, 2; George Washington Cable, *The Grandissimes: A Story of Creole Life* (New York: Charles Scribner's Sons, 1880), 99, 101, 182, 184, 253, 257, 447; Lafcadio Hearn, *"Gombo Zhèbes.": Little Dictionary of Creole Proverbs, Selected from Six Creole Dialects* (New York: Will H. Coleman, 1885; reprint Bedford, MA: Applewood, n.d.), 39, n. 2; *Picayune's Guide to New Orleans,* 2nd ed. (New Orleans: Picayune, 1900), 66; Catherine Dillon, "Voodoo, 1937–1941," transcript, Northwestern State University of Louisiana, Watson Memorial Library, Cammie G. Henry Research Center, Federal Writers' Project, folders 118, 317, and 319, sec. "Louisiana," 4, sec. "Marie the Mysterious," 3:1, 4:8, 5:7, 9, 18A-18B, 20, 6:5A, sec. "St. John's Eve," 27, sec. "Voodoo Openings," 21–24; Claude F. Jacobs and Andrew J. Kaslow, *The Spiritual Churches of New Orleans: Origins, Beliefs, and Rituals of an African-American Religion* (Knoxville: University of Tennessee Press, 1991), 83–84; "Idol Worship in Massachusetts," Palmyra, Missouri *Marion County Herald,* 14 December 1884, 6; Mary Alicia Owen, "Among the Voodoos," in *The International Folklore Congress 1891: Papers and Transactions* (London: David Nutt, 1892), 242; Owen, "Voodooism," 313–317; Anderson, "Research Journals," vol. 3, 101–3, 143; vol. 4, 192–3, 234; Hudson, *Southeastern Indians,* 126–127; "Dance of the Voodoos," *The Times-Democrat,* June 24, 1896, 2; Helen Pitkin, *An Angel by Brevet: A Story of Modern New Orleans* (Philadelphia: J. B. Lippincott, 1904), 194–196, 204–206, 208, 210–211, 267–270, 273–286; Harry Middleton Hyatt, *Hoodoo-Conjuration-Witchcraft-Rootwork,* 5 vols, Memoirs of the Alma Egan Hyatt Foundation (Hannibal, MO: Western Publishing Company, 1970–1978), 773–775, 1295–1309; Robert Farris Thompson, *Face of the Gods: Art and Altars of Africa and the African Americas* (New York: Museum for African Art, 1993), 161; Robert Farris Thompson, *Flash of the Spirit: African and Afro-American Art and Philosophy* (New York: Random House, 1983), 108, 117–131, 166–167; Hans-W. Ackermann and Jeanine Gauthier, "The Ways and Nature of the Zombi," *Journal of American Folklore* 104 (1991): 467–469; Lyle Saxon, "Voodoo," *The New Republic,* 23 March 1927, 136; Zora Neale Hurston, "Hoodoo in America," *Journal of American Folklore* 44 (1931): 319, 359, 362–363; Joshua Clegg Caffrey, *Traditional Music in Coastal Louisiana: The 1934 Lomax Recordings,* with a foreword by Barry Jean Ancelet (Baton Rouge: Louisiana State University, 2013), 102–103, 180–1811, 239–40; Harold Courlander, *The Drum and the Hoe: Life and Lore of the Haitian People* (Berkeley: University of California Press, 1960), 321; Dédé, interview by McKinney and Arguedas, 2–3; Jeffrey E. Anderson, *Conjure in African American Society* (Baton Rouge: Louisiana State University Press, 2005) 32–33, 58; Carolyn Morrow Long, *A New Orleans Voudou Priestess: The Legend and Reality of Marie Laveau* (Gainesville: University Press of Florida, 2006), 106, 114–116.

The spirits of the dead were also important to the spiritual world of Voodoo. Mrs. Robinson, the Voodoo priestess interviewed by Robert McKinney in 1936, gave perhaps the most insight into the Mississippi River valley Voodoo concept of the place of ancestral spirits when she took McKinney and fellow Federal Writers' Project worker Hazel Breaux, who was white, to a series of graveyards and explained to them various methods and purposes for calling upon the dead. After writing names—apparently of enemies—inside colored shells at the front of some tombs, placing a nickel into another sepulcher, and calling out in front of another, "Help us, defend us, let us command all of them, let us conquer all," they stopped at the last resting place of one Gaston Bonnafon, a nineteenth-century Democratic Party operative who later found himself imprisoned for operating an illegal lottery.[74] There, Robinson spoke to the wife of Bonnafon, swearing to bring the whiskey the dead woman liked next time she visited. At the grave of a Dr. Faget she had known when he was a young child, she promised to bring apples. Breaux later mentioned that during this or a subsequent visit, Robinson had left a helping of *congris,* composed of cow peas and rice, under a concrete flowerpot at the same tomb. In the midst of her activities, she explained to the FWP employees that one should always reward the spirits with what they like whenever they favor you. Upon an earlier occasion, she had explained that the deceased like the same things as they had while alive. At the tomb of her godfather, Clement St. Cyr, she shouted that he had to grant her wish. In short, if Mrs. Robinson was a typical practitioner, Voodoo treated the dead as very much a part of everyday life who were glad to help those who treated them well and could even be pressured into service by those to whom they had been connected in life.[75]

While Robinson's account indicates that believers commonly relied on the spirits of those they had known in life, others were more widely respected. According to Robert McKinney, for instance, a wall vault tomb he visited with Mrs. Robinson was "filled with red brick crosses," presumably resembling those that believers (and tourists) drew on Marie Laveau's grave until recent years when access to St. Louis Cemetery No. 1 has been severely restricted.[76] As one drew the cross, explained McKinney, he or she was to make a wish. Robinson averred that the tomb's inhabitant always granted such requests. The vault belonged to a Voodoo priestess Robinson called "La Beaute Comptesse,"

Candles in a wall tomb from St Louis Cemetery Number 2 in New Orleans Louisiana.

but at the time, many mistakenly believed it belonged to Laveau, another indication that it was widely discussed, albeit inaccurately. Less spectacularly, the group noted that someone had left a lottery ticket at the tomb of Dominique You, a pirate in life. Robinson interpreted this as a sign of good fortune, indicating that she shared a common understanding with the unknown person who had visited the sepulcher previously.[77]

At least one spirit of the dead gained special prominence. By the 1930s, Marie Laveau was treated more like a minor deity than a typical ancestor. Mrs. Robinson and a white coworker, Mrs. Dereco, stated that the long-dead queen helped supplicants obtain money if they would take a pint of milk to Congo Square and pour it three times into holes there. While doing so, they were to say, "Marie Laveau, this is for you, for money, to get plenty of money. Open the door in necessity."[78] The statement is reminiscent of calls to Lébat and may

The grave of New Orleans's most famous Voodoo practitioner, Marie Laveau. Photograph taken ca. 2001.

well reflect a close association between the priestess and divinity that some informants reported. Even more telling, Robinson considered Laveau's spirit important to the process of gaining control over evil spiritual beings. According to her, after selling one's soul to the devil, the supplicant should then pray both to him and to the Voodoo Queen. As part of the prayers, one should ask

Laveau to kill him or her if ever he or she turned on Satan. The testimony of Lala Hopkins likewise situates Marie Laveau in a highly honored place among the dead. Hopkins reported that she placed flowers on the priestess' grave and prayed to her for assistance. A Federal Writers' Project worker also noted Laveau's picture prominently displayed in Hopkins' home.[79]

Though precise details of the role of the dead in Voodoo come from only a handful of sources, the importance of human spirits to the religion can be independently confirmed by the importance of graveyard dirt to the supernaturalism of the area. During 1938 and 1940, folklorist Harry Middleton Hyatt twice visited the Crescent City, collecting several accounts of graveyard dirt used in hoodoo. Although in most cases, he noted little information on the precise role of the spirits of the deceased, in one instance, he recorded that soil taken from what his informant called "a sinner-man's grave" could be utilized to protect oneself from harm. The fact that the person buried in the grave was of key importance indicates that at least in some supernatural work, specific spirits of the dead played key roles in the effectiveness of the graveyard dirt.[80]

Moreover, the concept of using spirits of the dead through the medium of graveyard dirt is very much in keeping with West Central African prac-

Graveyard dirt, human bones, and other magical items used by an Ngunza priest for supernatural work. Photographed in Brazzaville, Republic of the Congo.

tices. Roch Mampouya, a minster from Brazzaville who practices the modern manifestation of traditional religion known as Ngunza, uses dirt from specific graves to restore marriages and to help incarcerated people gain their release. As he explains it, the spirits lead him to the best graves for the job at hand, and he calls on the spirits within them to work on his behalf. Such practices would likely have been as intelligible to a nineteenth-century Voodoo priest or priestess as they are to a modern Ngunza practitioner.[81]

WHY SOME GODS AND NOT OTHERS:
AFRICA, HAITI, LOUISIANA, AND HISTORY

So, what can one say with confidence about the origins of the Voodoo gods? Of those deities whose presence in the Mississippi River valley has been confirmed by independent sources, five have clear-cut spiritual ancestors who inhabit the Vodun religion of the Bight of Benin region of Africa. Though less certain, Dambarra Soutons appears to be of the same extraction. If one also includes the Joe Feraille of folksong among their number, then there were seven total deities confirmed from the area. Simbé/Grand Zombi, meanwhile, appear to hail from West Central Africa, and the same is true of the name *zombi* as a class of spirits. Jean Macouloumba likely arrived from the same geographical region. These yield a total of two or three, depending on whether one judges Simbé and Grand Zombi distinct deities or one. Spirits of the dead cannot be definitively connected to any one part of Africa as they exist across most of the sub-Saharan portion of the continent.

Among the many gods claimed for the religion whose existence cannot be verified, Vériquité, Charlo, Mama You, and the unnamed images reported in the first half of the nineteenth century seem the most likely to have existed. If genuine, Vériquité was almost certainly the North American manifestation of a deity from modern Benin. The little evidence available suggests a Congolese or Yoruba origin for Charlo. Mama You cannot be tied to any one region. The images are problematic because those who described them did so incompletely and with little context. Those remaining unverified are difficult to connect to any particular portion of the continent, further calling into question their existence.

Altogether, the tally of definite and likely points of origin stands at eight or nine for the Bight of Benin and three or four for West Central Africa. The prominence of spirits of the dead may indicate additional West Central African influence because ancestor veneration was particularly prominent there, but the fact that ancestral spirits are part of religions throughout the sub-Saharan portion of the continent renders any such assumption problematic. What is clear, however, is that while the Bight of Benin appears to have contributed the most deities to the faith, it was certainly not the sole origin of the religion.[82] The situation parallels that of Haiti, where believers link *nanchons* of *lwa* with specific African homelands. Moreover, the relative positions of spirits from the Bight of Benin and West Central Africa are roughly equivalent to that found in Haiti. Among believers in the Caribbean nation, the Rada *lwa* of the Bight of Benin are the most prominent *nanchon*. Second in importance are the Petwo spirits, who are predominantly from West Central Africa.[83]

Along with the sheer number of Haitian immigrants to southern Louisiana, such similarities raise the question of whether scholars should understand Mississippi River valley Voodoo as an outgrowth of Haitian Vodou instead of a direct import from Africa. Of the confirmed Louisiana deities, Miché Agoussou, Monsieur Danny, Papa Lébat, and Vériquité are easily recognized as the North American manifestations of Haiti's Rada *lwa* Agasou Gnenen, Danbala Wèdo, Legba, and Ayizan Velekete, respectively.[84] Monsieur D'Embarras, Joe Feraille, Assonquer, Mama You, and the unnamed female figure with serpentine legs may have Rada counterparts as well. The Mississippi River valley spirit most likely to have a Haitian counterpart from outside the Rada *nanchon* is Simbé/Grand Zombi, whose counterpart (or counterparts) would be found within the Simbi and/or Gede families. Charlo could be the minor *lwa* known as Charles Nago, and Jean Macouloumba might be one Aloumba or Grann Aloumba. Neither identification is close to being certain, however. Such commonalities suggest that Haitian influence on Voodoo, at least in Louisiana, was significant.[85]

A tendency to minimize the importance of some African deities in both Haiti and the Mississippi River valley bolsters evidence supporting the connection. For example, Sakpata, a divinity of the earth, illness, and healing and one of the most prominent spirits of West African Vodun had no known presence in the Mississippi River valley and had little visibility under that name in Haiti, though there is a *lwa* named Bosou, which was one of the alternate names for Sakpata in what is now Benin. The same can be said of Xevioso, a major god of thunder and lightning in what is now Benin. Though he appears in Haiti, he is relatively minor, and his presence has gone unrecorded in the Mississippi River valley. While the relative absence of such deities may indicate Haitian influence, the Mississippi River valley's sparse records or similar conditions during the slave trade could be the culprits as well.[86]

Table 2. Voodoo Gods and Haitian Equivalents

Mississippi River Valley Name	Mississippi River Valley Name	Found in Haiti	Haitian Name	Haitian Characteristics
Vaudoo or Voodoo Magnian	Powerful deity	No		
Unnamed female deity	Statue of a female deity with lower limbs resembling serpents; possibly linked with the worship of Vaudoo	Possibly	Possibility 1: Lasirenn Possibility 2: Less likely Ezili	Possibility 1: Mermaid *lwa* sometimes associated with Our Lady of the Assumption, St. Martha, and Saint Philomena Possibility 2: Lwa representing love, beauty, motherhood, and other qualities connected with femininity; associated with Mater Dolorosa and other representations of the Virgin Mary
Unnamed female deity	Statue of a female deity who resembled either a rag doll and/or a cross between an Egyptian mummy and a centaur	Unknown		
Simbé	Reportedly a Voodoo spirit called upon during the Civil War to aid the Confederacy; may be the same as Grand Zombi	Likely	Possibility 1: Simbi Possibility 2: Jan Zombi Possibility 3: Praise name of another deity	Possibility 1: Healing *lwa* associated with freshwater and coasts, represented by St. Christopher Possibility 2: Ferocious minor spirit of a historical Haitian revolutionary Possibility 3: Another deity

Table 2. Voodoo Gods and Haitian Equivalents (*continued*)

Mississippi River Valley Name	Mississippi River Valley Name	Found in Haiti	Haitian Name	Haitian Characteristics
Héron	Unknown, though context suggests it is possibly a name for a deity	No		
Miché Agoussou, Mon Agoussu, Vert Agoussou, or Yon Sue	Deity of love, represented by St. Anthony or St. Peter	Yes	Agasou Gnenen	Healing *lwa* associated with bodies of water; represented by large crabs
Assonquer, Onzoncare, or On Sa Tier	Deity of good fortune; represented by St. Paul	Likely	Possibility 1 (preferred by American *manbos*): *Lwa* known as Osanj, Ogou Ossange, or Osanyin	Possibility 1: Retired warrior *lwa* and healer
			Possibility 2 (preferred by Haitian *manbos* and *oungans*): *Lwa* known as Ozanfè or Konzonfè	Possibility 2: Similar to Ogou but a *lwa* of the wires or metal in the ground
				Possibility 3: Minor spirit associated with Saint-Marc
			Possibility 3: A Haitian oungan seemed to recognize the name as one belonging to a spirit in Saint-Marc.	
Monsieur Danny, Daniel Blanc, or Blanc Dani	Deity of discord; possibly also connected with storms; represented by St. Michael	Yes	Danbala Wèdo	Serpent *lwa* representing fertility and associated with St. Patrick

Table 2. Voodoo Gods and Haitian Equivalents (*continued*)

Mississippi River Valley Name	Mississippi River Valley Name	Found in Haiti	Haitian Name	Haitian Characteristics
Papa Lébat, Laba, Liba, Legba, Papa La bo, Lela, or Limba	Keeper of entrances; opens communication with deities; represented by St. Peter or St. Anthony	Yes	Legba	*Lwa* of gateways, crossroads, and highways who opens communication with the other *lwa;* associated with St. Peter
Monsieur D'Embarras or Dambarra Soutons	Deity of death	Likely	Likely Ayida Wèdo	If Ayida Wèdo, a serpent *lwa* and wife of Danbala Wèdo, representing fertility and the rainbow and associated with the Miraculous Mother
Grand Zombi	Important Voodoo spirit, whose name means roughly the same as Voodoo Magnian, making it likely that the terms refer to the same being	Likely	Possibility 1: Simbi Possibility 2: Jan Zombi Possibility 3: Praise name of another deity, possibly Danbala Wèdo	Possibility 1: Healing *lwa* associated with freshwater and coasts; represented by St. Christopher Possibility 2: Ferocious minor spirit of a historical Haitian revolutionary Possibility 3: Another deity
Zombis	Multiple spirits with unknown powers; possibly another name for the spirits of the dead or a general name for deities	Yes	*lwa*	General term for Vodou deities
Eomny	Represented in Massachusetts by a molded figure of a woman with very long arms, a rounded face, and "ample drapery"	No		

Table 2. Voodoo Gods and Haitian Equivalents (*continued*)

Mississippi River Valley Name	Mississippi River Valley Name	Found in Haiti	Haitian Name	Haitian Characteristics
Samunga	Called on by Missouri practitioners when gathering mud	No		
Grandfather Rattlesnake	Uncreated serpent spirit from the dawn of the world	Yes	Danbala Wèdo	Serpent *lwa*, representing fertility and associated with St. Patrick
Old Sun	Creator	Yes	Bondye	Supreme creator god
Old Boy and Wife	A devil and his wife, the latter of whom gives venom to snakes	No		
The Moon	Female divinity; understood as a skinned frog who volunteered to light the world; controls the growth of plants and movements of waters	No		
Vériquité	Depicted in sources as being involved in a love spell; represented by St. Joseph	Yes	Ayizan Velekete	*Lwa* of temples, public places, entrances, and roads, associated with images of Christ being Baptized by John the Baptist
Charlo	Child spirit	Possibly, though most Haitian *manbos* and *oungans* did not recognize it	Possibly Charles Nago	Child *lwa*

Table 2. Voodoo Gods and Haitian Equivalents (*continued*)

Mississippi River Valley Name	Mississippi River Valley Name	Found in Haiti	Haitian Name	Haitian Characteristics
Colombo or Jean Macouloumba	Unknown	Possibly, though Haitian *manbos* and *oungans* were divided	Possibly Aloumba or Grann Aloumba	*Lwa* from the Jérémie area; white and old; trembles and cannot stand
Pichotee (of uncertain authenticity)	A spirit who reveals danger	No		
Uncle or Unkus	Spirit of the air, represented by St. George or a sand-filled bucket in which candles or American flags are set	No		
Great One (of uncertain authenticity, but perhaps identical to Monsieur Danny)	Connected with storms and snakes	Unclear	Bears a resemblance to Danbala Wèdo and Ayida Wèdo	Serpent *lwa* representing fertility if Danbala Wèdo and Ayida Wèdo; connected with fresh water and rainbows; associated with St. Patrick
Great Moccasin (of uncertain authenticity, but perhaps identical to Monsieur Danny)	Gaining power	Unclear	Bears a resemblance to Danbala Wèdo and Ayida Wèdo	Serpent *lwa* representing fertility, if Danbala Wèdo and Ayida Wèdo; connected with fresh water and rainbows; associated with St. Patrick
Kangaroo (of uncertain authenticity)	Stops petitioners from worrying	No		

Table 2. Voodoo Gods and Haitian Equivalents (*continued*)

Mississippi River Valley Name	Mississippi River Valley Name	Found in Haiti	Haitian Name	Haitian Characteristics
Jenipee (of uncertain authenticity)	Marriages	No		
Death (probably identical to Monsieur D'Embarras)	Causes deaths for petitioners	Unclear but its function exists in Haiti	Specific deity is unclear, though its function exists	Various *lwa* can harm others
Joe Feraille	Mischievous character from Louisiana folk songs who may be connected with Voodoo	Yes	Ogou Feray	*Lwa* of fire, metallurgy, and armies; associated with St. Philip, St. George, and St. James the Greater
Mama You	Represented by St. Mary, mother of Jesus	Possibly	Possibility 1: Name seemingly recognized by Haitian oungan Possibility 2: Lasirenn, according to an oungan	Possibility 1: Large-breasted female *lwa* that manifests in Gworoch Possibility 2: Mermaid lwa sometimes associated with Our Lady of the Assumption, St. Martha, and Saint Philomena
Spirits of the dead	Aid or harm the living	Yes	*lèmo*	Spirits of the dead who aid or harm the living
Animistic spirits	Various roles	Yes	Various	Multiple *lwa* manifest as animals, plants, and in the landscape

Sources: "Idolatry and Quakery," *Louisiana Gazette,* 16 August 1820, 2; Hebblethwaite, *Vodou Songs,* 206, 212–213, 226–227, 233–235, 237–239, 243, 253–256, 257, 273, 291–292; 303; "Curious Charge of Swindling," *Daily Picayune,* 3 July 1850, 2; "Obtaining a Statue Under False Pretenses," *Daily Delta,* 3 July 1850, 3; "The Virgin of the Voudous," *Daily Delta,* 10 August 1850, 2; "Tribulations des Voudous," *L'Union,* 1 August 1863, 1; George Washington Cable, "Creole Slave Songs," *Century Magazine* 31 (1886): 815–817, 820; Mambo Vye Zo, *Serving the Spirits,* 174–175; Tann, *Haitian Vodou,* 100, 101, 104; Mary Washington, interview by Robert McKinney, transcript, Northwestern State University of Louisiana, Watson Memorial Library, Cammie G. Henry Research Center, Federal Writers' Project, folder 25, 8; "Marie Leveaux," transcript, Northwestern State University of Louisiana, Watson Memorial Library, Cammie G. Henry Research Center, Federal Writers' Project, folder 25, 2; George Washington Cable, *The Grandissimes: A Story of Creole Life* (New York: Charles Scribner's Sons, 1880), 99, 101, 182, 184, 253, 257, 447; *Picayune's Guide to New Orleans,* 2nd ed. (New Orleans: Picayune, 1900), 66; Catherine Dillon, "Voodoo, 1937–1941," transcript, Northwestern State University of Louisiana, Watson Memorial Library, Cammie G. Henry Research Center, Federal Writers' Project, folders 118, 317, and 319, sec. "Louisiana," 4, sec. "Marie the Mysterious," 3:1, 4:8, 5:7, 9, 18A-18B, 20, 6:5A, sec. "St. John's Eve," 27, sec. "Voodoo Openings," 21–24; "Idol Worship in Massachusetts," Palmyra, Missouri *Marion County Herald,* 14 December 1884, 6; Mary Alicia Owen, "Among the Voodoos," in *The International Folk-lore Congress 1891: Papers and Transactions* (London: David Nutt, 1892), 242; Mary Alicia Owen, "Voodooism," in *The International Folk-lore Congress of the World's Columbian Exposition, July 1893,* Archives of the International Folk-Lore Association, vol. 1, ed. Helen Wheeler Bassett and Frederick Starr (Chicago: Charles H. Sergel, 1898), 313–317; "Dance of the Voodoos," *The Times-Democrat,* June 24, 1896, 2; Helen Pitkin, *An Angel by Brevet: A Story of Modern New Orleans* (Philadelphia: J. B. Lippincott, 1904), 194–196, 204–206, 208, 210–211, 267–270, 273–286; Jeffrey E. Anderson, "Research Journals," 4 vols. (Field notes, personal collection, 2015–2017), vol. 4, 101, 127, 128, 139, 153, 164, 192–193, 205–206, 282–283, 292–293; Harry Middleton Hyatt, *Hoodoo-Conjuration-Witchcraft-Rootwork,* 5 vols, Memoirs of the Alma Egan Hyatt Foundation (Hannibal, MO: Western Publishing Company, 1970–1978), 773–775, 1295–1309; Hans-W. Ackermann and Jeanine Gauthier, "The Ways and Nature of the Zombi," *Journal of American Folklore* 104 (1991): 467–469; Lyle Saxon, "Voodoo," *The New Republic,* 23 March 1927, 136; Zora Neale Hurston, "Hoodoo in America," *Journal of American Folklore* 44 (1931): 319, 359, 362–363; Joshua Clegg Caffrey, *Traditional Music in Coastal Louisiana: The 1934 Lomax Recordings,* with a foreword by Barry Jean Ancelet (Baton Rouge: Louisiana State University, 2013), 102–103, 180–1811, 239–40; Harold Courlander, *The Drum and the Hoe: Life and Lore of the Haitian People* (Berkeley: University of California Press, 1960), 320–321, 325, 327; Dédé, interview by McKinney and Arguedas, 2–3; Jeffrey E. Anderson, *Conjure in African American Society* (Baton Rouge: Louisiana State University Press, 2005) 32–33, 58; Carolyn Morrow Long, *A New Orleans Voudou Priestess: The Legend and Reality of Marie Laveau* (Gainesville: University Press of Florida, 2006), 106, 114–116.

Despite the similarities, there are important differences between the gods of the Mississippi River valley and of Haiti. At the most basic level, the names differ in pronunciation. In cases like *Legba* and *Lébat,* the distinction is minimal. On the other hand, *Monsieur Danny* is not recognizable as *Danbala Wèdo* without the benefit of historical context. In addition, the Mississippi River valley pronunciation strongly resembles the name of the deity's African counterpart, *Dan* or *Da,* sometimes recorded as *Dañh-gbi,* which roughly translates as "life-giving snake." On the other hand, the name *D'Embarras* or *Dambarra* does sound quite similar to *Danbala,* but the African and Haitian experts who provided insights on the Louisiana spirit's identity drew a distinction between it and Monsieur Danny and Danbala.[87]

Perhaps just as important is the absence of prominent Haitian deities in the Mississippi River valley and vice versa. While divinities like Monsieur Danny/Danbala and Legba/Lébat held roughly the same importance in both the Mississippi River valley and Haiti, such was not the case for others. Key *lwa,* including but not limited to Agwé, Zaka, Bawon Samdi, and Ezili Freda—have no recorded existence in the Mississippi River valley.[88] The presence in the Mississippi River valley of other *lwa,* like Lasiren and Ogou Feray, seems likely, though they were far less visible than one would expect had they come directly from Haiti. Even the general term *lwa* is completely absent from the primary sources that address Voodoo along the Mississippi. Considering the comparative dearth of documentary evidence in the Mississippi River valley, the absence or relatively minor status of divinities in the area when compared to those of Haiti provides more suggestive evidence. Assonquer, for instance, was among the most commonly mentioned spirits in the New Orleans area but is far from prominent in Haiti to the extent that his identification remains uncertain. If the spirit does indeed descend from the Yoruba Osanyin, however, Assonquer's importance in Mississippi River valley Voodoo mirrors the importance of Osayin in West Africa. Likewise, Jean Macouloumba has no clear equivalent in Haiti but does possess a probable West Central African pedigree. Even Grand Zombi was much more prominent in the New Orleans area than among Haitians and held a status even greater than that possessed by Zombí in Cuba.[89]

While the contributions of different African regions to the pantheon of Voodoo are clear and relatively easy to ascertain, determining the precise role of Haiti in the migration of the African deities to North America is far more difficult, not least because there are almost no sources that discuss Voodoo before the influx of Haitians during the early nineteenth century. By the time nineteenth-century observers began to describe the faith, the population of the region had been drastically reshaped both by Haitian immigration and by the ever-growing numbers of Anglo-Americans flocking to the wealth promised by the Mississippi River and Gulf trades. Moreover, it was these latecomers, who knew less about the area's religious and spiritual practices than the Creole whites and Blacks whose ancestors had arrived at the beginning of the previous century, who produced many of the sparse sources on which scholars depend. While Haiti did not contribute unique deities as did the Bight of Benin or West Central Africa, it doubtlessly bolstered the Voodoo already practiced along the Mississippi and contributed its own interpretations of the divinities already in place. The direct influence of Haitians on nineteenth-century Voodoo would certainly have been strong, maybe more so than the Africans who arrived during the colonial era. Regardless of the relative weight of the different influences, the gods of the Mississippi River valley differed in many ways from those of the Haitian and African faiths that influenced Voodoo.

That the pantheon was not a static carryover from either Haiti or West Africa should come as no surprise. One would expect the traumatic disruption of enslavement to impact all aspects of Africans' lives, including their understanding of the beings who inhabited their spiritual world. Cataclysmic turmoil, however, is not necessary to explain the differences. African traditional religions, like other polytheistic faiths, are exceedingly open to transformation. Some of the most popular deities in modern Benin and Togo are recent arrivals. Habadadzi Antoine of Lomé, Togo, for example, described a powerful and benevolent vodu known as Lahadikunde as having come into his country from Ghana. In Benin, among the most popular deities is Thron, a spirit who brings good fortune and protects his followers and the society in which they live. He likewise originates in Ghana. It is also common to encounter divinities whom priests describe as Muslim, and one can occasionally see temples that honor deities drawn from Hinduism. Changes to the pantheon are by no means all recent, however. Scholars have argued, for instance, that deities as central to modern Vodun as Dan, Mawu, Xevioso, and Sakpata were unknown or associated only with particular locales prior to the mid-eighteenth century. In addition to illustrating the potential for change prevalent in the religion, the apparent late arrival of such divinities may well help to explain why some are absent from the Mississippi River valley. Such change is also common in West Central Africa, where traditional ancestor veneration has developed into the modern Ngunza religion, which centers on the worship of anticolonial leaders. In short, change—not stability—is the rule in Voodoo and its African and Haitian relatives.[90]

The Vodun Thron Church of Papa Djrado Blomankpon Blodedji Nan-Yeme Ahidazan Azansien Justin in Benin. Thron is relatively new to Benin but has become immensely popular because of his reputation as a helpful deity that never harms those who follow him.

3

THE VOODOOS
AND THEIR WORK

Between the gods and their followers were a variety of ministers and their assistants. While the most famous of these was Marie Laveau, there were dozens of others whose names have survived in the documentary record. Their precise duties and the full range of their activities have been obscured by the passage of time, the secrecy of believers, and the racial attitudes of the authors who wrote about them. Much does survive, however, allowing us to gain a broad if incomplete understanding of just who served as leaders, what leadership entailed, and how ministers earned their livings.

THE MINISTERS

Queens, Kings, and Dauphins

The best-known title for Voodoo's female leaders was *queen.* By the twentieth century, New Orleanians often applied the label to any female practitioner of Voodoo or hoodoo, but during the nineteenth century, it appears to have had a more precise meaning. Lafcadio Hearn, for instance, wrote in an article memorializing the life of Jean Montanée that "Swarthy occultists will doubtless continue to elect their 'queens' and high priests through years to come."[1] Though the precise definition of the title underlying Hearn's comments remains obscure, his offhand comment appears to state that the title paralleled that of high priest, implying that it was held by single individuals at a time and that it was of high authority. Other nineteenth-century sources support just such an interpretation. George Washington Cable, whose writings on Voodoo were brief but detail filled, likewise affirmed that the office was an elected one and remained with its holder as long as she lived. He went on to describe Marie Laveau as its most famous bearer, stating that in his own day an otherwise obscure Malvina Latour held the office. While appointments as queen may have had the potential to last a lifetime, it appears that such was not always the case. According to an 1869 account of St. John's Eve for instance, Marie Laveau had stepped down as queen because of her age, allowing for the election of a new queen in her place. Interestingly, however, additional sources report her as presiding over the ceremonies in succeeding years.[2]

The development of the office of queen was likely tied to the St. John's Eve Ceremonies. According to the 1869 account, for instance, the gathering was the venue for the coronation of Marie Laveau's successor. Cable latter added that the queen was responsible for designating when what he called "midnight forest rites" would take place, going on to state that by his time, the date the queen chose was invariably St. John's Eve. Though Federal Writers' Project workers and others demonstrated that Cable was incorrect in his beliefs about the frequency of Voodoo rituals, virtually all accounts of St. John's Eve describe it as being presided over by a queen.[3]

While *queen* was by far the most commonly referenced title in the surviving records, they occasionally referred to other royal and noble terms. Missouri, for instance, had a King Alexander. Coincidentally, some also referred to Jim Alexander of New Orleans by the title of *king*. A prominent nineteenth-century New Orleans priestess was known as Marie Contesse or Comptesse. One twentieth-century practitioner who honored the deceased at her grave described her as "La Beaute Comptesse," almost certainly meant as French for "the Beautiful Countess," perhaps implying that this particular Marie had adopted a noble title, which may or may not have implied a particular status in comparison to a queen.[4] Another leader referred to herself as the *dauphin* of her congregation, according to an 1850 news article. This particular title, derived from a French term designating the heir to a monarch, might have indicated the holder possessed a second-in-command position.[5] Such an interpretation is rendered more likely in light of an 1873 French-language article that described one Caroline as the presiding priestess during a St. John's Eve Ceremony. This Caroline the article described as "la princesse," a term similar in meaning to *dauphin,* and explained she was acting in place of the ailing "reine," meaning "queen," Marie Laveau. It went on to state that she was, in fact, "l'héritière présomptive à la couronne," meaning "the presumptive heiress to the crown."[6]

Royal labels conferred in connection to celebrations and other rituals have been a common feature throughout much of the African Diaspora. Scholar Elizabeth W. Kiddy has noted their prevalence in Brazilian festivals, for instance. Paralleling and perhaps contributing to the Louisiana milieu, royal titles for important figures have long been prominent in Haiti as well. For instance, an alternative title for the *oungenikon,* the leader of songs and dances during Vodou gatherings, is *reine-chanterelle,* meaning "queen chorister." Individuals also adopt royal or imperial titles to reflect their prominence. One modern example is Eric Pierre of La Gonâve, Haiti, who as of 2017 presided over the island's largest *ounfò* and had adopted the title of *empereur.*[7]

The use of such titles was certainly a continuation of African traditions. In Benin, for instance, hereditary monarchs—albeit usually kings in this case—continue to fill the highest ministerial ranks in West African varieties of Vodun, and their influence could be profound. Eighteenth-century King Agaja of Dahomey, for instance, reportedly fundamentally changed the religion of his homeland by promoting Fa divination derived from Yoruba tradition over local practices of consulting the ancestors when seeking spiritual guidance. Kings are similarly important to the traditional religion and magic of many other African peoples from whom African Americans descend. An excellent example is the King of Mbaya who is reputedly of such spiritual potency that the president of the Republic of the Congo visits him in order to receive the supernatural power to rule.[8]

Other Leaders

In the case of male leaders, the title of *doctor* was the norm. Evidence for this fact can be found among the contributions of the Federal Writers' Project. Marcus Christian, an African American participant, produced a manuscript entitled "Voodooism and Mumbo-Jumbo" that addresses both male and female practitioners. While much of his focus was on Marie Laveau, he also spent considerable time discussing male practitioners, to most of whose names he appended the honorific medical title. Among those he mentioned were Dr. John, Dr. Yah-Yah, Dr. Jack, Dr. Beauregard, Dr. Alexander, Dr. Sol,

Dr. Brown, and Dr. Lewis. The only male practitioners he described without the title—other than those involved in the city's distinctive Spiritual churches, who held ecclesiastical titles—were one Don Pedro, an unnamed "voodoo king," and the 1930s practitioner Prophet Joseph Rajah Lyons, M.S. Unlike royal titles, however, *doctor* does not appear to have been linked to any particular ceremony. Instead, it more likely was adopted by the practitioners themselves as a way to project authority, a choice doubtlessly influenced by the fact that much of their business consisted of the production of herbal remedies.[9]

If queens and the occasional king were the typical leaders of ceremonial life, they did not act alone. Within the congregation of believers were several other specialists. It appears that queens, for instance, had assistants. A twentieth-century Voodoo practitioner named Oscar "Nom" Felix described Marie Laveau as having "workers," a designation that he seemed to attach to their ability to perform magic or participate in ceremonial activities. He also stated that they "would wait on her and serve her all the time," indicating their subordinate role in this particular context.[10] During a 1939 FWP interview, two informants reminisced about Laveau, stating that she "had her own class of associates" and described a Ben Lazime as her "assistant" and two others as some of her "helpers."[11] Whether all three filled the same role is unclear, and it is possible that *assistant* and *helper* were distinct formal offices. They reported that Lazime, for instance, was a diviner who would "read your life" from one's leavings after drinking water from a glass. Unfortunately, the informants provided no such information on the two helpers. Evidence suggests that others had similarly specialized roles within Voodoo congregations. When interviewed by FWP workers, for instance, Charles Raphael stated that he performed as a singer at weekly ceremonies hosted every Monday by Laveau in the house of a lesser-known practitioner named Mama Antoine. He went on to explain that an accordion player named Zizi accompanied him and his fellow singers and that there were a group of dancers who appear to have been equally distinct from the congregation as a whole. The conspicuous role of the dancers was evident in the much larger annual St. John's Eve Ceremony as well. There were almost certainly others involved in the musical aspect of ceremonies. Two other FWP informants, for instance, mentioned tom-toms providing the dancing rhythm at the St. John's Eve Ceremony, and one can safely assume that they had skilled players. Another interviewee confirmed that drummers worked with Marie Laveau and James Alexander.[12]

Believers who had attained a status that enabled them to perform magic held their own titles. One of these, mentioned in an 1886 article by George Washington Cable, was a *monteure*. In modern French, the word resembles one meaning "editor," but in context, it appears to have meant something along the line of "worker" in the day's Louisiana French. Indeed, *worker* seems to have been a common title for practitioners of hoodoo in the lower Mississippi River valley and its environs. Though the word could be found outside the region, it was usually in such constructions as *root worker*. In fact, approximately 61.5 percent of the unambiguous uses of the term came from the Mississippi River valley area with the largest number of those originating in Memphis, Tennessee, and the New Orleans area.[13]

Becoming a Leader

Becoming a minister in Voodoo could happen in various ways. Initiations, called openings, along with instruction from experienced ministers appear to have been normative, however.[14] By the twentieth century, multiple types existed. The version one underwent appears to have depended upon the aspect of the religion that one was pursuing at the time. For instance, there appear to have been different procedures for preparing initiates to practice harmful hoodoo from those who aspired to benevolent deeds alone.[15] Whatever the exact nature of initiations or the variations they presented, they were logical aspects of the faith, which included hidden knowledge and operated within a culture hostile to its tenets. Moreover, such specialized or perhaps progressive initiations are common among African Diasporic religions. Followers of Haitian Vodou, for example, include various levels of practitioner, including uninitiated congregants, *ounsis* who have undergone the *kanzo* ceremony that places each under the protection of a particular *lwa*, others who have mystically married specific *lwa*, and those who have been elevated to the priesthood as *oungan* and *manbo*. [16]

As is true in Africa and the Caribbean, there were ways to become a religious minister outside of formal initiation. Birth was one potential route to leadership. Zora Neale Hurston claimed that there were three generations of Marie Laveaus through whom the mantel of priesthood passed with the last being the granddaughter of the first. Though there is considerable uncertainty that there truly was a succession of Marie Laveaus, birth appears to have played a role in other ways. A prime example is Hurston's statement that two of the practitioners with whom she spoke claimed to be related to Laveau.[17] Harry Middleton Hyatt indirectly testified to the importance of being a relative of Laveau when he asked an informant about a supposed nephew of Laveau, "Is he really her nephew? I mean, he isn't a fake or anything?"[18] Even today, one encounters claims of descent from Marie Laveau among those who seek to revive the Voodoo of history.[19]

As elsewhere in the United States, birthplace and ancestry appear to have been important indicators of spiritual acumen outside of immediate parentage, as illustrated by the prominence of two of Laveau's contemporaries, Jean Montanée and Jim Alexander. The former was of African birth, and according to an 1859 description, his face bore "the distinctive marks of his tribe."[20] Another article from an 1885 issue of *Harper's Weekly* describes him as having been born in Senegal, probably of Bamana ethnicity. Though these writers stopped short of explicitly stating that his African birth had imbued him with supernatural prowess, the fact that both accounts follow statements about his nativity by describing him as a "performer of miracles" in the eyes of his supporters and as "the most extraordinary African character that ever obtained celebrity within her limits," respectively, clearly indicate that his birth was important to his reputation.[21]

Another practitioner for whom birth played a significant role was James Alexander, likewise a key figure in New Orleans Voodoo as indicated by an 1871 account of a dispute between him and Laveau over an unspecified aspect of their faith. The article, which appeared in the *Daily Picayune,* referred to Alexander as "the great physician, who is supposed by his disciples to hold in his hands the issues of life and death."[22] Alexander, according to a Federal Writers' Project informant named N. H. Hobley, was three quarters Native American and one quarter African American. Another source indicated that he was sometimes known as Indian Jim and described him as resembling a Native American as part of a list of what the informant apparently considered Alexander's other praiseworthy features, which also included possession of fine clothes and a white wife. Though neither specifically credited his American Indian descent for his power, the fact that they emphasized his ancestry in their praise of his abilities and person indicates that it was in some measure important to his practice. Moreover, other prominent Voodoos, such as Missouri's King Alexander, claimed Native American ancestry, further indicating that descent from American Indians was a useful trait for a successful career.[23]

Even when practitioners could not assert spiritual power through circumstances of birth, they sometimes were able to claim it through association with other prominent Voodoo clergy. This spiritual kinship was most evident regarding those who claimed friendship with Laveau or other prominent leaders. A prime example was Charles Raphael, who claimed—with justice, based on the existing evidence—to have served as a singer in Laveau's weekly ceremonies. Not only was this distinction an apparent badge of honor for Raphael, but he also described fellow practitioner Oscar Felix as a fake based on the assertion that he had never known the renowned priestess. The alleged fake, on the other hand, claimed that he had known her ever since he was "old enough to remember" and stated that as a child, he had sung at her ceremonies.[24] Nathan Hobley, who denied working hoodoo but claimed the profession of divine healer, maintained that he had known both Marie Laveau and Jim Alexander but asserted that the latter was "more clever and could do things that she couldn't."[25] He went on to describe Alexander's ability to heal and to assert that Laveau relied on him to help her own clients. Similarly, Lala Hopkins claimed to have learned her craft from Marie Comptesse whom she stated was the greatest of all Voodoo practitioners, going on to say "Marie Comtesse taught me all ah know. Dat makes me know what Marie Laveau knows. Cause Marie Laveau taught Marie Comtesse." Shortly thereafter, Hopkins went on to assert, "What Ah don't know ain't to be known."[26]

Descent is likewise an important part of Mississippi River valley Voodoo's Caribbean and African relations. In Haiti, lineage, both physical and spiritual, is an important bond that ties congregations together, and some claim such links to specific bodies of believers as authenticators of their practice. In Benin, Vodun ministers sometimes assert their standing and authenticity by referencing other prominent leaders with whom they associate or have sanctioned their practice. Meyè Lokossou, a priest who lives near Comé, Benin, for instance, displayed a document from Daagbo Hounon Houna II verifying that he had undergone the proper rituals for the priesthood and appeared understandably proud of the accomplishment. Likewise, Laté Anagonou Ayolomi II, King of the Kotafon, emphasized his links to other kings as a means of further bolstering his already considerable prestige.[27]

Possession of items imbued with supernatural powers was another route to leadership in the religion. For instance, one 1869 article claimed that a major source of Marie Laveau's power was what it called, "a powerful fetish in the shape of a large doll-like idol from Africa."[28] She does not appear to have been unique, however. According to Mary Alicia Owen, Missouri Voodoo practitioners believed that one way to obtain supernatural power was to acquire what she called "cunjer-stones." She described one that fell into her possession as being small, black, and shaped like a kidney. These seemingly insignificant rocks, according to her, allowed one to bypass any barriers to the profession, stating, "it is initiation, it is knowledge, it is power."[29] Similarly but on a less universal scale, Jean Montanée claimed that some shells he possessed were African and allowed him to tell the future. Possession of magical items as a source of spiritual power has parallels in Africa as well. For instance, after a Beninese ceremony for a guardian divinity known as Zangbeto witnessed by the author in 2015, the organizer drew him aside to show him the source of his power, which took the form of a horn decorated with cowries. It was most probably, like Laveau's fetish, a representation of a deity.[30]

For those not lucky enough to have a powerful spiritual lineage, possess an item of power, or know those capable of initiating them, one could seek out power through various forms of self-initiation. According to the writings of Mary Alicia Owen, this option appears to have been normative in late nineteenth-century Missouri. King Alexander, for example, specified that what he called the "strength of head" necessary to practice Voodoo was to be obtained through self-initiation involving the preparation of ritual drinks, isolation from others, and spiritual dreams.[31] Another belief was that selling one's soul to the devil was an effective means of gaining access to the supernatural powers associated with hoodoo, albeit not necessarily ministerial status in Voodoo. Two Memphis practitioners described formulae of executing such pacts, which required obtaining black cat bones for the purpose of obtaining invisibility and musical skill as well as the sale of one's soul. A common feature of such doings was the boiling of a black cat alive. Hyatt recorded a similar practice in New Orleans. Fortunately for the cats but less so for historians, most of those interviewed by Hyatt either claimed never to have undertaken the ceremony or at least implied that they had not. Hyatt also recorded a different style of soul selling in Vicksburg, Mississippi, during which the acquaintance of an informant supposedly visited a crossroads at midnight. When he arrived, he turned around three times and then offered his soul to the devil, gaining the power to "do anything he wanted."[32] Zora Neale Hurston, meanwhile, claimed to have participated in an event in Marreo, Louisiana, during which participants went to a crossroads at midnight, sat upon the ground, and prayed to the devil for assistance. According to her, this ritual served in place of an initiation. Though Hurston stopped short of specifying that any souls were bartered for supernatural power, the event's resemblance to the ceremony Hyatt reported in Vicksburg makes it likely that it did.[33]

Clothing

The clothing worn by leaders in the context of rituals set them apart from the average attendee. For example, according to one Federal Writers' Project informant, a major ceremony that took place on St. John's Eve each year saw the female participants clothed in long, belted cotton dresses. Males, meanwhile, wore pants without shirts. None wore shoes. Interestingly, the witness claimed that this was the only occasion on which he saw Marie Laveau wear a type of head cloth known as a *tignon,* which was otherwise common headwear for nineteenth-century African American New Orleanians. The wearing of light clothing as during the St. John's Eve ceremony seems to have been significant in other contexts as well. In an initiation ceremony witnessed by FWP workers, the male officiant similarly was clad only in pants, and he instructed the initiates to remove all of their outer clothing and shoes. While no witnesses explained the precise import of the removing of one's outer clothing and shoes when preparing to encounter a deity, it remains a practice common in West African Vodun to the present, and doing so was almost certainly an indicator of respectful submission.[34]

Other occasions called for different attire. A few witnesses claimed that some dances required nudity, though that may well have been an exaggeration for the entertainment of listeners.[35] A more reliable statement from a supposed eyewitness—the informant who spoke of Marie Laveau's attire at the St. John's Eve festivities—describes women dancing while wearing large handkerchiefs, which male counterparts had tied around their waists. Two inhabitants of the Thomy Lafon Catholic Old Folks Home, Eugene Fritz and John Alfred, likewise mentioned the use of handkerchiefs in dances in an FWP interview. In their account, however, the handkerchiefs were tied around women's necks during St. John's Eve ceremonies. Another informant spoke of women dancing while wearing brassieres and a band around their waists, but his somewhat ambiguous description may well describe dancing for a purpose other than the practice of Voodoo.[36]

Female Leadership

One oft-remarked aspect of Voodoo by scholars and popular authors alike was its female leadership. Indeed, the prominence of women in Voodoo has been well established. Nineteenth-century accounts of Voodoo in New Orleans, for instance, almost invariably emphasize the importance of women. Typical of the writing of the time was an 1860 article describing the forcible breakup of a ceremony by city police, which recorded the participants as five "disreputable free women of color . . . and a slave girl."[37] Participation, however, does not necessary imply leadership roles, but that women filled such positions is evident from the sources. The prominence of the likes of Marie Laveau and Marie Comptesse likewise attests to the centrality of female leadership. That women remained key figures into the twentieth century is also evident from the fact that Lala Hopkins was the most famous practitioner of her day.[38]

The leadership of women extended beyond the luminaries of the faith. For example, Mary Alicia Owen's "Among the Voodoos," includes the names of nine prominent practitioners of hoodoo, five of whom were women. A review of those Voodoo ministers mentioned in Catherin Dillon's unpublished "Voodoo" manuscript, a long work undertaken by the Federal Writers' Project that drew its information from a wide range of news articles, books, and Federal Writers' Project interviews, indicates a similar predominance in favor of women in the Crescent City. Harry Middleton Hyatt recorded a more profound imbalance among those twentieth-century practitioners of Voodoo and hoodoo he interviewed in New Orleans, Louisiana; Memphis, Tennessee; Mobile, Alabama; and Vicksburg, Mississippi. For every one male practitioner, there were approximately three women.[39]

On the other hand, by no means were women necessarily the only authorities in the faith. Of the six Louisiana workers Zora Neale Hurston claimed to have studied with, only one was female. Likewise, though one FWP worker described Lala Hopkins as the most famous Voodoo of her day, he also noted that her contemporary, Oscar Felix, was a "medicine man and high priest." Moreover, the writer later described Hopkins and Felix presiding over initiation ceremonies in roughly equivalent roles.[40] In earlier days, while many regarded Marie Laveau as the preeminent Voodoo minister, her contemporaries,

Jean Montanée and Jim Alexander, certainly outstripped all but her in prominence.[41] In Missouri, meanwhile, King Alexander was, according to Owen, "the head-man in the Voodoo circle that meets after church is over in the African Methodist Church."[42]

In short, while it would be inaccurate to describe Voodoo as a women's religion, one must account for the fact that females were certainly a majority of both its laypersons and ministers. Through the antebellum era, the numerical imbalance in the lower Mississippi River valley was likely simply an extension of the fact that the free people of color who were at liberty to organize and participate in Voodoo ceremonial life were disproportionately female. During the colonial period and beyond, relationships between white men and women of African descent were common and not particularly frowned upon. Those women who were owned by their lovers sometimes found themselves emancipated, leading to a growing and disproportionately female population of free people of color. It should come as no surprise that Marie Laveau's father was a product of just such a relationship, perhaps between his mother and prominent New Orleanian Charles Laveau Trudeau. While this system of interracial relationships continued to persist and develop, the Haitian immigration of 1809 reinforced the pattern of free African American women's numerical dominance by introducing a total of 1,805 adult free Blacks to the city, with only 428 men among that number.[43]

While the demographic and social situation in the lower Mississippi River valley undeniably contributed to the importance of women in Voodoo, it must be noted that women were important leaders among the faith's African ancestors and Caribbean cousins. Priestesses, called *mambos* or *manbos,* have long been common in Haitian Vodou, though they have never been as numerically dominant as the priestesses of the Mississippi River valley. Plus, scholars like Alfred Métraux have considered the roles of male and females in the priesthood as more or less equivalent, a considerable difference from the gender roles assigned in many religions. Likewise, women are also prominent in the priesthoods of various African religions, including the Vodun of Benin and its neighbors. In addition, among the Fon and related peoples, women hold a reputation for supernatural power, which sometimes reputedly manifests itself in harmful witchcraft. The best explanation for women's importance is that it was an amplification of African and African Diasporic gender roles in an environment with a strongly feminine sexual imbalance.[44]

MAGICAL LIFE

Many a writer has described Voodoo as no more than magic. As much of the preceding should make clear, they were incorrect. Still, their misinterpretation of the religion is somewhat understandable since supernaturalism was very much a part of the faith. Unfortunately for historians, however, magical practices are quite open to change because of their results-oriented nature. By the twentieth century, when detailed descriptions of Voodoo's magical formulae became increasingly common, hoodoo had come to resemble the conjure of elsewhere in the South. Despite the resemblance, however, it retained many features that kept it unique.

For one, its terminology was distinct. The term *gris-gris,* common in Louisiana from the colonial era on, was not to be found outside the lower Mississippi River valley and a strip along the Gulf of Mexico near the river's mouth.[45] Likewise, early references to the term *hoodoo*—including its first known use in 1849—also came from the Mississippi River valley, though by the late nineteenth century, its use had spread across the nation.[46] Along the same lines, while collecting folklore in the Mississippi River valley prior to World War II, Harry Middleton Hyatt was the first to note the term *nation sack* used in the area. As described by his informants, these were bags carried exclusively by women who wore them on belts around their waists. Nation sacks could be used to hold money or lucky items, or they could also be dedicated to particular ends, including gambling success, escape from legal trouble, or protection against spells designed to force one to move. Hyatt noted that the term was unknown along the East Coast but was common in Memphis and could sometimes be heard in New Orleans and Mobile. Katrina Hazzard-Donald disputes the existence of items called *nation sacks,* arguing that Hyatt and others simply misunderstood informants who spoke of *nature sacks,* which she claims referred to bag charms known across the American South. The problem with her interpretation, however, is that if Hyatt was mistaken, his error was curiously specific geographically. Moreover, the uses of the nation sacks described by Hyatt were considerably more varied than the nature sacks proposed by Hazzard-Donald, who stated that they were designed to control men's ability to become sexually aroused. [47]

The paraphernalia of hoodoo was distinctive as well, particularly in New Orleans. Hyatt, in fact, found it so different that he devoted a 145-page section of his five-volume work to the area. Prior to visiting the city, Hyatt was already familiar with its reputation as a supernatural center and avoided going there early in his studies so that he could gain experience in the collection of conjure lore first. While a reputation for being unique is not the same as actually being distinctive, Hyatt's extensive study of conjure and hoodoo made him the foremost authority on the subject in his day. In short, he was more qualified to judge than any of his contemporaries.[48]

After completing research trips to New Orleans, Hyatt determined that it was Catholic influence in the city that made hoodoo unique, an understanding embodied in the title he gave the section that addressed its distinctiveness: "Shrines: Altars—Candles—Saints: New Orleans Area."[49] While conducting interviews in Mobile, Alabama, he learned from a Rev. Young that candles were in use both in New Orleans and along the Gulf Coast by African Americans who had been influenced by Catholicism, a Christian denomination in which candles are prominent features of spiritual life. Young likewise added that he had not encountered the use of candles elsewhere. These candles came in all colors, and as other informants would explain, they were an important part of rituals, including magical ones. Some uses of candles in the New Orleans and Mobile areas were to calm users, remove magical ailments, cause business failure, remove or cause bad luck, undo or cause the loss of energy, strengthen or destroy relationships, and grant wishes.[50]

The theoretical basis behind the burning of candles appears to have been nearly identical with what one finds in Catholicism. According to Greg Dues' *Catholic Customs and Traditions,* Christians had begun to burn candles on the graves of martyrs and other respected dead by the second century and before representations of the saints within the next hundred years. By the Middle Ages, they began to appear on altars. When burned by individuals outside of religious services, candles indicate that the lighter requests a favor from the blessed dead or from God, and the slow melting of the wax is a form of symbolic sacrifice while the supplicant awaits spiritual action.[51]

Numerous examples indicate that hoodoo practitioners often burned candles in ways that would have been familiar to any Catholic. For instance, a Doctor Sims explained to Hyatt that one could place a green, a black, and a yellow candle around a figure of St. Anthony, burning them each morning until the candles had completely melted. Doing so would "relieve you or your mind."[52] Federal Writers' Project workers likewise testified to Catholic candle practices

Lala Hopkins prepares candles for watching Federal Writers' Project employees who were posing as aspiring hoodoo workers. State Library of Louisiana.

that had made their way into Voodoo. For example, two New Orleans Voodoo practitioners explained to Robert McKinney that a hoodoo doctor could win back a woman's wayward lover by using a pin to engrave her name on a brown candle and then burning it atop an altar. One of them went on to explain that particular colored candles corresponded to specific saints. Even burning tapers on graves could be found in hoodoo lore by the early twentieth century. One spell designed to kill an enemy—as recorded by McKinney—required cooking a rooster, taking its head and feet to the grave of a person who had possessed an evil character in life, and then burning a black candle that had been placed in the beak of the bird. To be sure, such rituals were far

A shrine to Dan, the Beninese serpent deity, near the palace of Dada Daagbo Hounon Houna II in Ouida, Benin. This direct representation of the deity's form is rare outside of Africa.

from orthodox Catholic activities, but they demonstrate just how strong the influence of this Christian denomination was. Moreover, a host of references to other Catholic paraphernalia used in hoodoo—including incense, holy oils, holy water, Bible verses, and medals—litter the sources.[53]

The Catholic influence extended even to practitioner's understanding of the deities who aided their supernatural deeds. Several of the gods found in New Orleans had known correspondences to saints. Believers, for instance, sometimes considered Papa Lébat the same being as St. Peter and deemed the mysterious spirit called Mama You identical to the Virgin Mary.[54] The exact reason for such correspondences is unclear, but it seems likely that they developed during the era of slavery as Africans struggled to come to terms with

Danbala Wèdo, the Haitian serpent *lwa,* as St. Patrick in the *ounfò* of Emil, called "Hountor," in Source Matelas, Haiti. In New Orleans, practitioners believed Monsieur Danny was the same as St. Michael.

their status as bondspersons in a land dominated by French and Spanish Catholics. In some cases, specific saints and deities were probably linked because of shared characteristics. Lébat's frequent identification with St. Peter likely has to do with his position as the deity who opens the path of communication with the gods, paralleling St. Peter's status as keeper of the keys of heaven. The fact that Catholic iconography frequently pictured Peter with a set of keys may well have provided a visual cue that accelerated the identification. In Haiti, where saint-*lwa* correspondences are similarly normative, Danbala is tied to St. Patrick, whom legend describes as driving the snakes from Ireland and who often appears in religious art with serpents at his feet. In New Orleans, however, Monsieur Danny appears to have been linked to Michael the Archangel. Most likely, this identification developed out of the exalted status of both beings as well as artistic renderings of Michael locked in combat with a serpentine devil.[55]

Ounfò of Eric Pierre, Empereur in La Gonave, Haiti, showing *lwa* represented by saints.

What is clear is that the identification of African gods with saints did not happen immediately and does not appear to have been fully in place until the late nineteenth century. The first references to Voodoo deities in New Orleans, for instance, tie them to specific images, one resembling a woman with serpentine legs and the other a combination of a mummy and a centaur. While newspapers called the latter the "Virgin of the Voudous," its description does not sound at all like the Virgin Mary. Clearly, neither of these has any apparent link to Catholic iconography. By the time Helen Pitkin wrote her Voodoo-themed novel, *Angel by Brevet,* published in 1904, she was able to confidently state that certain deities were identical to saints. That this development was already in place by the late nineteenth century is evidenced by Federal Writers' Project records that indicate Marie Laveau used an altar on which the figures of saints featured prominently. Moreover, Marie Dédé, who knew Laveau as a child, described the way in which the famous priestess served specific deities, naming their saint equivalents in the process.[56]

This tendency toward god-saint correspondence is widespread in African diasporic religion and is common in Haitian Vodou, but unlike in the Caribbean nation, there is no clear evidence that the Christian God was incorporated into the Voodoo pantheon. In Haiti, Vodou practitioners refer to the Supreme Being as Bondye, from the French for "Good God." In their understanding, he is the omnipotent and omnipresent creator and master of the universe, a unique power who rules over humans, *lwa,* and other spirits. In keeping with African concepts of God, however, he is aloof and has little direct dealings with humans, who rely on the subordinate deities for spiritual succor. So strong is the resemblance to African concepts of the Supreme Being that

Table 3. Selected Gods with Catholic Equivalents in the Lower Mississippi River Valley

Name	Saint	Characteristics
Monsieur Danny	St. Michael	Deity of discord; possibly also connected with storms
Papa Lébat	St. Peter or St. Anthony	Keeper of entrances; opens communication with deities
Miché Agoussou	St. Anthony or St. Peter	Deity of love
Assonquer	St. Paul	Deity of good fortune
Vériquité	St. Joseph	Depicted in the sources as being involved in a love spell
Uncle or Unkus	St. George	Spiritual Church spirit; possibly connected with Voodoo
Mama You	Virgin Mary	Unknown

Sources: Cable, *The Grandissimes,* 99, 101, 135, 182, 184, 257, 272, 311, 447, 453–456, 468; Pitkin, 185–213, 260–292; Hurston, "Hoodoo in America," 319; Maria Dédé, interview by McKinney and Arguedas, 2.

scholar Leslie Desmangles suggests that Bondye is not so much a syncretic or creolized deity but is an African god called by a name derived from French.[57]

In the Mississippi River valley, however, Bondye does not appear to have existed in a context distinct from Christianity. For instance, Marie Laveau was a regular attendee at Catholic masses, which one must conclude she considered the proper occasions to worship God. Zora Neale Hurston likewise identified Voodoo practitioners as also being Catholic, Protestant, or as having no affiliation in her "Hoodoo in America," which hints that Laveau's view of the situation was not unique. Nevertheless, the presence of Catholic prayers in Voodoo ceremonies indicates that while practitioners may have treated the worship of God as a rite best carried out in a church, they did not necessarily segregate their Christian beliefs from their understandings of Voodoo. Ultimately, the distinctions between Haiti and the Mississippi River valley regarding the Christian God's place in Voodoo may well have represented little more than a slight degree of difference that hinged on naming more than actual function. After all, in Haiti and earlier in Africa, the key distinction between Voodoo and Christianity was the centrality of the lesser spirits to ritual and everyday life in the former, not the basic concept of a supreme being.[58]

New Orleans's hoodoo was also distinctive in the degree to which it incorporated Catholic saints with no known deity correspondence. Among those called upon was St. Raymond, to whom practitioners burned candles and prayed for monetary success and to meet household needs. One informant extended his purview to include protection for those engaged in illicit alcohol sales. St. Expedite, meanwhile, could supposedly provide a wide range of benefits to his servitors, including protection from police, the ability to travel wherever one wished, success at finding jobs, fortune at gambling, victory in court cases, the return of errant lovers, and luck. St. Rita was a patron of women, particularly but not exclusively by responding to their requests in matters of the heart. An unnamed Federal Writers' Project informant also explained that at least one hoodoo practitioner she knew of called on St. George for anything she wanted. Another stated that Marie Laveau kept a statue of St. Marron on an altar in her home.[59]

In some ways, the doings of these saints resembled those encountered in Catholicism, but in other ways they did not. Praying and burning candles to saints is common practice in folk Catholicism. Along those lines, one of the various St. Raymonds of Catholic belief was associated with money because

Saint Expedite at Our Lady of Guadalupe Church. Courtesy of Catherine Wessinger.

of his devotion to ransoming Christian slaves from Muslim corsairs. St. Rita was particularly connected to women because of her experience as a forced bride of a husband who brutalized her during the early years of their marriage. In contrast to such commonalities, one of Hyatt's informants stated that one should rap on the floor when praying and burning candles to St. Expedite. In a manner atypical of Catholic spirits, St. Expedite would supposedly respond with raps of his own. Significantly, rapping was a common aspect of Voodoo ceremonies in general. Similarly, one informant claimed that the saint required an offering of milk or white rum before he would go to work, a practice more reminiscent of West Africa or Haiti than the Vatican. Even the placement of his image near the entrance to one's home, a location stipulated by some servitors, had African overtones, resembling the placement of Legba images in West African Vodun. Like St. Expedite, Raymond could be the recipient of offerings of alcoholic beverages. Some also considered him willing to harm enemies if properly entreated. Along similar lines, St. Rita supposedly not only worked on women's behalf but was actively hostile to men and sometimes even brought bad luck to women with husbands. In New Orleans hoodoo, St. George, rather than rescuing maidens, could drive away unwanted husbands.[60]

One outlier among the saints called upon by hoodoo doctors was Black Hawk, who was well attested to have been incorporated into New Orleans supernaturalism by the first half of the twentieth century. Voodoo priestess Lala Hopkins relied upon him to "bring evil" on others, for instance.[61] Another practitioner, called Madame Maika in the Federal Writers' Project records, likewise treated Black Hawk as a dangerous spirit sent to harm victims.[62] Hyatt's informants were a bit more specific. One described him as "one of the old evil saints" who in life "did not believe they had a god." Another stated that he was "one of those mean saints" who had not believed in the Gospel, the Creator, and life after death. To call upon him, the informant explained, one should pray to the devil instead of God.[63]

It is tempting, albeit possibly mistaken, to assume that Black Hawk made his way into hoodoo through New Orleans Spiritual churches, a collection of congregations that originated in the early twentieth century and that place a heavy emphasis on interaction with saints and spirits of the dead. While some Spiritual congregations continue to incorporate him into their beliefs, they usually treat him as peaceful and protective, not malevolent, and tend to believe that he was introduced to the Crescent City by Leafy Anderson, the founder of New Orleans's Spiritual churches.[64] Black Hawk had a presence in the supernatural beliefs of the city well before Leafy Anderson moved there from Chicago during the early twentieth century. During 1871 and 1876, prominent Spiritualist James M. Peebles, visited the city, speaking on his religion and apparently introduced its inhabitants to his interpretation of the historical Native American leader named Black Hawk, whom he described as foregoing violence and embracing peace in the afterlife. Spiritualism was one of the major influences on the origin of Spiritual churches, and as it has in a variety of Afro-Caribbean faiths, it likely left its mark on Voodoo as well. One of the more obvious traces of Spiritualism was that those who were knowledgeable about Voodoo sometimes used the word *séance* to describe one of the religion's ceremonies. *Séance,* French for "session," was the term adopted by Spiritualists to denote their central ceremony in which they summoned and spoke with the spirits of the dead. Marie Déde, who had been friends with Marie Laveau's granddaughter as a child and had witnessed some of the Voodoo Queen's rituals, described both small indoor gatherings and large outdoor group rituals using the Spiritualist term. Dédé may well have been unusual in her use of terminology, but her word choices indicate that at least some of those with more-than-average familiarity with Voodoo linked it—consciously or unconsciously—with Spiritualism.[65]

On the other hand, it is possible that the Spiritual churches coopted and rehabilitated a Voodoo saint. For instance, Nathan Hobley, who had been an acquaintance of Jim Alexander and supposedly Marie Laveau, stated that the latter "invoked the spirit of Black Hawk" for a white client whom she visited each week.[66] Hobley, who reported that he had arrived in New Orleans on January 30, 1880, would have only known her for the last year and several months of her life, but even if he was mistaken about which Voodoo priestess he had known, he clearly intended his description to predate Alexander's death in 1890, more than two decades prior to Leafy Anderson's reported introduction of Black Hawk to New Orleans. Moreover, he claimed that during his acquaintance with Laveau and Alexander, he worked as an agent for Laurence D. Scott, by which he probably meant DeLaurence, Scott, and Company, one of the earliest spiritual supply companies. According to Hobley, he sold images of Black Hawk on behalf of the company to Laveau, Alexander, and another practitioner named Sol. One problematic feature of his identification of customers, however, is that the current manifestation of his erstwhile employer, the DeLaurence Company, claims 1892 as its founding date.[67]

In short, while some certainly understood Black Hawk as a hoodoo saint who was quite different from the peaceful protector of the Spiritual churches, his precise point of entry into Voodoo supernaturalism remains murky. He may well have migrated from Spiritualism during the nineteenth century or perhaps entered independently because of Voodoo's preexisting belief system, which looked to the spirits of the dead as sources of supernatural aid. It is even possible that the pictures of Black Hawk sold by Nathan Hobley and possibly other agents of early spiritual supply companies were the origin of the "mean saint" who seemingly had nothing in common with his historical namesake or his Spiritual church parallel. While this latter explanation might seem odd, it is in keeping with the examples of the coastal West African deity Mami Wata, who supposedly developed from European depictions of mermaids, and the process by which Haitians identified the *lwa* Papa Legba with St. Peter on the basis of lithographs showing the latter holding the keys to heaven. Like so much else about Mississippi River valley Voodoo, the details of Black Hawk's advent will likely remain a mystery.[68]

While non-African influences were prominent in hoodoo, they were not ever present. Many spells and charms associated with Voodoo had few, if any, Catholic elements. For example, of fifteen spell formulae collected upon one occasion by Robert McKinney of the Federal Writers' Project from New Orleans practitioner Madame Ducoyielle, only four have any link to Catholic belief. Moreover, three of these four are references to the devil, the enemy of the Christian God. Another group of magical formulae collected over a nine-day period from Madame Ducoyielle and a friend during late 1936 was similarly short on Catholicism. Of the nineteen spells recorded, four called for the use of candles, and one required holy water as an ingredient. One of those that utilized candles also referenced the need for an altar upon which to burn them. Ducoyielle was not unique, however. Lala Hopkins supplied McKinney and two companions with a collection of twelve formulae following one of the FWP workers' initiations into the practice of hoodoo, none of which has any features that could be described as Catholic in origin.[69]

Likewise, the active force behind many charms had no identifiable link to Catholic practices. The honored dead and lesser spirits often filled the role sometimes occupied by the Christian God and Catholic saints. For example, Ducoyielle prescribed pouring milk into holes in Congo Square while calling out to Marie Laveau. Upon another occasion, as she prepared to share spell formulae with a FWP worker, she placed a glass of wine atop a table as an offering to Madame Jean, a spirit about whom she had dreamed, and to Gaston Bonnafon.[70]

The deities of Voodoo also found themselves intimately involved in pragmatic supernaturalism. For instance, while instructing FWP workers in the working of spells, Ducoyielle found it necessary to take her charges to a cemetery in order to continue their education. As the group prepared to set out, she had the government employees each light a candle and make a wish. Meanwhile, she called out, "Labat ouvre la port," a request for the deity elsewhere known as Lébat to open the door, presumably to success in their pursuit of spiritual power. She followed her cry with, "Go spirits, open the way for us.

Lala Hopkins performs a ritual for Federal Writers' Project workers. State Library of Louisiana.

Pass before us."[71] Lala Hopkins likewise provided them with a spell that combined the Catholic feature of candles with distinctly non-Christian elements of animal sacrifice and supplication of a deity whom she called Onzoncare, known elsewhere as Assonquer.[72]

Another distinctive aspect of the magic worked by Voodoo practitioners was the tendency for some amulets to be specifically bound to their possessors. The best examples of these were what were known in Missouri as luck balls. Folklorist Mary Alicia Owen described two informants wearing them in the form of small bags on a string hung from the left shoulder and looping the body under the right arm. This particular type of charm was unique to its possessor, and its loss could create acute anxiety in its owner. According to Owen, believers consider their souls to be bound up in them. King Alexander, the prominent nineteenth-century hoodoo worker of the St. Joseph area, produced another at Owen's behest for her friend and colleague Charles Leland. Over the course of a lengthy ceremony, Alexander fashioned the amulet and imbued it with a spirit, which he named Charles Leland, presumably because it was spiritually linked to its future possessor. Though Missouri's luck balls were the best documented types of these charms, they could be found elsewhere in the Mississippi River valley. In 1869, New Orleans's *Daily Picayune* reported that Voodoo doctor Jack Goine had a charm to which his life was bound. He had kept it hanging from a nail at the head of his bed until it fell when the nail gave way, precipitating his death and the short news article that reported it. Jean Montanée appears to have possessed one as well and carried it with him at all times. Journalist Lafcadio Hearn described it as being two small bones wrapped in black string.[73]

The use of various body parts of cattle, such as hearts and tongues, were other examples of items common in the Mississippi River valley but rare elsewhere. The 1869 article reporting the death of Jack Goine describes the charm to which his life had been bound as a crepe-draped, herb-filled beef heart. Numerous similar examples appear in Hyatt's *Hoodoo—Conjuration—Withcraft—Rootwork.* A New Orleans practitioner, for example, explained that to keep hostile parties from speaking out against a person being prosecuted for crimes, one should place their names in a beef tongue, apparently after cutting it open. While inserting the names, the practitioner was to pierce the tongue with nine new needles, pins, and tacks. Once the operation was complete, the worker was to salt and freeze the whole. Ground beef and steaks also appeared in some formulae, and other portions of cattle used in Mississippi River valley hoodoo included lard, gall, blood, and liver. Moreover, within Hyatt's collection, formulae from the Mississippi River valley that include cattle body parts are between six and seven times more numerous than similar recipes from elsewhere. In short, spells featuring beef tongues, hearts, and similar items, while common in the lower Mississippi River valley, were virtually unknown elsewhere.[74]

Several other details that were uncommon among the supernatural traditions of other regions were found in New Orleans. For example, a 1773 trial record indicates that alligator hearts were once supposedly in use to kill enemies.[75] Another distinctive feature of lower Mississippi River valley supernaturalism was the employment of brick dust for magical ends. Author George Washington Cable recorded its use in the home of an elderly Marie Laveau, stating that the floor was "worn with scrubbing and sprinkled with crumbs of soft brick." Cable, however, interpreted the sight as a "Creole affectation of superior cleanliness."[76] During the twentieth century, however, Hyatt's informants explained its supernatural usage. According to one New Orleans informant, it was a key ingredient in a mixture with which businesspeople washed their floors in order to draw customers. Another source from the Crescent City described it as an agent with which one should scrub doorsteps in order to protect oneself from hoodoo. A Memphis resident also noted its use as an ingredient with which to draw a spirit to a specific type of coffin-shaped amulet, and an inhabitant of Vicksburg prescribed it as an ingredient in love charms.[77]

Some aspects of Mississippi River valley hoodoo items mirrored the distinctive impact of specific African ethnicities. The Senegambian origins of the words *gris-gris* and *zinzin* were prime examples, as was the West Central African genesis of *wanga*. In addition to terminological ties, Mary Alicia Owen's description of luck balls as being worn on one's side under the arm was uncommon in North America outside of the Mississippi River valley. During the twentieth century, scholar Wanda Fontenot noted similar placements of what she called single-string amulets while conducting research on traditional healers in Louisiana. Such charm placement hearkens back to traditions still common in Senegambia, where under-the-arm placement of charms remains one of the most popular today, a similarity easily explained by the strong presence of Senegambians during the early settlement of Louisiana under the French. The same is true of a healing practice still sometimes found in rural Louisiana in which strings are tied around body parts afflicted with illness or injury. According to some, when the string falls off on its own accord, the ailment is cured. The same practice is still found in Senegal, as well, where the strings are known as *talki* when tied around legs or arms and *luti* when bound around the waist or neck. Brick dust, though not itself distinctively African, was tied to the magical practices of the continent through its color. Though Cable did not describe the hue of the dust he observed, two of Hyatt's three informants agreed that it should be red. In one case, Hyatt noted that it symbolized blood, but the color was clearly rooted in the beliefs of many different African peoples for whom red was a color strongly associated with spirits. My information on current West African charm placement comes from personal observation in Senegal, where similar charms are an everyday part of life. The

The shop of Marabout Aliou Sy in Dakar, Senegal. Its selection of amulets, herbs, animal curios, and other magical items is typical of the spiritual marketplaces of Senegal.

same is true of the color red. Based on my observations in Senegal, Benin, Togo, and the Republic of the Congo and my conversations with a wide variety of these countries' citizens, it is safe to say that the color red remains the hue most commonly associated with the spirit world.[78]

By the late nineteenth century, times were changing as manufactured spiritual commodities made their way into traditional hoodoo practice. Evidence from George Washington Cable's *The Grandissimes* indicates that New Orleans may have witnessed an early advent of such spiritual products. At various points in the narrative, a pharmacist in the city is mistakenly believed to be a purveyor of magical goods. The merged roles of pharmacist and spiritual merchant, which Cable described in 1880 but set during the early nineteenth century, would become common prior to World War II. By 1910, at least one New Orleans pharmacy was producing commercial spiritual supplies, as evidenced by a notebook preserved in the New Orleans Pharmacy Museum that includes formulae for items associated with hoodoo, including one entitled "Hoodo Mixture." By the 1920s, the city's most famous spiritual supply shop, the Cracker Jack Drugstore, was selling similar goods.[79]

With the new businesses came new products. One such was Van Van, for which an early formula composed of oil of cinnamon, oil of lemon grass, oil of rosemary, and alcohol appeared in the Pharmacy Museum notebook. Within the next few decades, it had come to be a fixture of the lower Mississippi River valley. Hyatt reported that by his day, it was an oil and perfume used mainly for spiritual scrubs and washes. Among its many functions were to bring its user monetary success, draw loved ones back home, win money while gambling, repel evil spirits, and acquire other similarly positive benefits. By the time Hyatt collected data, knowledge of Van Van had spread beyond its point of origin and was recognized elsewhere in and near the Mississippi River valley, including Mobile, Alabama and Memphis, Tennessee. Moreover, on the only occasion he encountered it outside the area, his informant had once practiced hoodoo in New Orleans. Less common but no less distinctive was Four Thieves Vinegar, which Hyatt recorded in use among practitioners in New Orleans. Among its attributes was the ability to anger enemies' landlords and to make them unable to rent their buildings.[80]

With the appearance and growth of consumer hoodoo, how-to magical texts came to be a mainstay of spiritual supply shops across the nation, but once again, the lower Mississippi maintained its distinctiveness. One prominent text, *Les secrets merveilleux de la magie naturelle du Petit Albert*—better known simply as *'Tit Albert*—stands out because of its early appearance and persistent presence. Its use in New Orleans was noted as early as 1880, when it was mentioned in Cable's *Grandissimes*. Confirmation of its use appears in the records of the Federal Writers' Project. An informant, recorded as Mrs. J. Fortune, reported that Marie Laveau, as well as lesser-known Voodoo practitioners Joseph Melon and Felice Francois, used the *'Tit Albert* in their practice. Twentieth-century practitioners Lala Hopkins and Charles Raphael also discussed the use of the book. So strong was its reputation that it appears that at least some practitioners had come to consider "Tete Albert" a spirit by the years preceding World War II. According to Carolyn Morrow Long, another French work, *Le Poule Noire* or *Black Pullet,* was of similarly venerable heritage. Both the *'Tit Albert* and *Le Poule Noire* probably entered hoodoo during the colonial period by way of French supernaturalism. Cheap editions of both works appeared in France around the turn of the eighteenth century and reached its colonies, including Saint-Domingue, over the succeeding decades. Their likely adoption by Voodoo during the colonial era places them among the earliest spiritual commodities associated with African American supernaturalism, perhaps even predating the appearance of hoodoo supply shops and definitely anticipating the spiritual products boom of the late nineteenth century and beyond. Nevertheless, they remained in use until at least the early twentieth century.[81]

By the twentieth century, new how-to works had appeared that drew their inspiration from the preexisting hoodoo and Voodoo beliefs of the area. The most famous of these was a book entitled *The Life and Works of Marie Laveau,* which included a collection of petitions to an unnamed deity along with accompanying magical formulae. By Federal Writers' Project worker Robert McKinney's day, it was available from the Cracker Jack Drugstore, but it had been around for some time before. Based on the writings of FWP worker and historian of Voodoo Catherine Dillon, the book came to the attention of the broader public in 1927 during a mail fraud investigation. Shortly thereafter, Zora Neale Hurston included much of its contents in her "Hoodoo in America," where she misleadingly treated it as traditional lore. Another text was *Black Hawk's Works,* and it was more mysterious. Though no known copies survive, Lala Hopkins described it as having black pages with white text and stated that it was used for "dirty work." In both cases, the books were unique to the Crescent City and virtually unknown outside of it until much later.[82]

TEMPORAL BENEFITS

For leaders, Voodoo was both a religion as well as a career. As is true of the minsters of most faiths, their followers supplied their upkeep in a variety of ways. According to FWP informant John Smith, a Voodoo priestess he described as Marie Laveau but who was almost certainly a considerably younger woman charged $1.50 to white men who would attend dances she held in a white cabin at Spanish Fort. Another informant stated that when she was a girl during the 1860s or 1870s, the Voodoo practitioners who hosted the St. John's

Eve gathering at Lake Pontchartrain would charge one dollar to enter a pavilion over the water that they used. An additional interviewee likewise claimed that Voodoo practitioners charged twenty-five cents for entrance into what he said Marie Laveau called the "Hoo-doo Creole" dances held at the intersection of St. Bernard Street and Robertson Avenue. Former associate of Laveau, Charles Raphael, stated that a group of wealthy whites periodically hired the Voodoo Queen to conduct ceremonies for them at a restaurant on Robert E. Lee Boulevard. In contrast to the modest sums charged at the other events, these women reportedly paid ten dollars to each dancer who took part. If one assumes that at least five dancers participated, the total would have likely approached or surpassed the equivalent of $1,000 in 2020 dollars.[83]

Those seeking initiation as practitioners could likewise expect to pay a price. According to Zora Neale Hurston, Samuel Thompson initially asked $350 for instruction—a figure worth well over $5,000 in 2020—before eventually settling for the much lower price of simple sincerity. When Federal Writers' Project workers spoke with two female practitioners about initiation in 1936, one of them suggested that an initiation would cost around $5.00. While not a great sum at a bit over $93.00 in 2020 dollars, it was not exactly pocket change during the Great Depression. When they later met with the man who was to officiate, they were able to negotiate his fee down to $2.15, plus $1.00 for the purchase of items necessary for the ceremony. Lest one take the fees associated with initiation as somehow lessening the authenticity of the rituals, it is important to remember that similar expenses are common among both African traditional religions and their descendants.[84]

The most lucrative source of income for most practitioners, however, was the practice of magic. According to an 1887 article in *The Century*, for instance, a group of disgruntled workers on a sugar plantation determined to get rid of an unpopular overseer by hiring a hoodoo worker from New Orleans to remove him from the scene. Reportedly, the Voodoo initially asked the sizeable sum of $30 for his efforts but eventually settled for only $2.50, which would be almost $68.50 in 2020 dollars. It must be noted, however, that even this seemingly small sum would have been hard to come by for a plantation laborer in those days. According to the author who reported the incident, all the magic worker did was dust the overseer's doorstep with a white powder and place upon it two crossed black hairs. Examined simply through the lens of profit, the magic worker likely made a reasonable sum for his expense in time and material. King Alexander of Missouri similarly settled for modest profits, reportedly charging a dollar to make a luck ball. The famed Jean Montanée, meanwhile, reportedly asked routinely many times the fee quoted by the Missouri practitioner and once made $50.00 selling a single potion.[85]

Prices remained high in the twentieth century, as evidenced by a list of spells and prices collected by Hazel Breaux and Robert McKinney during their time with the Federal Writers' Project. Those who desired to, as the document put it, "get a woman" could hope to do so for as little as $5.00. Causing a marriage to happen, however, was considerably more expensive, requiring an expenditure of $50.00. The costliest works, however, were those designed to cause the deaths of victims, induce madness, or cure the insane. Such undertakings cost $500 each, a sum worth around $9,000 in 2020 terms.[86]

Evidence suggests that the income of some practitioners could be anything but modest. John Smith, for instance, claimed that the woman he described as Marie Laveau "had fine jewelry and wore it all the time."[87] He went on to elaborate, stating that she wore diamond earrings, a diamond pen, and various rings. According to another Federal Writers' Project informant, Raymond Rivaros, Laveau charged for her supernatural deeds and reputedly "got plenty of money" for causing the disappearance of a white grocer.[88] One Mary Washington averred that whites were the Voodoo Queen's sole clientele because she charged so much that African Americans "couldn't afford to pay her."[89] Carolyn Morrow Long, Laveau's premier biographer, suggests, however, that oft-repeated tales of the Voodoo Queen's wealth may well have been overblown. In 1855, for instance, she was unable to prevent her home being seized for debt. On the other hand, Long notes, Laveau occasionally offered sizeable security bonds for women accused of minor crimes. The largest of these bonds was $500 in 1850, roughly the equivalent of $16,685 in 2020. Moreover, Laveau was a slaveowner, a status sought by virtually anyone who could afford it but that even most white southerners never actually attained. Over the course of her life, she and her domestic partner, Christophe Glapion, bought and sold eight slaves. While she seems to have experienced times of hardship, she also had times of plenty, presumably but not definitively because of her professional Voodoo work.[90]

Much less ambiguous was the economic standing of Laveau's contemporary, Jean Montanée. According to journalist Lafcadio Hearn's account of New Orleans's second-best-known practitioner, Montanée was quite well to do. As described by Hearn, he was the owner of considerable land and was at one time worth a minimum of $50,000, a figure equivalent to more than $1 million today. Though the journalist went on to say that the Voodoo had lost much of his wealth to dishonest businessmen and gambling on the lottery, he was extraordinarily successful for a man reportedly kidnapped from Senegal by Spanish slavers as a child. Recent research has backed up Hearn's account. Carolyn Morrow Long has demonstrated, for example, that Montanée was actively involved in investments in land and slaves from 1845 to 1860, by which later date he possessed real estate alone worth $12,000. It does indeed appear, however, that his fortunes declined following the onset of the Civil War.[91]

Despite the success of Jean Montanée, it is clear that many practitioners did not attain wealth. According to Mary Alica Owen, King Alexander of Missouri owned only two garments and those ill-fitting and worn. Likewise, the practitioners interviewed by the Federal Writers' Project during the 1930s and early 1940s rarely showed signs of great prosperity. Even Lala Hopkins, called by Robert McKinney "the most famous present day hoodoo queen" during the late 1930s, lived in what he described as a "single cottage house." He went on to add that her furniture was "very old."[92]

While Voodoo might not have won wealth for all of its successful practitioners, it reliably brought standing. Lala Hopkins, despite her apparently modest means, was nevertheless renowned as a practitioner of what a fellow hoodoo woman called "bad work." When this colleague of Hopkins offered to take Robert McKinney and two journalists to meet her, she insisted that no one must know of the visit. To that end, the group made its way to Hopkins' home well after dark, so late in fact, that Hopkins had gone to bed before they arrived. While her reputation was far from positive, it was obviously powerful. King Alexander, likewise, was "a Voodoo doctor or cunjurer of great power and influence," according to Owen, despite his evident lack of assets.[93] To see that such renown could be enduring, one needs look no further than the continued fame of the likes of Jean Montanée, as Dr. John, and Marie Laveau or the longstanding rituals performed at the grave of Marie Comptesse in St. Louis Cemetery No. 2. Moreover, such repute frequently extended well beyond the bounds of the Voodoo faith, as attested by examples like the 1937 article, "Voodoo Yet Rules Faithful Disciples of Dead Sorceress," which proclaimed that Laveau's "gray ghost haunts the city in which she imperiously ruled the voodoo rites."[94]

Ultimately, while many a Voodoo might have found a strong motivation in the money or power associated with his or her profession, believers came to these spiritual leaders for reasons other than to simply confer wealth or status. Many, perhaps even most, sought them out simply as professionals who could aid them in quests for fortune, love, revenge, or anything else they judged unobtainable by everyday means. For numerous believers, however, Voodoos were something much more. Voodoo's queens, doctors, dauphins, and kings were links to the spirit world and thereby leaders in a ceremonial life beyond the simple pursuit of pragmatic ends.

4

WORKING WITH
THE SPIRITS

The clergy of Voodoo were more than purveyors of magical goods and services. Like the ministers of other religions, they led their followers in corporate ceremonies of worship and petition. As with almost everything surrounding the faith, the record of the individual ceremonies is far from complete. Nevertheless, there is much that has survived. For instance, careful study can provide one with a general outline of the places where such gatherings happened. Moreover, one can divide the rituals of the Louisiana version of Voodoo into groups based on whether they were initiations, part of an annual cycle of holy days, or common ceremonies that took place on a weekly or monthly basis. Outside New Orleans, however, little more than a bare outline of the religious community's ceremonial repertoire has survived.

RITUAL AREAS

Some of the most consistent accounts of ceremonial life describe where the rituals took place. The best journalistic account of a Voodoo ritual space appeared in the July 30, 1850, Tuesday evening edition of the *Daily Picayune*. The article described the examination of a Voodoo priestess named Betsy Toledano, a free woman of color who had been arrested for holding unlawful assemblies of slaves and free people. Police, attracted by the sound of singing, broke into her home. One of the rooms, they found, was decorated with colorful prints of Catholic saints and contained a variety of ritual items. Many earthenware bowls, each containing gravel, pebbles, a paving stone, or a flint stone were prominent features of the room, as were vases and goblets containing liquids that the police were unable to identify. Though Toledano did not explain the liquids, she did state that the stones were used to prevent lightning strikes. According to her, she scattered the smaller stones across the floor and placed the larger ones in the water-filled bowls in order to keep the house safe. She also added that a colorful seashell necklace she wore during the examination allowed her to control the rain. An earlier article described her as possessing banners, rods, and wands, presumably for use in her gatherings.[1] Toledano explained that she learned about the practice of Voodoo from her grandmother, who had come from Africa.

Though Betsy Toledano claimed no connection to Haiti, the description of her ritual paraphernalia and space could as easily fit a modern Haitian Vodou temple, or *ounfò,* as it did an antebellum New Orleans Voodoo house.[2] Compare the above to part of a description of a Haitian ritual space provided by Harold Courlander in his 1960 book, *Drum and Hoe:* "Inside the hounfor was an impressive display of sacred objects and decorations . . . There was a large plate of *loa* stones, and various protective charms stood near by. Flags and sabres were stacked against the wall, and set about in various places were several assons, iron crosses, Catholic lithographs, chains and iron bars for the *loa* Ogoun, candles set in bottles, and an old forged double bell of African design."[3] A key difference between the Haitian model and that of New Orleans is that Toledano's ritual area was part of a private home rather than a temple in its own right. The fact that slaves gathered at Voodoo ceremonies without white supervision was an obvious reason to keep the holy space concealed. The similarities and reasons for difference are obvious, but determining whether they indicate direct descent from Haiti, parallel development from African originals in Catholic-dominated areas, or a combination remains open to interpretation.

The practice of conducting rituals in private homes continued well after the demise of slavery. During the later 1930s or early 1940s, for instance, Federal Writers' Project workers recorded an account of a ritual space belonging to an unnamed "old lady" who practiced hoodoo. The brief description states that she worked in a room in her house where she had an altar, images of saints, and candles. Maud H. Wallace, an employee of the FWP, was a firsthand observer of a similar room in the home of Lala Hopkins. She described it as a small, dirty area with a disorderly assemblage of furniture and knick-knacks. More importantly, its walls were adorned with what Wallace called "religious pictures," and an altar resided in the corner. The lone item upon the altar was a picture of Marie Laveau that its owner had clipped from a newspaper.[4] During the late nineteenth century, Laveau herself supposedly used different places in her home for rituals but also hosted ceremonies—"horrible seances and dances," according to one witness—in her back yard.[5] The interior space centered on two areas, according to Charles Raphael, who claimed to have known Laveau when he was a teenager. In the front part of her home, she had an altar for work designed to benefit followers and clients. Upon it rested statues of St. Peter and St. Marron, the latter described by the informant as a "colored saint." Another informant, Marie Dédé, who had likewise known Marie Laveau, added that she sometimes held dances in this room, kept flowers and "all kinds of saint pictures" on her altar, and had a large statue of St. Anthony, which likely represented Miché Agoussou, in a corner. This statue she would sometimes turn upside down in her back yard, probably to compel its spirit to take action in cases of clients seeking love. Though intended for positive work, this front room was off limits to visitors unless they had what she considered important business. In the back of her house was a second altar used for harmful work. It was surmounted by statues or a bear, a lion, a tiger, and a wolf, and it was dedicated to what Raphael called the "spirit of the snake." This spirit was evidently Monsieur Danny or another deity whose name has not survived the passage of time.[6]

While a great many rituals took place in private homes, not all of them did. Marie Laveau, for instance, supposedly held dances thrice a week in a one-room cabin near Lake Pontchartrain. Others took place outside. Congo Square was a site for evening dances according to some sources. St. John's Bayou was also a popular location for Voodoo gatherings.[7]

CEREMONIAL LIFE

Common Gatherings

Small-scale ceremonies were performed in home ritual spaces. Unfortunately, no systematic account of what these entailed exists, and many of the earliest reports, which appeared in newspapers, are so brief that little is to be learned from them. A typical instance of a journalistic description appeared on July 20, 1851, and reported on a free person of color witnessing a ceremony that consisted of twenty-four mixed race women dancing in a circle around a twenty-fifth who had placed herself, naked, in the center of the gathering. An 1854 article was even more vague, stating that one such "African heathenish rite or mystery" consisted of an all-night affair in which naked men and women engaging in a "wild sort of a Indian dance" in a room with a boiling cauldron at its center.[8]

At one time, such rituals may well have had a variety of names depending upon their purpose, but by the twentieth century, they tended to be known collectively as séances, a term adopted from Spiritualism, or *parterres*, meaning "layouts," from the frequent practice of placing offerings upon a white cloth spread on the floor of the meeting place. These were intended as feasts for the spirits, and according to one participant, they tended to share certain features. Particular foods, for instance, always appeared. Among them were *congris* composed of rice, cow peas, apples, oranges, and red peppers. In the corners of the room were placed lighted candles, the color of which could be red, green, blue, or brown, depending on the purpose of the ceremony. According to the participant, however, white candles never appeared. An accordion provided the instrumental music in at least some cases, and singers and dancers completed the ensemble.[9]

Many ceremonies dispensed with the white cloth. According to an 1891 article from the *Times-Democrat*, for instance, it was once common for followers of a priestess named Zourinous to dance at midnight around a hollow tree in Congo Square, placing money and other offerings inside of it. These rituals reportedly continued for a considerable but indeterminate period until a sailor used a marlin spike to violently halt the meeting and steal all of the spirits' monetary offerings.[10] Two generations later, an informant named Joseph Morris confirmed aspects of the *Times-Democrat*'s account but ascribed the activities in Congo Square to Marie Laveau. As the earlier report indicated, however, the ceremony included dancing and the placing of offerings into a hollow tree. In Morris' account, the contributions consisted of liquor, jambalaya, and fifteen cents. The last of these, on their own or appended to additional monetary offerings, was a common sum in accounts of transactions connected with Voodoo. One Federal Writers' Project interviewee explained that the fifteen cents were for what he called the "hoodoo 'risen,'" and they appear to have invariably been reserved for the use of the spirits rather than those who served them. Oscar Felix, who claimed to have sung at Laveau's ceremonies, likewise linked her to the hollow tree in Congo Square. He added some interpretive details, as well, stating that the fifteen-cent offerings represented the Trinity of Father, Son, and Holy Spirit, presumably because it could consist of three nickels. The food as well as the money also served the social function of providing sustenance for the poor, who would take it from the tree the next day. In contrast to others who described ceremonies in Congo Square, FWP informant Theresa Kavanaugh stated that *parterres*—in which tablecloths placed on the ground held chicken, cake, wine, and bowls of gumbo—took place there as well.[11]

What may have been a similar gathering reportedly took place at what was known as the Wishing Spot located along Bayou St. John outside the city. According to FWP informant Josephine Jones, the ceremonies centered on a stump around which people would bow and kneel to wish, pray, clap hands, and sing at various points during the week. Peak involvement took place on Fridays at noon, 3:00 p.m., and midnight— when hundreds would arrive, sometimes gathering around the stump in crowds up to ten rows deep. The details of this account are somewhat muddled. At one point, the informant seems to say that these gatherings happened well after Marie Laveau's death but at other times seems to say they took place in Laveau's day. The confusion likely resulted from the fact that she was not herself a witness and was simply relaying what her elderly grandmother had told her about them.[12]

Though there does not appear to have been a single day each week devoted to Voodoo ritual by all practitioners, many did meet or perform ceremonies on particular days of the week or month. For instance, believers would visit the tomb of Marie Comptesse in St. Louis Cemetery No. 2, on the first Mondays, Wednesdays, and Fridays of each month. There, they would make cross marks, burn candles, and leave offerings of money to request favors. During the first half of the twentieth century, a group of Voodoo ministers met each Friday in a New Orleans hall where they would be joined by fishermen. Prior to the meeting, they drove out evil beings by washing the corners of the room with whisky and then sprinkling the liquor across the floor. Once the guests arrived, they would pay $5.15 each, with the fifteen cents "paying the floor" as an offering. The ministers would then rub the bodies of the fishermen with an oil that would protect them and bring them luck. Marie Laveau reportedly held her services on Wednesdays and Fridays, according to Marie Dédé. Information supplied by Charles Raphael indicates that Laveau also held *parterres* on Monday evenings in the home of a lesser priestess called Mama Antoine. Another unnamed Federal Writers' Project informant likewise confirmed that Laveau's ceremonies were typically on Mondays, Wednesdays, and Fridays.[13]

Some informants elaborated on the Friday gatherings. One man, Raymond Rivaros, stated that Laveau called her Friday gatherings "rehearsals," and that she never allowed anyone to enter her house with anything crossed. Charles Raphael added detail, claiming that the Voodoo Queen dedicated these gatherings to harmful work. Raphael stated that they featured red, blue, green, brown, and black candles. In apparent contradiction to information he elsewhere gave about her altar for evil work, he stated that she used no altar on these malevolent Friday gatherings, and he described those present as shaking, singing, and dancing what he called the "Pe Chauffe," elsewhere associated with St. John's Eve, and the "Chanson de Dance," a performance in which people are each called when it is time to dance in the middle of the floor. Another informant, Edward Ashley, claimed to have attended one of the Friday night gatherings and described the events as centered around asking a man he called "the boss" questions while the latter was possessed by the devil. The questioned man would lay on a board with a seven-layer cake at his head, each layer adorned with seven candles. As each person left the gathering, he stated, Laveau rubbed liquid upon him or her. The reliability of Ashley's account is somewhat suspect, however, because he also described lightning flashing through the room during the ritual.[14]

While it may well be that each practitioner engaged in unique weekly ceremonies, at least one worker from the late nineteenth century reserved Wednesdays for his healing and other benevolent rituals. Charles Dudley Warner, a white writer for *Harper's Weekly,* reported on one such event, noting with surprise that he was not the only Caucasian in attendance. Moreover, unlike many Voodoo gatherings, the one he attended took place at noon. On the other hand, like many smaller gatherings, it was an indoors event. As with the work area of Marie Laveau, this unnamed practitioner's ten-by-fifteen-foot ritual space was occupied on one side by a buffet or bureau used as an altar. A statuette of the Virgin Mary with lighted candles to either side was its chief adornment, and it was accompanied by cruets and some small, unidentified objects. Two additional candles rested on a shelf below. On this lower shelf and the floor before the altar were offerings: plates filled with various fruits; dishes containing sugar, sugar plums, and orris root; and bottles of brandy and water. Among or in front of these were two more candles and an earthenware bowl. Prior to the start of the ceremony, the chief minister crouched to one side of the assemblage and his wife on the other.[15]

As with many other Voodoo ceremonies, this one began with three raps on the floor. Next followed a recitation of the Apostles' Creed and prayers to the Virgin, all in French. The priest's wife then began to sing the "Dansé Calinda" with a refrain of "Dansé Calinda, boudoum, boudoum!" while her husband arose, poured some brandy to either side of the brown bowl, and drank some himself. He then began a shuffling dance that gradually accelerated. While doing so, he poured brandy and another liquid into the bowl and set it aflame. He then proceeded to dip the various offerings into the burning liquid, apparently with no harm to himself, and distributed them to the eager hands of the attendees. As the dance continued, pieces of burning offerings gradually littered the floor, while the priest continued to dance. At some point, reported the journalist, the chant switched to the "Canga," the words to which were as follows:

Eh! eh! Bomba, hen! hen!
Canga bafio té
Canga moune dé lé
Canga do ki la
Canga li.

While dancing, the priest filled his mouth with liquid, which he then sprayed onto the heads and faces of those nearby. During this portion of the ceremony, attendees approached the priest and knelt for healing, each holding a lighted candle. These candles the priest put out by placing them in his mouth. He then dipped his hands into the burning bowl, washed each one's head, lifted them to their feet, and spun them around. After about an hour and a half had passed, the ceremony closed with the priest's wife taking up a collection.[16]

Warner's description should not be taken as a wholly accurate representation, however. For one, the chants he quotes in his 1887 article appeared only the year before in two articles by noted author George Washington Cable. In the case of the "Dansé Calinda," it is entirely possible that Warner saw a performance of what Cable wrote about. The "Canga," on the other hand, was reported by Cable to have been witnessed nearly a century earlier at a Vodou gathering in colonial Saint-Domingue. While it could be that Warner had seen its Louisiana incarnation, it seems more likely that he simply found himself unable to recall the songs he heard and therefore substituted the songs recorded by Cable in order to fill in the gap left by the unfamiliar and forgotten chants. On the other hand, the account must not be dismissed out of hand. The ritual offerings strongly resemble those of well-attested parterres of later decades, and the altar and candles resemble those described as belonging to the ritual space of Marie Laveau. The spitting of alcoholic beverages is likewise a common feature of Haitian Vodou. Perhaps most important, the ceremony Warner described strongly resembled initiatory rites witnessed by Federal Writers' Project workers many years later.[17]

Initiations

Like most African traditional religions and their New World descendants, Voodoo was an initiatory faith. Fortunately, accounts of initiation ceremonies exist in various states of completeness and reliability, including several that can be found in Zora Neale Hurston's "Hoodoo in America" and *Mules and Men.* She claimed to have experienced initiations at the hands of Voodoo practitioners named Albert Frechard, Father Simms, and Dr. Barnes, among others. The complexity of these ranged from a simple ritual calling on the devil for help working magic to a complex ceremony of lighting and snuffing candles performed before a picture of St. George and a piece of brain coral.[18] The most elaborate of all began with multiple meetings with a man she called Samuel Thompson in "Hoodoo in America" and Luke Turner in *Mules and Men.* On the fourth of these, he reportedly asked her to sit before an altar upon which rested incense and candles, placed a snakeskin across his shoulders, and stood behind her with his hands on her head. After speaking in a language she did not comprehend and going through what she called "violent retching of his body," he told her to remain in place until she felt she needed to move and to then leave without speaking.[19] She was to return the following Thursday at 11:00 a.m. Hurston reported that when she returned, the two of them arranged nine candles upon Thompson's altar, dressing them, presumably with oil, and placed them on top of nine tumblers. The tumblers were divided into groups of three, which contained honey, syrup, and holy water, respectively.

These were then arranged in a semicircle on the altar. At this point, Thompson instructed her to prepare herself by sleeping in her right stocking for three nights and keeping herself clean in mind, body, and spirit. He also stipulated that she was to silently offer herself to a spirit he called the Great One. Hurston was to return at the end of nine days, bringing with her three snakeskins required for what was to follow.[20]

Upon her reappearance before Thompson, he reportedly took the snakeskins, attaching one to a piece of green cloth and lying it over a couch. He made a crown from another. According to Hurston, she then lay upon the couch with a pitcher of water at her head for the Great One. She claimed that she lay there for sixty-nine hours, finally arising on March 19—which was St. Joseph's Day—to be led through running water and then returned to the couch. Thompson and two other men then painted lightning symbols down her back in red and yellow, dressed her in new clothing, and painted eyes on her cheeks and the sun on her forehead. Next, Hurston, Thompson, and five other Voodoo leaders mixed their blood in wine and drank of it, and at noon, Hurston took her place before an altar topped with a communion candle with her name on it, five cakes with icing, honeyed bread, serpent-shaped breads, spinach and egg cakes, okra, veal, wine, flowers, thirty-six yellow tapers, and a bottle of holy water. All was performed in silence according to the version of the events given in "Hoodoo in America."[21]

The silence was broken by Thompson's prayer to the Great One that the spirit accept Hurston as his devotee. Once the spirit apparently indicated its acceptance, Thompson lifted the veil Hurston was wearing, placed the snakeskin crown upon her head, and lit the many candles on the altar. The group then drank a glass of blessed oil and ate the items on the altar. At 10:00 p.m., they left the city, driving for an hour into the countryside in order to sacrifice a black sheep. In preparation, Hurston had written a repeated request to the Great One on nine sheets of paper. These she stuffed into the slit throat of the animal as it lay dying so that it could transmit her prayer to the spirit. They concluded by burying the sheep. They dug earth from beneath it, which they transferred into a mound above it.[22]

Unfortunately, Hurston's works are not known for their reliability. Both "Hoodoo in America" and *Mules and Men* are marred by plagiarism, sensationalism, and at least occasional invention. Hurston's initiations do not strongly resemble the few more reliable descriptions collected in later years. More important, her field notes for the initiation have either not survived or never existed. What little independent evidence of her research survives consists mainly of letters to acquaintances and provides only vague details, which sometimes conflict with the accounts in her publications. Likewise, of the Voodoo practitioners she claimed to have met, none have been conclusively verified to have existed. When Harry Middleton Hyatt conducted research in the area less than a decade later, he unsuccessfully sought out Luke Turner. At one point, he asked a Madame Murray of Algiers, Louisiana, about him and briefly described some of the ceremonies Hurston had recounted. Murray did not comment on Turner one way or the other but spoke of the reputed ceremonies, stating, "Well, we don' do stuff [like that]. Ah think—ah dunno whut that is."[23] Another female practitioner in the area stated that she had never heard of Turner.[24] To be sure, the former informant may simply have never encountered such a ceremony, and it is possible that the name *Luke Turner* was a pseudonym for a genuine Samuel Thompson. In addition, while Hyatt was unable to locate Turner, he did encounter a hoodoo practitioner named Dr. Sims in Washington, DC, who had once lived in New Orleans and stated that he performed initiations using altars and candles. He may well have been the same man Hurston called Father Simms in "Hoodoo in America."[25] While the absence of corroborating data certainly does not prove Hurston's accounts false, it does require that scholars remain skeptical of them.[26]

A more reliable and complete description of an initiation comes from the files of the Federal Writers' Project. Unlike Hurston's reported initiations, it was attended by more than one witness and was followed up by further initiations attended by additional witnesses. FWP employees Robert McKinney and Hazel Breaux arranged the ceremony with two practitioners—"hoodoo queens" McKinney called them—the Mrs. Robinson known as Madame Ducoyielle, an African American, and her white associate, Mrs. Dereco. Robinson and Dereco initially demanded that what they called an *opening* take place after McKinney and Breaux posed as aspiring hoodoo workers with the former later stating that he wanted to practice evil magic while Breaux claimed that she wished only to do good. When the would-be initiates asked what the ceremony entailed, the two Voodoo practitioners explained that it was "a drink or feed to the spirits" who would then aid the future hoodoo workers.[27]

The queens set the ritual sixteen days in advance for December 9, 1936, a Wednesday, chosen because it was the most auspicious day of the week for openings. They spent the time between the decision to proceed and the ceremony itself teaching McKinney and Breaux various aspects of hoodoo. Among the lore learned by the FWP employees were that crossing any parts of one's body prevented spirits from assisting him or her and that a wide range of hoodoo formulae existed, including, but not limited to, spells designed to help them obtain money, win love or sex, kill, or improve their luck. Also included in their instruction were details about calling on the saints by lighting candles and knocking three times each on their statues in the nearby St. Raymond's Church. Robinson also explained that those who devote themselves to evil must work primarily in cemeteries and spent a day teaching McKinney and Breaux how to make offerings of money and food to the dead and how to seek their aid to harm enemies and obtain wishes.[28]

Two days before the scheduled ceremony, the group made final preparations. As part of the lead up, the queens introduced McKinney and Breaux to Oscar Felix—later to become a Federal Writers' Project interviewee himself and called "Nom" by Robinson and Dereco. He would perform the ceremony. Nom asked for a fee of $5.00, which he reduced to $2.15 following negotiations with the FWP workers. McKinney and Breaux also provided a dollar for the queens to buy necessary supplies, consisting of rice, cowpeas, sweet oil, colored candles, "chicken corn," popcorn, small apples, basil, bird sea, and "lucky beans."[29]

The opening itself was an elaborate affair. Those present included Robinson and Nom, along with the two Writer's Project workers, Breaux and McKinney. In their presence, Nom prepared a carefully arranged *parterre* atop a rectangular white cotton cloth placed on the floor against one wall. First, in a central position on the edge of the cloth touching the wall and furthest from the initiates, he put a picture of St. Peter, described by the authors as being the one who "opens the way to heaven."[30] Though Breaux and McKinney did not appear to have realized it at the time, Peter was also Lébat in Voodoo belief. Next, Nom situated lit candles, one white and one green, to the right and left of the cloth, respectively. Then followed the placement on the cloth of bottles of cider and raspberry soft drink; unlit colored candles; plates of steel dust, orris root, dried basil, broken stage planks, bird seed, powdered cloves, and cinnamon; a box of ginger snaps; bananas; apples; a bag of sugar; a jar of olive oil; a camphor branch; a tall glass holding a sprig of basil and a mixture of gin, sugar, and water; a bottle of Jax beer; and two granite pans of *congris*, which in this case was the dish better known today as red beans and rice. Nom also placed

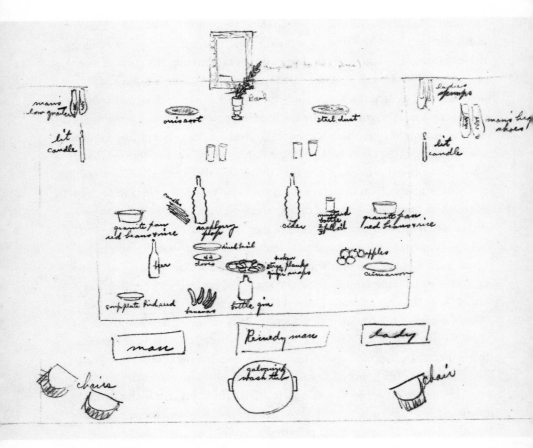

Drawing of a *parterre* for an Opening Ceremony performed by Oscar Felix. Northwestern State University of Louisiana, Watson Memorial Library, Cammie G. Henry Research Center, Federal Writers' Project, folder 44.

a court notice beside the picture of St. Peter. After completing this arrangement, Nom took off his coat, vest, shirt, and shoes. He also instructed the initiates to remove any coats, shoes, socks, and/or stockings they were wearing. Nom sat the shoes against the wall on either side of the picture of St. Peter.[31]

Once properly attired, the three knelt, knocked three times on the floor to call the spirits, and recited the Lord's Prayer. Robinson, meanwhile, observed from nearby. Afterward, the officiant continued to pray and to sing in French while drinking gin. All the while, he made motions with his hands, frequently spit gin into them, and rubbed it on his face. McKinney, who recorded the account of the opening, considered him to be in a trance, which was likely an expression of spirit possession, as would have been common in the corresponding rituals of Haitian Vodou and many other African diasporic faiths. During this process, Nom began to dance. Then, he picked up Breaux and McKinney, one after the other, and turned them "under his arm" three times each.[32] Nom, an elderly man, later lifted McKinney and Breaux onto his back and turned them each around three more times. While all this took place, McKinney and Breaux were told to ask the spirits for the power to work evil and good, respectively. Following the dances, Nom rubbed the legs of McKinney and Breaux with a compound composed of most of the items from the cloth, which had been combined in a large washtub nearby. Nom then passed the lit candles over his visage and through his mouth several times. He gave the white candle to Breaux, instructing her to burn it on three different occasions while asking for what she desired. McKinney, meanwhile, received a red candle broken into three pieces, which he was to use to work evil. Like Breaux, he was to burn it while asking for the fulfillment of his desire. Nom then bit the end off the lit green candle and told the writer to light it at that point in order to upset his enemies. After distributing the candles, the officiant rubbed the insides of the initiates' shoes, first with a mixture of steel dust, basil, and cinnamon, and then with the mixture from the washtub, concluding the procedure by spitting into McKinney's shoes and washing Breaux's stockings in gin. As the ceremony neared its close, Nom first offered gin to both initiates, who refused to drink but placed the bottle to their lips, and then washed Breaux's hair in the liquid in a manner reminiscent of a *lave tet,* meaning "head washing," associated with Haitian Vodou initiations and designed to prepare initiates for possession by the *lwa.* Finally, the Voodoo priest distributed items from the cloth to the newly-minted practitioners, telling them how to use or sell them, and received his payment.[33]

There was not, however, simply one form of opening. McKinney arranged one that he called a St. Peter Opening for the morning of Friday, February 26, 1937, so that two employees of *Life* magazine, a Mr. Henle and a Mr. Peckles, could photograph it.[34] These newcomers posed as gangsters bent on making "a racket out of hoodoo in New York City."[35] As before, Nom Felix was to be the principal officiant, and once again, the initiates negotiated his fee down from $5.00, persuading him to perform the ceremony for $2.00 as long as they purchased all the necessary supplies. Mrs. Dereco opened her home for the event, and McKinney and his companions provided her with a dollar to purchase the needed items. This time there was no period of instruction prior to the ceremony.[36]

The opening itself began in a manner similar to the one encountered by Breaux and McKinney the previous year. The layout resembled that of the previous opening but was this time arranged on the floor of Mrs. Dereco's home before McKinney and his acquaintances arrived. On the altar, as McKinney called the *parterre,* were arranged containers holding basilic, olive oil, seeds of paradise, bird seed, cinnamon, holy water, *congris* (cowpeas and rice, in this instance), sweet oil, bergamot oil, cakes, beer, gin, steel dust, and a picture of St. Peter. Most of these were present in the earlier ceremony, though it had also included many materials not used in this one. Likewise, both Dereco and Robinson were present along with Nom.[37]

Unfortunately for the integrity of the ceremony and the record of it, Henle and Peckles were disruptions from the start. Their request to photograph the ceremony, ostensibly to prove the genuineness of their initiation, angered Nom and made him suspicious of their intentions. Though he eventually agreed to proceed, he would not do so until he had inspected the license plates on his clients' car to assure himself that they were the New York gangsters they claimed. As the ceremony was to begin, Nom partially disrobed, while McKinney and the journalists merely removed their coats. The undressing sparked further commotion as the *Life* reporters began to laugh. McKinney attempted to aid their attempts to stifle their mirth by jumping and making wild motions to distract those present from the laughter, which McKinney had also taken up. According to the Federal Writers' Project worker, Dereco and Robinson interpreted their actions as spirit possession, prompting Peckles to fall on the floor and pretend he was shouting. This highly disrespectful display delayed the ceremony considerably. Even after it began, the initiation was marred by periodic laughter from McKinney, Henle, and Peckles. Peckles made matters worse by repeating, "I say there the spirit has me. I am unable to keep from making this noise. Oh the bloody spirit!" McKinney found this particularly amusing because of the speaker's English accent.[38]

Despite the boorish behavior of his clients, Nom pressed on, beginning by having the participants kneel and pray. He then went into a trance, poured gin on the initiates' heads, and blessed them by praying in French. Nom danced and sang as during the prior ceremony, but he did so alone on this occasion.

After a time, he pronounced his clients "blessed to do what ya want" and closed by passing lit candles through his mouth and "making signs" on the heads of the participants. Nom's part in the day's activities ended when he ordered Henle, who had been photographing the ceremony, never to take his picture again and not to show his face.[39]

The day was not done, however, as a second initiation, called a Black Cat Opening had been prepared by Lala Hopkins and her husband in a back room of Dereco's home. Hopkins, anxious to get started because of the delays to the previous ceremony, was standing before a tub of boiling water when the initiates entered the darkened space. The ceremony was further disrupted because, according to McKinney, Dereco had not purchased the needed materials. Still, Hopkins had the novice hoodoo doctors stand around a table in the middle of the room and began by praying, "Stars above, saints, everybody, hep dese boys to do what dey want to do. Let dem be successful in dere undertaking."[40] Then, the officiant had them kneel beside the table, placing and then lighting a green candle in the center of it. A black candle, Hopkins explained, was appropriate for this type of opening, but was simply not available. She then prayed once more, asking the spirits to give McKinney and company the power to do "bad work" and to conquer. The initial stage of the opening ended with Hopkins instructing Dereco to fetch an egg, a glass, and a piece of straw from a broom for later use.[41]

The ceremony began in earnest when Hopkins shook and proclaimed that the spirit was on her and that the supplicants would receive what they desired. She prayed to the candle, asking the flame to divide into five points if the participants would receive the power they sought. To the surprise of McKinney and the journalists, it did so. Next, the egg supplied by Dereco, which rested on a piece of paper inside a glass took its place on the table. Atop the egg, Hopkins placed the piece of straw, pointing it away from the participants before praying to the "bad spirits," asking that they make the straw indicate who would be successful in their work. McKinney described himself as very startled when the straw pointed to each initiate in turn, beginning with him. No one laughed during this ceremony.[42]

As the event drew to a close, the three men paid Hopkins $1.25, and Hopkins gave the men a charm and some instruction in magic. The charm consisted of three black cat bones enclosed in a bag along with steel dust, a piece of horse's hair, and something she called "returning powder." The last of these may well have been a manufactured item of the kind sold by hoodoo drugstores of the day. Finally, Hopkins provided the now-thoroughly-impressed men with instructions on how to perform several spells designed to protect one's home from evil spirits, kill enemies, obtain good luck, and otherwise utilize spiritual forces to do their bidding.[43]

Two weeks after the St. Peter and Black Cat openings, McKinney, accompanied by Hazel Breaux, spoke with Hopkins again. Breaux, this time, feigned a connection with the supposed gangsters of the previous ceremonies and expressed an interest in malevolent work. During the course of the conversation, the Voodoo adept performed the straw and egg divination that she had previously demonstrated during the previous opening. Her goal was to determine whether or not Breaux would be successful as a hoodoo queen. When the straw refused to move, Hopkins stated her conclusion that Breaux was herself a hoodoo victim in need of an uncrossing opening, a ceremony that the FWP would fail to document.[44]

Though no other sources contain the rich detail provided by the FWP papers, earlier documents described Voodoo ceremonies similar to the openings encountered by McKinney and Breaux. For example, an 1854 article that appeared in the *Daily Delta* vaguely described Voodoo dances, stating that the centers of the rooms in which these took places would be occupied by boiling cauldrons containing herbs for making charms and casting spells. Though the author of the news article drew parallels with stereotypical images of European witches, each of the openings described by the FWP workers contained a cauldron or tub used for just the purpose referenced by the *Daily Delta* article. An account from 1863 also mentions the use of liquids in a ceremony, including an attempt to persuade a witness to drink it. A different report of the same event described the presence of a cauldron filled with liquid. Similarly, newspaper accounts frequently reference dances taking place in some level of underdress, frequently outright nudity. Though nakedness was not a part of the openings experienced by McKinney and Breaux, removal of some clothing was. Moreover, it is quite possible that accounts of nudity were simply exaggerations. The 1863 account referenced above, for instance, noted that while witnesses described nude dancing at the ceremony, law enforcement officers who broke it up stated that none of the participants was actually naked. Some of the greatest corroborative detail comes from an illustration by E. W. Kemble in George Washington Cable's 1886 article, "Creole Slave Songs." Though the image portrays what the article simply calls "the Voodoo dance," it bears a striking resemblance to the first two openings experienced by McKinney and Breaux. At the center of the ritual is a square cloth, laid with offerings and burning candles at each corner. A male Voodoo practitioner dances near the center of the image, just off the edge of the cloth. To the right, a priestess seated in a chair atop a slightly raised platform presides over the gathering, roughly replicating the placement of Oscar Felix and the Voodoo women of the later ceremonies.[45]

Annual Sacred Days

Two holidays, at least, were sacred to Voodoo practitioners. The one that we know least about was November 1, All Saints Day. According to Marie Dédé, each year on this date, Marie Laveau would visit St. Louis Cemetery Number 1, taking a black box with her. This receptacle she would supposedly place atop her parents' tomb and sit there silently all day. When night fell, she would return to her home. Unfortunately, Dédé's testimony is the sole extant witness to this apparently solitary ceremony, which evidently honored and/or petitioned the dead.[46]

In contrast to the small and secretive initiations as well as Laveau's somewhat mysterious All Saint's activity, the annual St. John's Eve/Day ceremonies on June 23 and/or 24 could be large and sometimes public affairs, especially by the later 1800s.[47] As scholar of Marie Laveau, Carolyn Long, has noted, St. John's Eve was not dedicated solely to Voodoo ceremonies. In contrast, it was an occasion for nighttime celebrations across the Crescent City by people of many backgrounds.[48] Nevertheless, that it was a key holiday in the New Orleans Voodoo year is well established. An 1875 article that appeared in *Appleton's Journal* purportedly described a St. John's Eve ceremony of fifty years prior. The informant, a "Professor D——, of New Orleans," stated that as a boy of fifteen, he had witnessed a ritual on St. John's Eve in an abandoned brickyard. According to the professor's account, he had accompanied a slave named Phoebe to the location, gaining entrance with what appeared to have been a secret knock on the gate, followed by a brief conversation with an elderly man who was evidently guarding the ceremonial grounds. Shortly thereafter, the two met the presiding officer of the ceremony, whom the author called Sanité Dédé, who was none too happy with his presence. Rites followed in a large shed nearby in which two large fires atop squares of brick at either end of the building and smaller flames along each wall lit the scene. Around sixty participants arrived, clothed in white with similarly colored kerchiefs around their heads, the women having an additional knotted Madras handkerchief over the white one. Near one of the large fires was an altar containing stuffed black and white cats, a cypress sapling, and a black doll wearing a dress embellished with various signs and symbols and a necklace of snake vertebrae from which hung a single alligator tooth covered in silver.[49]

The ceremony began with the playing of a drum, with one man beating the head with sticks while two other musicians played along its wooden sides using sheep and large bird bones as drumsticks. A couple of feet away was a young man playing a rattle made from a calabash filled with pebbles. Following a signal of some sort, four initiates formed a semicircle in front of Dédé, who then sprinkled them with liquid from a calabash she held. Immediately afterward, the drummer reached behind the doll on the altar, bringing out a snake of red and black coloring, which he passed over the heads and placed around the necks of the initiates. As he did so, he repeated the words "Voudou Magnian" with each pass. After these initial steps, the drummer returned to his playing and was joined by a banjo player, while tables were set up for a feast.[50]

The supper ended when the drummer sounded a "long, fierce call" on his instrument. Once more he brought forth the snake, moving it around the gathered crowd and dancing with it, initiating a call-and-response of "Voudou, voudou, Magnian." He ended his dance by throwing the unfortunate serpent into one of the large fires. The musicians renewed their playing, and the congregation began to yell. This activity apparently triggered spirit possession. A woman took up an undulating dance resembling the motions of a serpent, and within moments, the other women present began to do the same. According to the professor, the drummer chanted the following:

> Houm! Dance Calinda,
>> Voudou! Magnian,
>> Aie! Aie!
>> Dance Calinda!

The witness's experience ended when he hastily departed shortly thereafter, prompted by the sudden extinguishing of the flames that lit the room.[51]

If accurate, Professor D——'s account would make it the first Voodoo ceremony described in detail by a witness. Unfortunately, it is problematic because of its uniqueness. Unlike postwar ceremonies, the one witnessed by the professor was a secretive affair, more closely resembling in that way the initiations recorded by Federal Writers' Project workers than the St. John's Eve ceremonies of the late nineteenth century. Of course, antebellum African Americans had a greater motive for secrecy, especially when such ceremonies involved prohibited gatherings of slaves. In addition, later St. John's Eve gatherings took place near water, while the one attended by the professor does not appear to have. Such distinctions can be explained in several ways. First, it may be that Professor D—— was a writer of fiction rather than ethnography. Another option is that the passage of five decades had addled his memory, causing him to confuse an initiation with a St. John's Eve ceremony or to recount it in a way that made it appear more distinct from later ones than it actually was. Perhaps he was more or less accurate. For instance, secrecy was certainly more important during the antebellum period than it would be after the Civil War, and if initiations had been incorporated into a St. John's Eve gathering, the Voodoos would have had an additional motive for concealing their doings. Moreover, the passage of time was just as likely to alter ceremonial life as it was individual memory. It is entirely plausible that the location of an annual ceremony would shift from within the city limits to a rural location over time and with changes in leadership.

An 1872 account from the *New Orleans Times* provides some details, supposedly by an eyewitness, of a ceremony that occurred on the evening of June 23 of that year. The author indicated that the location of the ritual changed from year to year but that on this particular occasion, it took place on Lake Pontchartrain near Bayou Tchoupitoulas and that he traveled there by boat down Bayou St. John to the lake, arriving sometime after 8:00 p.m. Shortly after he had reached the location chosen for the celebration, approximately 300 assembled, with females composing a slight majority of the attendees. Approximately two thirds of the group were African American or mixed race, but the other third were whites.[52]

According to the journalist, the ceremony began with the arrival of Marie Laveau and ten attendants, who reached the scene in a skiff and were greeted with cheers. The Voodoo Queen began by speaking to the crowd in a creole dialect that the author described as Gumbo French and started a chant during which she sang, "Saiya ma coupé ca," and was answered with "Mam'selle Marie chauffez ca."[53] At about 11:00 p.m., the queen ordered a fire constructed on the very edge of the lake, with each attendee adding a piece of wood and making a wish as he or she did so. Once it was blazing, someone in the congregation placed a cauldron atop it. To it were added several ingredients, beginning with water from a beer barrel. Next, an old man put salt into the water and was followed by a young woman who sang as she added black pepper. Then, the two joined Laveau in adding pieces of a freshly sacrificed black snake. According to the author, each part represented a person of the Trinity. All once again sang, "Mam'selle Marie chauffez ca," and Laveau killed a cat, placing it in the pot. The mixture was further augmented with a bound, live rooster, following another repetition of the song. After those present once more repeated the refrain, Laveau ordered them to disrobe—to what extent is unclear—and join hands in a circle around the cauldron. This done, the Voodoo Queen emptied a bag filled with white and colored powders into the pot, singing a song in creole French after doing so. The crowd responded by singing, "C'est l'amour, oui maman s'est l'amour," which can be translated "This is love, yes mother this is love."[54]

By this point, it was midnight. Noting the time, Laveau instructed those present to enter the lake, which they did, remaining there for half an hour before returning to shore. Once back on land, they sang and danced for about an hour, at which point the queen delivered a sermon. After she finished, the group broke up for a period of recreation. Following the suspension of the ceremony, which lasted half an hour, Laveau prompted someone to sound a seashell horn to signal the resumption of the ceremonies. Singing began once more, and after a time, Laveau announced that the crowd could now eat. The horn once again marked a shift in the ceremony. The group returned to the cauldron, the fire under which was extinguished by what the reporter described as "four nude black women, with white handkerchiefs on their heads." As the women extinguished the flames, the crowd returned to the "chauffez ca" chorus. Once the flames were out, those present transferred the contents of the pot to the barrel in which the water had been brought. Laveau explained that the mixture would be saved for the next year.[55]

Once the barrel was filled, the ceremony wound down. The queen had the participants dress, and the seashell sounded once more, calling the crowd to her. She delivered a second sermon, had the congregants kneel to pray, and blessed them. The final chorus, a repetition of "c'est l'amour," rang out as the sun began to rise, and Laveau gave her final instructions, saying, "Here is day, we must welcome it with song, and all go home."[56]

The general outlines of the version of St. John's Eve depicted in the 1872 article appeared in many other accounts. Three years before, a short article entitled "Voodooism" appeared in the New Orleans Commercial Bulletin, describing June 1 as the key date in the Voodoo calendar, marked by the religion's most important rituals and involving the election of a new queen. It went on to describe the season as marked by "Midnight dances, bathing and eating."[57] Though it falls short of specifically identifying St. John's Eve and seems to suggest that June 1 rather than the 23rd or 24th was the key date, the correspondences are a bit too great to dismiss it altogether. An 1871 description from the Daily Picayune likewise paralleled the 1872 account by locating the ceremony along Lake Pontchartrain, describing the crowd as multiracial, and emphasizing the singing aspect of the ritual. It similarly stated that the celebration continued until dawn. In contrast, however, it described the ceremony as taking place on June 24.[58] Clearly, like most spiritual traditions, St. John's Eve developed over time and could appear quite different over the passage of years, but by the late nineteenth century, it had clearly become a nighttime ritual characterized by feasting and associated with water.

Many years later, accounts collected by the Federal Writers' Project corroborated aspects of the earlier newspaper reports. According to Eugene Fritz and John Alfred—residents of a retirement home who claimed to have attended, but not participated in, a St. John's Eve ceremony at Lake Pontchartrain—the dancing took place on a boat. Laveau, they stated, was present and directed the activities from the center of the group as would a drum major. The music was supplied by a group of male drummers who sat in a circle to the side and played what the informant identified as tom-toms. Both women and men took part, with the women wearing short, low-cut dresses and the men clad in short pants, light shirts, and three-inch-wide leather belts. The dancers, reported Fritz and Alfred, would march out to the sound of drums and begin by stomping their feet, moving one out to the left and other to the right. After doing so, they would shake downward and then upward whenever the drums would sound loudly. They would then dance so that their "bodies would look like a turning top."[59] The two men described what was probably spirit possession, stating that the female participants would fall to the floor screaming and shaking. They added that even white women in the crowd of observers would "do funny things," while watching the dance. Some of the dancers would even jump into the lake to cool down. After the main event, Laveau supposedly had private parties in a nearby hut for white men and mulatto women, which the account seems to imply were something other than strictly religious rituals. Somewhat confusingly, however, the two elderly men stated that these events took place on June 21.[60]

Other observers who informed the Federal Writers' Project workers confirmed some details and added others. Charles Raphael stated that dancers on the barge threaded their way through seven or eight large bottles arranged in a circle while balancing candles atop their heads. During these performances, small pots of fire both provided illumination and acted as votive lights for the spirits. This dance he called the Fe Chofe, which ties it to the chant of "Mam'selle Marie chauffez ca" from the 1872 news article. Raymond Rivaros confirmed Raphael's account of the bottles and added that the dancers, male and female, would jump over them as well as weave among them. He also stated that the music was provided by a single drum and an accordion and that the participants sang a song called "Jolie Pounse," but he agreed that Laveau stood and directed the activities. He likewise confirmed Fritz and Alfred's statement that the dancers would jump from the barge into the water, after which they would "cut" the liquid with knives, scissors, and hatchets.[61]

A man who went only by the name of Pops confirmed the shaky dance mentioned by Fritz and Albert. He also said that the barge contained saint statues and an altar with flowers. Laveau and the female dancers wore purple dresses, and the Voodoo Queen also had a rope around her waist. The men wore white and purple and carried candles. Pops also stated that he once got cake, champagne, and liquor from Laveau's barge. Cake also appears in an account by William Moore, who related that on one June 24 or thereabout, he once went to see Laveau. According to him, she had an altar under a large tree in the forest near Lake Pontchartrain, upon which those seeking the aid of the Voodoo Queen were to place a cake. Then, each person disrobed until clad in a single piece of clothing and lay with others face down on the ground in a large circle at which point Laveau would appear wearing a very thin gown to dance around them until she collapsed in exhaustion. One might be inclined to dismiss Moore's account as describing something other than St. John's Eve/Day. The absence of the barge and group dancing is certainly distinctive. Moreover, Moore himself stated that his memory was failing and that he was unsure of the date. Plus, he described Laveau in terms one expects to hear regarding a much younger woman, stating, "And she was fine, too, I mean to tell you. She was a beautiful woman." On the other hand, he adamantly averred that he was an eyewitness and also stated that the ceremony began with the words, "Siama cope. Siama cope," undoubtedly the "saiya ma coupé sa" of the 1872 news account. The solution is probably simply that Moore, a seventy-six-year-old in 1940, who described himself as at least near adulthood when he attended, had confused a younger woman for Laveau, who would have been around eighty years old had he seen her.[62]

An account by Oscar Felix, who had performed the opening ceremonies for Breaux and McKinney a few years before, supports Moore's account that at least some of Laveau's St. John's activities were on land. As he described it, St. John's Day was a time of celebration ashore. Eating cakes, chicken, and red beans and rice and drinking liquor were central to his memories of the event. The religious aspect of the rituals centered on an altar with a large log cross behind it. Atop the former would be a picture of St. Peter, whom Felix stated was there for protection. Three large candles burned to each side and in front of the image. A large white cloth occupied the ground before the altar. Activities would begin when the leader of the ceremonies would place a picture of St. John upon the altar. All would then kneel before the altar and knock on the ground three times for hope, faith, and charity or Father, Son, and Holy Ghost. They would then sing in Creole French and praise St. John in a way that Felix said resembled "Mass in a regular church."[63] The Voodoo tradition would clearly diverge from Catholicism when what Felix called the Creole Dance began. As he described it, one man would dance with two women at a time. Each would have metal rings on their knees that would add a percussive sound to their movements. The man would turn each woman around then dance with first one and then the other. After completing their dancing, all present would kneel once more and recite the Our Father prayer, also known as the Lord's Prayer, to close out the religious aspect of the day. Casual eating, drinking, and enjoying each other's company followed.[64]

Felix's account, on its own, differs considerably from the 1872 news account and some of the Federal Writers' Project descriptions, but taken in conjunction with Moore's very similar description, the two may well indicate either that ceremonies on the lake became less common after the early 1870s or that the land-based events were specific to St. John's Day rather than the prior evening.

The sacred waterfall at Sodo, Haiti. The St. John's Eve bathing rituals of New Orleans are reminiscent of the washing that takes place in the stream beneath the waterfall.

Marie Dédé supplied a plausible reason for the former interpretation. According to her, the year after the news story appeared, a storm arose on June 24 while the celebration was in progress. Laveau herself nearly drowned but was saved after rescuers found her floating in the lake and brought her to shore. A brush with death of this sort could well convince one to avoid the water thereafter.[65]

Though numerous accounts of the ceremony exist, the question of its function remains very much an open one. At some level, at least, it was probably a celebration of spring. After all, as Carolyn Morrow Long has noted, New Orleanians of European descent celebrated St. John's Eve as just such a festival. Oscar Felix supplied his own interpretation, stating that participants celebrated on that day because they wanted to be like the saint, whom he stated "was a great man and always did what was right."[66] Similar celebrations take place in Haiti, where St. John the Baptist is celebrated with bonfires in his honor. New Orleans's ceremonies, which required participants to travel some distance to a spot on Lake Pontchartrain were likewise reminiscent of other Haitian and West African rituals related to water and the spirits that inhabit it. The most famous of these is the pilgrimage to the Sodo Waterfall and subsequent bathing in its water, though it developed too late to be an ancestor of Louisiana's St. John's Eve. According to Hounan Nïmantchee, head of Vodu in Togo, his country has an annual ceremony in June that is virtually identical to the type described by the 1872 news article. Another possible reason for the ceremony may be indicated by the practice of cutting the water, which was likely intended to protect the celebrants, their homes, or their city from destructive water-related disasters. Early twentieth-century sociologist Newbell Niles Puckett recorded similar practices in the folklore of African Americans elsewhere in the American South, reporting that it was common to chop the ground with an ax in order to cut storms in two. A similar logic might have well been at work on St. John's Eve. Of course, none of these explanations are mutually exclusive, and all might well have played their roles in motivating the celebration.[67]

Ceremonies outside Louisiana

Of course, the Voodoo outside of New Orleans had its own ceremonies, but as with much else, these were considerably less well documented than those of the lower Mississippi River valley. The best attested took place in Missouri, with the earliest substantial account found in former slave William Wells

Brown's 1880 work, *My Southern Home: The South and Its Peoples.* Brown stated that he once attended what he called a "midnight meeting" of Voodoo practitioners in St. Louis. Though he did not specify the date, he placed it in the context of a discussion of "superstition" as it existed forty years prior or about 1840. The ceremony, as he described it, took place outside around a small fire and included men and women of all ages. The officiants, however, consisted of one queen and two assistants. The ceremony began as the leaders arrived with one assistant carrying a cauldron and the other a box. The cauldron, having been placed upon the fire, was the focus of attention. The queen stood before it with what Brown called a "magic wand" in hand, and the remaining attendees formed a ring around her. She began her ritual actions by throwing an unknown material into the flames, which caused them to flare up and then subside into what Brown called a "veil of dusky vapors." Following what were most likely ritual motions and speech on the part of the queen, she had the contents of the box carried by the other assistant emptied into the cauldron. Brown describes the items it had contained as "frogs, lizards, snakes, dog livers, and beef hearts." Following this, the queen returned to her ritual actions, while members of the crowd took hold of each other's hands and danced around the fire until they were exhausted.[68]

Brown was dismissive of what he witnessed. In fact, the context of his passage is clearly condemnatory, his aim being to demonstrate that slavery was linked to an ignorance out of which African Americans had climbed by the late nineteenth century. On the other hand, there is no reason to think he fabricated it. One argument in its favor is that the presence of the cauldron resembles various descriptions of New Orleans Voodoo, including the carefully documented openings experienced by Federal Writers' Project workers many years later during which similar containers played important parts in the rituals. Still, the gap of forty years between the time he witnessed the ceremony and when he wrote about it renders it highly risky to embrace the description as an accurate depiction of Voodoo in St. Louis.

Another point in support of Brown's description is that others commented on similar ceremonies. For example, the title of an 1893 article that appeared in New Orleans's *Daily Picayune* proclaimed, "Voodoo Worship Exists in St. Louis." After describing the local version of the faith as requiring initiation through whipping, drinking various mixtures, and advancing through multiple stages of preparation, the anonymous author went on to state that disproportionate numbers of believers had been adults before the Civil War and that many had originally come from Louisiana. He or she then went on to state that believers held a ceremony during each quarter of the year, having recently done so at a location on Valentine Street and in the basement of an abandoned house on Eighth Street.[69]

The author added a somewhat detailed description of an event that took place on August 15 of that year in the Eighth Street location. According to the writer, parts of the event were stealthily witnessed by a group of African Americans, two of whom happened to fall into the basement when the rotten floor above gave way. Their testimony, transferred second-hand to readers, stated that the scene was lit by burning pine knots and dominated by a priest named Gumbo who stood before an altar upon which lay what appeared to be a sacrificial offering, a white rabbit in this case. The altar, which resembled a tree stump, was carved with images of animals and humans, and an iron urn from which burned a blue flame rested beside it. Four women and eleven or twelve men formed a ring around the priest. Both the officiant and the male participants were dressed in what the writer described as breech clouts, while the women wore short skirts, around the bottom of which were ornaments. Most were elderly. Some of the men were young, however, and had reportedly been undergoing initiation for the prior month.[70]

The ceremony, though interrupted by the arrival of unexpected guests, continued with the priest touching the sacrifice and then applying his fingers to the foreheads of those in attendance. According to the article, this act excited the worshippers, who formed a "long figure with parallel sides" with two women with a man between them at each end. Once they had assumed these new positions, Gumbo threw something that resembled tea leaves into an urn, which burned like incense and left all inclined to agreeable lethargy. The priest then pointed around the room, and each time he did so, one of the participants would begin to sway. After a time, they once again formed a circle, continuing the swaying motions in unison and taking up what the author described as a "hum or chant." The witnesses recognized no words and were unsure if the sounds were meant to be language. As the dance continued, Gumbo continued to point, and when he did so, flames seemed to emanate from his eyes, according to the writer. Each time, a dancer would collapse to the floor, unconscious, but would soon regain his or her senses to be helped up by the priest. At this point, the description ended, whether because it reached the end of the event or because the journalist thought further description too lengthy is unclear. Moreover, beyond the initiatory aspect of the ceremony, the writer ventured no guesses as to its purpose.[71]

The journalist mentioned one additional St. Louis ceremony, which reportedly took place at the Valentine Street location. A witness claimed that it consisted of dancing around a cauldron and that no initiates were present. Though an exceptionally sparse description, the presence of dancing around a cauldron appears to be quite similar to what Brown described and is reminiscent of various New Orleans ceremonies, including the openings described by Federal Writers' Project workers in which washtubs featured as prominent ritual paraphernalia.[72]

As is typically the case when examining Missouri Voodoo, some of the best information comes from the writings of Mary Alicia Owen. Her research focused on St. Joseph, Missouri, a city on the far side of the state from St. Louis but nevertheless connected to the Mississippi River valley because of its situation along the tributary Missouri River. One of Owen's key informants, the man she called King Alexander, described the religion's initiatory nature in the area, explaining that there were four degrees of Voodoo, regarding which either he or his chronicler gave only snippets of detail that do not clearly define what each degree entailed. In an essay called "Voodooism," Owen did record that as preparation for advancing through the degrees, one learned about the making of charms and the interpretation of dreams, a step in keeping with the magical training Breaux and McKinney would undergo in New Orleans several decades later. After this initial step, Owen recorded, one could potentially acquire power by obtaining a spiritually powerful object from someone else. The one Owen described was a large wolfskin bag containing a wide range of zoological curios. Those who gained their supernatural acumen in this manner were of low standing, claimed Alexander. To become a truly skilled practitioner, he averred, an aspiring priest had to progress through a series of trials designed to help him or her conquer himself or herself. These included fasting, eating repulsive items like live catfish, walking through graveyards at night, and undertaking similarly daunting tasks. After a period ranging from weeks to years of such trials, one who completed them would be ready to join a local society Alexander called the Circle.[73]

Elsewhere, Owen gave some indication of what the steps of the initiation entailed. These were not the elaborate affairs one would find in New Orleans and appear to have consisted initially of self-initiation. According to information she obtained from Alexander, the first step was to locate two saplings that the wind has caused to rub together until portions of their bark had been rendered smooth. This bark would then be harvested and boiled in water to make a quart of tea. Next, the tea would be blended with a pint of whiskey and the whole consumed, preferably at one sitting. Following a lengthy sleep to allow the effects to pass, the initiate would isolate himself or herself from others and fast for nine days. During this time, he or she would ponder over his or her new life and the power it would entail, sleeping frequently and paying close attention to any dreams, which would have spiritual significance. One or more of the visions would direct the initiate to an object imbued with spiritual force. This object the novitiate was to acquire as his or her source of power. Another practitioner of Owen's acquaintance, whom she knew as "Aunt" Dorcas, followed a similar pattern of gathering spiritually significant plant materials, followed by a nine-day wait prior to the start of prophetic dreams. The major differences were the plant itself, the requirement that its leaves be worn in a packet under the right arm, and the need to scatter the leaves in the four cardinal directions after the nine-day period. Likewise, there was no apparent stipulation of isolation in Dorcas's initiation.[74]

A period of tutelage under an established practitioner came after the initiation period. According to King Alexander, the teacher had to be of the opposite sex. In cases in which a member of the appropriate sex proved unavailable, the teacher would dress as the opposite gender on alternating days, which was the case when Alexander joined the Circle. The first lesson consisted of learning which numbers were powerful and which were unlucky. At the end of this opening period of instruction, the initiate would acquire a secret name under which he or she would work magic. The next steps of the novitiate consisted of learning herbal formulas and the workings of magic. First came instruction in remedies and poisons, which were not necessarily overtly supernatural, including the proper times to gather them and when to provide them to clients. Next came workings of a distinctly spiritual nature, including spells of various sorts to harm or help. According to Owen, master Voodoo and pupil typically sought inebriation after each period of instruction, drinking whiskey or swallowing tobacco smoke in pursuit of the desired result.[75]

Following the preliminary instruction, new practitioners would learn the lore of Grandfather Rattlesnake and the dances of Voodoo. Much of the knowledge associated with this chief spirit of Missouri Voodoo took the form of stories that illustrated his personality and told of his role in the working of the universe, tales heard and written down by Owen. The dances, meanwhile, were of four types. Owen reported most thoroughly on what she called the Grandfather Rattlesnake dance, which she described as functioning to communicate some of his wisdom and incisiveness to his devotees. At the heart of this ceremony was a live rattlesnake, freshly fed to make it sluggish and kept at a distance in the center of the dancers, who sometimes circled it and at other points jumped up and down, remaining otherwise stationary. According to Owen, participants were to some degree unclothed and had prepared themselves by consuming whiskey and tobacco smoke. She likewise states, somewhat questionably, that there was no rhythm to the dance, and that the only music was produced by participants, whom she said would "howl in any key, without words . . . the same as they do at a religious revival or camp-meeting."[76] The ceremony ended with a feast upon a black dog and sometimes a goat kid, supplied to dancers by a group consisting of two women and two men.[77]

Though the Grandfather Rattlesnake dance might appear of dubious authenticity, African and Haitian precedents lend it considerable plausibility. For instance, live snakes are very much a part of Beninese Vodun to this day, most prominently in the Python Temple of Ouidah, which houses dozens of snakes associated with the god Dan, and living pythons were important for centuries in various ceremonies of the once-independent kingdom. Likewise, though live snakes are not a prominent part of modern Haitian Vodou, Médéric-Louis-Elie Moreau de Saint-Méry, once an important official in colonial French Saint-Domingue, recorded that they were during the eighteenth century. According to him, adders appeared in at least some of the ceremonies, during which officiants kept them in cage-like boxes. They appear to have served as conduits for Danbala, helping him to possess devotees and enable the presiding priestesses—called queens by Moreau de Saint Méry—to utter prophecies. During the course of some ceremonies, believers also reportedly danced around a circle drawn on the ground by the lead priest into which initiates placed themselves. Just as important, Moreau de Saint-Méry asserted that the use of serpents in Vodou was tied to slaves from what is now coastal Benin, a key historical root of the religions found in both Haiti and the Mississippi River valley.[78]

In addition to the Grandfather Rattlesnake dance were three others. One that Owen called the "fire-dance" was performed to strengthen the body and appears to have centered around an actual fire from which sassafras and or maple wood were barred. Unlike the dance for Grandfather Rattlesnake, this one did not end in a feast, but Owen claimed they resembled each other in what she saw as a lack of organized ritual. Believers also gathered in woodland glades on full moon nights to hold ceremonies, which Owen appropriately called moon dances. Participants' chanting and rhythmic motion in a circle, she wrote, characterized these. She also stated that the Voodoos sacrificed black hens to the moon, opening their sides to let their entrails protrude and then releasing them to die, but it is unclear whether Owen considered this action part of the moon dance or a separate nighttime ritual. Finally, believers reported that the ghosts of dead conjurers also danced at the time of the full moon and that those who could locate them would learn their secrets. The sparse and somewhat uneven reporting by Owen is not surprising as she experienced only bits and pieces of the dances firsthand, collecting most of her information from witnesses.[79]

Owen also outlined what appear to have been marriage ceremonies between Grandfather Rattlesnake and female worshippers, a practice in keeping with the Haitian Vodou ritual known as *maraj lwa.* According to Owen's account, the serpent identified his bride, a female virgin, by causing her to smell like boiled gooseberries. Once her chosen status became evident, her fellow members of the Voodoo gathering would sacrifice a white goat kid in her presence. Owen interpreted the goat as a substitute for the human, whom she believed would have been herself sacrificed in earlier days. Interestingly, she states that both the woman and the kid were known as "the goat without horns," a term associated with supposed human sacrifice in Haiti. If this marriage indeed paralleled the Haitian practice of *maraj lwa,* then the young woman would from henceforth have had a special relationship with Grandfather Rattlesnake and would have been obliged to set aside a day to serve the spirit each week.[80]

Accounts of the religion's ceremonies outside the Mississippi River valley are rare and usually consist simply of using *Voodoo* as a synonym for *hoodoo* or *conjure.* Sometimes, what writers described as Voodoo were different religions entirely. In Florida, for instance, writers often conflated Voodoo with a distinct local faith that developed out of Cuban Santería.[81] Nevertheless, a few examples of what may well have been genuine Voodoo rituals do exist. One of these appeared in the same *Daily Picayune* article that addressed St. Louis ceremonies. The event in question reportedly took place in a predominantly Black suburb of Mobile, Alabama, and was observed by a St. Louis bookkeeper who had once lived in the area. After being attracted by sounds that he took to be evidence of an African American secular dance, he peered into an old house through a gap left by a loose board. Inside, he witnessed a group of men and women dancing in a swaying motion around a large iron kettle. All were naked, per the informant, and over the course of the ceremony, each took turns stepping up to the kettle to drop an item into it. Per the witness, these offerings consisted of a small alligator, a turtle, a lizard, and a cat's foot. As the ritual progressed, he stated, the participants became "wilder and wilder" before falling to the floor in what he called "catalepsy."[82]

As is typically the case in newspaper articles, one must take the account with a grain of salt. This account, in particular, includes the salacious detail of nude dancing and what white readers would judge to be bizarre offerings. On the other hand, the ceremony was remarkably similar to the one William Wells Brown described in Missouri and once again included the common feature of a large receptacle into which those present placed ritual items. Moreover, the proximity of Mobile to New Orleans and their shared history as parts of what had once been French Louisiana renders at least the broad outlines of the account plausible. At any rate, it would be more surprising to learn Voodoo was absent from Mobile than to find it there.

While any description of the ceremonial life of Voodoo would be incomplete, its vitality during the nineteenth century was clear. Its embrace by a substantial segment of the Mississippi River valley's population is all the more striking in that Voodoo was always suspect to the white ruling caste. The mocking descriptions one often finds in journalistic accounts of the faith reflect the prevailing, largely unquestioned racism of the nineteenth and early twentieth century. This same mindset is what allowed Henle and Peckles to laugh when given the rare privilege of participating in an initiation into the faith at the hands of its most prominent living practitioners. On its own, however, racism was not enough to dampen the African diasporic religion. The legal system could go much further than simple dismissal and denigration, however, frequently seeking to eliminate it altogether. While efforts to do just that were underway prior to the Civil War, they would intensify as the nineteenth century drew to its close and the twentieth progressed.

THE DEATH OF
A RELIGION?

In recent years, several scholars have addressed questions of Mississippi River valley Voodoo's African origins, ceremonial life, and leadership. One question that academia has largely sidestepped is whether or not it disappeared as a living religion.[1] With the highly visible presence of Voodoo imagery and souvenirs throughout those portions of New Orleans frequented by tourists, questioning its survival can seem counterintuitive. Indeed, sustained analysis of the question of Voodoo's survival has appeared only at the hands of historian Kodi A. Roberts. In his 2015 monograph *Voodoo and Power: The Politics of Religion in New Orleans, 1881–1940,* he persuasively argued that though it seemed to disappear as a distinct religion in the first half of the twentieth century, it actually survived under the guise of New Orleans's Spiritual churches. The truth of Voodoo's survival or lack thereof is more nebulous and open to interpretation, however. While much depends on how one defines the religion and delineates its boundaries, the faith of Marie Laveau, King Alexander, and Lala Hopkins is best understood as a historical religion rather than a living tradition, while today's New Orleans Voodoo is an emerging faith inspired by and seeking to reconstruct the older religion.

THE SUPPRESSION OF VOODOO

From early in Voodoo's history, city, state, and federal authorities did their best to suppress it. Historically, most of the legal actions that affected Voodoo had little to do with supernaturalism *per se.* Sometimes, criminal deeds that were only tangentially connected to Voodoo nevertheless impacted the religion. Such was the case with the well-known Gris-Gris Case of 1773. The crime itself was conspiracy to murder New Orleans-area slave owner Francisco Seimars de Bellile as well as an overseer, reportedly carried out by a group of three of Bellile's enslaved workers. Also caught up in the prosecution was an unwitting accomplice, Bernardo, who supplied the "crocodile"—presumably alligator—heart and gall necessary to produce a harmful "gri-gri." The leader of the plotters, Francisco, was himself an overseer and was infuriated that his colleague had physically punished him. The resolution of the case was unclear, but one of the alleged conspirators died in prison several months after the incident came to light. According to Laura L. Porteous, who summarized the case in a 1934 article, the other defendants likely went free. While this particular incident did not directly impact religious worship, it certainly undermined the practice of what would come to be known as hoodoo and helped further whites' belief that African spirituality was a threat not just to Christian ideals but to their very lives.[2]

A more common motive for stifling Voodoo during the nineteenth century was to exert control over the enslaved and their free descendants. One news article that explicitly linked Voodoo and illegal slave assembly appeared in an 1850 issue of New Orleans's *Daily Picayune.* Describing the religion's nighttime gatherings as characterized by "mystic ceremonies, wild orgies, dancing, singing, &c.," the author went on to state that not all were "dens of vice." He nevertheless concluded that none of them benefitted enslaved persons' "habits and morals."[3] This opinion found expression on multiple occasions, such as a raid on a Voodoo gathering in April of 1853, during which authorities arrested thirty to thirty-five enslaved females and free women of color. That this group was of mixed status was of particular concern to authorities who feared the city's large population of free persons of color might make common cause with the enslaved.[4]

Nevertheless, not all suppression of the faith and the related magical practices was directly tied to the control of people of color. One unusual case occurred during the Civil War, when pro-Union authorities broke up a Voodoo assemblage consisting of free Blacks and arrested some of them on the grounds that they were using their supernatural powers to aid the Confederacy. According to journalistic accounts of the incident, the accused reportedly feared that a Union victory would free the enslaved, threatening the free people of color's relative privilege.[5]

One of the most common criminal charges faced by practitioners of Voodoo and hoodoo during the nineteenth century and beyond has been fraud. Jean Montanée, for instance, found himself accused of such a crime in 1871 following an incident in which he reportedly claimed he could remove a skin discoloration from the face of female client. After receiving a gold watch in advance payment, he failed to eliminate the blemish, prompting the woman to call upon the police. Threatened with arrest for the alleged fraud, he promised to return the watch.[6] During the twentieth century, mail fraud—a federal crime—became a particular threat to prosperous practitioners.[7] A 1914 article in New Orleans's *Times-Picayune,* for instance, detailed the pursuit of one McKay, who had fled the city to evade arrest by the US Post Office Department. His crime had been sending letters across the South purporting to be able to cure supernaturally induced illnesses by removing living creatures, including alligators, snakes, and frogs, from the bodies of his clients. All that one needed to do to be cured was to mail him $7.50. Though the article reported that McKay had escaped, his wife was jailed. During the 1930s, a similar case involved Rockford Lewis, a prominent hoodoo worker in New Orleans. Robert McKinney reported that Lewis made in excess of $50,000 annually, an impressive sum totaling close to $957,000 in 2021 dollars. According to McKinney, Lewis was imprisoned for mail fraud in 1934, and he faced a potential second prison term in 1938 following further allegations of illegal doings. On the second occasion, he owed his narrow escape to solid legal counsel, part of which included advice that he pay an unnamed Louisiana politician a bribe of $1,500.[8]

On the other hand, while the religion itself was never explicitly outlawed, there were laws that directly targeted the magical practices associated with it. For instance, in 1902, one Julius P. Caesar found his lucrative practice broken up when New Orleans police arrested him for violating what a journalist described as "an ordinance against magnetic healers and fortune-tellers."[9] While such a law might seem rather innocuous and doubtless protected many from unscrupulous frauds, it also served to suppress supernatural practices of which white authorities disapproved, a fact evident in the a newspaper's account of Caesar's arrest. When detectives entered his practice, they found a female client in conversation with the practitioner. The woman, evidently questioned as to the motive for her presence, claimed that she was merely in the midst of a friendly visit, not seeking his services. That she felt the need to distance herself from Caesar's practices indicates that she recognized that she was at some level threatened, not protected, by the authorities. That the journalist reporting the event provided readers with her name further suggests that she was correct in her assessment. Even today, New Orleans's Code of Ordinances includes a ban on telling fortunes for profit as section 54–312. The same paragraph-long law also bans various practices associated with hoodoo, including conferring luck, eliminating domestic troubles, and finding missing valuables. Although the section concludes with a statement that the ordinance does not apply to any religious worship, the fact that it would necessarily impact Voodoo is undeniable.[10]

Even when Voodoo seemingly had no genuine connection with an alleged crime, it was sure to appear in accounts of one when journalists could draw a connection, however tenuous. In June 11, 1881, for instance, Missouri's *Windsor Review* carried a brief account of a Mandeville, Louisiana, couple who had tortured a child under their guardianship by holding him in front of a fire for having stolen a piece of bread. As an apparent explanation for their brutality, the author described the perpetrators as "professors of the voudou art." The journalist's motive for including such apparently irrelevant information was almost certainly simply to make an already disturbing story a bit more shocking. Similarly, the 1924 notice of the arrest of alleged arsonist Odis L. Herron appeared under the title "Negro 'Hoodoo Doctor' Held as Fire Bug Suspect." While it is entirely possible that Herron was a professional hoodoo practitioner, the foundation of the claim appears to have been simply that police discovered a substantial amount of magical paraphernalia in his lodgings. Moreover, the article makes no direct claim that the arson and hoodoo were connected, but it certainly implies it.[11]

Almost universally, sources chronicling the suppression of Voodoo and hoodoo are emphatically unsympathetic to the practitioners and their plight, especially prior to the twentieth century, but that does not mean there was not resistance to attacks on religious freedom. Records of opposition are rare, but they do exist. For instance, in 1850, no less a personage than Marie Laveau approached the Orleans Parish Recorder to accuse a watchman of having fraudulently acquired a "statue of a virgin." While she did not immediately obtain its return, what appears to have been the same image was released to an unnamed woman following payment of an $8.50 fine the following month. Whether it eventually made its way back to its proper owner or not remains unclear, but its reacquisition was at least a partial victory.[12]

At approximately the same time that Marie Laveau was battling for the return of her religious image, another leader of the faith fought charges of encouraging illegal slave assemblage on the grounds of her constitutionally guaranteed freedom of religion. Having suffered in some capacity from three different raids on Voodoo gatherings between June and August, Betsy Toledano, a free woman of color and Voodoo priestess, emerged as the principal spokesperson for the faith. In one appearance before the Orleans Parish Recorder, she maintained that she had the right to hold Voodoo meetings in her home, emphasizing that her faith was indeed a religion and that it had been passed down to her through her grandmother "from the ancient Congo queens." Moreover, though she confessed that portions of Voodoo were mysterious to outsiders and were, indeed, sometimes secretive, she emphasized that they were not immoral. She even took the time to explain the spiritual and supernatural importance of some of the articles found in her home. The journalist who reported her plea for justice was evidently impressed, reporting that she made her argument "with no lack of words or weakness of argument." The authorities, however, chose to ignore the case's constitutional ramifications and focus on the narrow aspect of slave assembly.[13]

The law did not work alone.[14] The dominant white culture's hostility toward Voodoo interacted with concerns about the dangers of harmful sorcery shared by those of both European and African descent to render the religion increasingly frowned upon within the African American community. An 1869 notice in the New Orleans Daily Picayune, for instance, stated that the friends of a man found dead on Burgundy Street in New Orleans suspected his death to have been occasioned by witchcraft or Voodoo sorcery.[15] When communities suspected practitioners of supernaturally harming others, the consequences could occasionally prove deadly. Such was the case with Dave Farmer, whom an 1877 news article described as a Black "Missouri Voudou" and a "conjuror." He lived outside the small town of Bucklin. Farmer had reportedly moved there after the community of Brunswick, Missouri, forced him to leave following what the author vaguely described as "deviltries." After taking up his new abode, however, he quickly found himself an object of suspicion after three people in the community died. On a Tuesday evening, approvingly reported the newspaper, the son of one of the supposed victims removed chinking from between two of the logs in Farmer's cabin and mortally wounded its inhabitant with a shot fired through the aperture.[16] Approximately ten years later, similar fears inspired the lynching of Andrew Edwards in Meriden, Louisiana. A disturbingly cursory notice of the murder stated that fellow African Americans killed the elderly man because they suspected him of "being a 'voudou.'"[17]

That the same aversion to the religion and its associated magical practices was alive and well during the twentieth century is evidenced in the voluminous interviews and other documents chronicling the faith generated by the Federal Writers' Project. One less-than-approving informant, Alexander Augustin, for instance, stated that practitioners thanked St. John for the power to work with the devil.[18] An elderly women named Della Greenfield displayed similar sentiments when she stated that though she remembered her younger days when everyone spoke of Marie Laveau, she knew little about her because she "didn't 'filiate with her stripe."[19] Emile Labat expressed much the same opinion of the Voodoo Queen—and indirectly, her religion—saying, "Black magic, superstition, credulity, sorcery, trickery were her weapons."[20] In light of such legal and communal pressure, the fact that the religion was alive—if perhaps not quite well—into the 1940s is a testament to its durability.

THE DISAPPEARANCE OF THE LIVING TRADITION
AND THE SURVIVING LEGACY

Despite its longevity, Voodoo was certainly on the wane by the time the Federal Writers' Project recorded so much valuable information about it, and fear of persecution had spread throughout the community by that time. While six decades before, Marie Laveau was seemingly unconcerned with the fact that she was widely recognized as the Voodoo Queen, her spiritual heirs were much more reserved. Voodoo practitioner Oscar Felix's markedly negative reaction to having his picture taken by researchers associated with the Federal Writers' Project posing as gangsters was a prime example. Though Felix, suspicious and angry, eventually agreed, he did not consent until he believed he had proven to himself that they were indeed the gangsters they claimed to be rather than a threat to his practice. Less dramatically but just as telling, many of New Orleans's hoodoo and Voodoo workers were quite reluctant to speak to others about their craft. For instance, in 1936, when FWP worker Jacques

Villere visited what he called a Voodoo drugstore with aspiring African American writer Robert McKinney, he had to gradually draw the reluctant proprietor into conversation about his trade by claiming to be a beginning practitioner himself, despite the fact that the business owner and McKinney were already well known to each other.[21]

Though Voodoo survived well beyond the days of Marie Laveau and Dr. John, ultimately, active suppression and cultural hostility took their toll. Writing in 1990, Ron Bodin suggested that Voodoo had long before disappeared from New Orleans. As he put it in his short book, *Voodoo: Past and Present,* "by the 1920s it was difficult to find any trace of the once thriving and tightly organized Voodoo society in Louisiana."[22] He went on to state that "the formal, structured 'religion' disappeared" following African American efforts to obtain power by joining the dominant social structure and improved access to education. Outside of Louisiana, the situation was even more dire. The last significant evidence for a living tradition of Voodoo in the upper Mississippi River valley, for instance, was a late nineteenth-century article about it by Mary Alicia Owen. While Owen noted that rituals, including communal dances, continued to take place, she was the last to do so. In Louisiana, however, Bodin claimed somewhat paradoxically that a form of Voodoo survived in the magical practices that most modern scholars describe as hoodoo.[23] Scholar of religion Albert J. Raboteau likewise described the faith as flourishing in times gone by. According to him, it was vibrant only until the late nineteenth century, and while it survived in some form into the twentieth century, it had lost such important features as its pantheon and theology, key aspects of what sets a religion apart from other supernatural beliefs.[24] Popular accounts of the religion have not entirely escaped such conclusions. For example, an unusually well-researched how-to guide, *The New Orleans Voodoo Handbook* by Kenaz Filan, includes a chapter entitled "The (Re)Creation of 'New Orleans Voodoo,'" suggesting a historical break of some sort. The content of the chapter implies the same, focusing on specific individuals who helped shape the twenty-first-century city's blend of both tourist-oriented and sincere African diasporic religion.[25]

SPIRITUAL CHURCHES AS CONTEMPORARY VOODOO

On the other hand, some have argued that Voodoo survives in the guise of an African American Christian spiritual movement. Zora Neale Hurston in her

1931 "Hoodoo in America" identified the Spiritual churches of New Orleans as repositories of the belief system she called *hoodoo,* which she described as identical to the religion called *Voodoo* by whites. Once common in New Orleans but greatly reduced by the destruction of Hurricane Katrina, they were described by photographer and author Michael P. Smith as "founded on traditions deriving from native African spirit worship (and its New World offspring, Voodoo), south African Zionism, native American Indian belief, fundamental Christianity, and an almost medieval Catholicism."[26] Hans Baer, author of *The Black Spiritual Movement,* similarly describes them as a combination of "elements from Spiritualism, Catholicism, Black Protestantism, and Voodooism and hoodoo," a portrayal repeated by Margarita Simon Guillory in her 2017 work *Spiritual and Social Transformation in African American Spiritual Churches: More Than Conjurers.*[27] Such congregations emphasize healing, communication with spirits, and other forms of supernaturalism while also venerating Catholic saints, honoring the Bible, and otherwise incorporating a blend of characteristics from different types of Christianity in America. Their strangeness to outsiders and disproportionately African American composition made it easy for those who encountered them in New Orleans to equate them with the better-known Voodoo for which the city was already famous.[28]

After visiting New Orleans in 1928 when such churches were booming, Hurston claimed that eleven of twelve congregations in New Orleans had been coopted by Voodoo practitioners. Though she stated that not all Spiritual churches practiced Voodoo—as usual, called *hoodoo* by Hurston—she explained their tendency in that regard by stating, "Spiritualism, as a technique for communication with the dead, has a ready appeal to the black," and went on to add that a "spiritualistic name protects the congregation."[29] Of course, the documents collected by the Federal Writers' Project clearly demonstrate that Voodoo was certainly alive at the time she wrote and existed as a distinct religion alongside the Spiritual churches, a fact that she did not dispute.

Experts on Spiritual churches have followed Hurston's lead to acknowledge the institutions' evident debt to Voodoo. Michael P. Smith, for instance, noted their shared emphasis on healing and obtaining advice from spirits. Hans Baer identified as common features their adoption of Catholic elements, use of magic to shape destiny, practice of bibliomancy, and utilization of John the Conqueror root and other magical items. He also briefly discusses a reportedly shared veneration for the nineteenth-century Native American

Bishop Barbara Gore in St. Benedict Spiritual Church of New Orleans's Lower Ninth Ward in 2001. Though many interpret such institutions as simply manifestations of Voodoo, the Spiritual churches have a distinct history.

leader Black Hawk of Illinois, whom both Baer and author Jason Berry identify as being introduced to New Orleans by Leafy Anderson, a key founder of the city's Spiritual churches. Anderson had relocated to the city in or around 1920. In addition, Baer also notes that it is common for those who are not members of such bodies to equate them with Voodoo and even for some members of Spiritual churches to acknowledge that others claiming to be coreligionists practice it. He went beyond acknowledging similarities to state that Spiritual churches were often "a respectable cover" for Voodoo, explaining, however, his view that the latter had "degenerated from a religious system to a simple magical system" that had then become just one component of what he refers to as the Spiritual movement.[30] Like Baer, scholars Claude F. Jacobs and Andrew J. Kaslow, authors of the preeminent study of the congregations in New Orleans, add that tracing the churches to Voodoo was one of two common explanations of their origin—a viewpoint embraced by a few church leaders. Stephen C. Wehmeyer, though not claiming the New Orleans churches were Voodoo, has persuasively argued that their respect for spirits of the dead and the presentation of feather-garbed images of Native Americans reflect distinctly West Central African precedents.[31]

Kodi A. Roberts went further, arguing that Voodoo flourished during the period when most observers described it as a rapidly disappearing faith and that it survives today in the form of Spiritual churches. His book is a well-argued study and relies heavily on primary sources collected by the Federal Writers' Project. According to Roberts, Spiritual churches had not been simply taken over by Voodoo practitioners, as Hurston had claimed. They were instead manifestations of a new model of Voodoo introduced into the city by Leafy Anderson when she founded New Orleans's Spiritual church tradition. Anderson, he states, conferred upon Voodoo the legitimacy associated with organized Christian churches.[32]

The transformation of religions, of course, is certainly nothing out of the ordinary. The Christianity one finds in Southern Baptist congregations, for instance, looks quite different from what one would encounter in Roman Catholic circles, and both differ significantly from Pentecostalism. A similar parallel from an African context is the Ngunza faith of the modern-day Republic of the Congo. Though many describe it as a traditional religion, it differs considerably from the precolonial faiths of the region. Though it embraces the ancestor veneration of earlier iterations of the region's spirituality, it now focuses specifically on two twentieth-century anticolonial figures: Simon Kimbangu (1887–1951) of the former Belgian Congo and André Matsoua (1899–1942) of the former French Congo. Followers of the faith treat these two men as deities. The faith has also incorporated notable elements of Christianity, with ministers often referring to their congregations as churches and adopting pulpits, cruciform symbols, and other trappings of Christian denominations. At the same time, its followers frequently include Kimbangu and Matsoua alongside God the Father as part of a divine trinity.[33]

While the similar histories of Ngunza and the Spiritual churches convey the plausibility of Hurston and Roberts's conclusions, analogy is not the only evidence of connection between Voodoo and the New Orleans churches. Jacobs and Kaslow, like Baer, point out common features they shared, including the prominence of spirits of the dead and the practices of healing and divina-

The Ngunza church of Roch Mampouya in Brazzaville, Republic of the Congo. Note the prominent Christian imagery in an institution that focuses primarily on the spirits of deceased freedom fighters.

tion. Spirit possession is likewise common in both the Spiritual churches and various African diasporic faiths. Historical documents also connect practices associated with hoodoo with Spiritual people. A witness claimed Mother Kate Francis, a Spiritual church leader who flourished in the 1920s and 1930s, once pulled a live rattlesnake from under a woman's arm. Elsewhere, one anonymous Federal Writers' Project worker stated that interviewees tended to fear Francis because of her open practice of hoodoo. During a 2001 service that I attended at St. Benedict Spiritual Church, leaders in the congregation recommended the use of spiritual products like those employed in hoodoo whenever needed for the good of others and spoke of using floor washes for protection of the home, a practice common to the supernaturalism of the Mississippi River valley and beyond that hearkens back to a host of West African liquids infused with botanical, mineral, and/or zoological materials to make washes and potables for protection and other beneficial ends. They also incorporated images of Jesus, saints, and Native Americans into their services, the latter reminiscent of practices associated with both Haitian Vodou and nineteenth-century New Orleans Voodoo.[34]

To argue against the influence of Voodoo within Spiritual churches would be foolish, but Roberts's contention that the latter simply represent a new model of Voodoo goes a bit too far. To some extent, the longstanding identification of the two faiths likely rests on an equally persistent tendency to conflate any religions that exist outside the mainstream. This penchant is particularly prevalent among authors discussing African diasporic faiths. An example appeared in a 1981 article in the *Journal of Forensic Science,* entitled "Forensic Sciences Aspects of Santeria, a Religious Cult of African Origin." The article opens by stating, "'Voodoo' and 'obeah' are terms used to describe religious practices of African origin," and then it goes on to designate Santería as falling into these broad categories.[35] A similar approach can be seen in journalist Rod Davis' *American Voudou,* which treats *voudou* as a generic term that can be "used to refer to almost any of the New World theologies emanating from the Yoruba religion and kingdoms."[36] One sometimes even finds non-African faiths inaccurately defined as forms of Voodoo. This tendency was especially common prior to the mid-twentieth century in writings such as healthcare author John Lee Mattox's "Modern Voodooism," which treats practices from lands as distinct as New Zealand, China, the Philippines, and Californian Native America as types of what he called *Voodooism.*[37]

Just as significant, Spiritual churches can trace key aspects of their origins outside of Voodoo. Among the other forces that shaped them were Catholicism, Black Protestant Christianity, and Spiritualism. The last, according to Hans Baer, was the "springboard for the present Black Spiritual movement."[38] Spiritualism, which most trace to claims of communication with the dead advanced by sisters Margaretta (1833–1893) and Kate Fox (1837–1892) of Hydesville, New York, beginning in 1848, developed into a religion during its sensational rise to popularity during the mid-nineteenth century. Claiming at least one million members in the United States alone and perhaps many times that number during the same time that Voodoo flourished in the Mississippi River valley, it gradually faded in importance during the twentieth century. It was not simply an American phenomenon, spreading to much of Europe, Latin America, and the Caribbean following the 1857 publication of *The Spirits' Book* by a French author writing under the name Allan Kardec (1804–1869). Within a few years of the Fox sisters' reports of contact with the dead, New Orleans had active believers among both its Black and white populations. Significantly, Afro-Creole Spiritualists generally drew a sharp distinction between their beliefs and Voodoo, which they considered a form of superstition at best and evil witchcraft at worst. In keeping with their low view of the African diasporic faith, they eschewed the use of gris-gris, performing ceremonial dances, and participating St. John's Eve gatherings.[39]

Claude F. Jacobs and Andrew J. Kaslow likewise recognized the multiple influences on the Spiritual churches in New Orleans and persuasively argued that Spiritualism was indeed key to its origins. Though they pointed out that late twentieth-century Spiritual church members knew little of the older Spiritualist movement and that those who did often disavowed any connection, they also concluded "that there were strong connections between the two belief systems in the churches' formative years during the 1920s."[40] Among the evidence they supply are guest-speaking by a prominent Spiritualist in what was probably the first congregation in New Orleans, Leafy Anderson's Eternal Life Christian Spiritualist Church Number 12, and strong similarities between early statements of purpose between Spiritual congregations and Spiritualist organizations. In addition, prior to the 1940s, Spiritual bodies in New Orleans generally referred to themselves as Spiritualist congregations.[41]

Just as important as the spiritual roots were the geographical ones. The reputed founder of the Spiritual churches, Leafy Anderson, was not from

New Orleans and likely had little if any prior contact with Voodoo. Conflicting reports describe her as being born in either Wisconsin or Virginia. At some point, she moved to Chicago, where she founded the Eternal Life Christian Spiritualist Church in 1913, traveling to a new home in New Orleans several years later where she established Eternal Life Christian Spiritualist Church Number 12 in 1920 at 2719 Amelia Street. From this original church sprang New Orleans's many other Spiritual congregations. Moreover, while it appears that Anderson lived approximately forty-four miles outside New Orleans in Raceland, Louisiana, for some time between residences in Chicago, she does not appear to have been the origin of the Voodoo and hoodoo influences outsiders so strongly associate with the Spiritual churches. Even Hurston, writing only four years after Anderson's 1927 death, reported that Anderson's former congregation was notable in that its members did not practice hoodoo.[42]

More importantly, most members of Spiritual churches in New Orleans have denied historical links to Voodoo. In an account of Kate Francis removing living creatures from the bodies of clients, the informant, a friend and former servant of the minister, made the point that these had not been acts of hoodoo. By removing the rattlesnake, the informant explained, she removed the sins of a "woman of the streets." Alligators, meanwhile, came out of a man who incorrectly believed he merely had rheumatism but had actually been hoodooed.[43] The informant elsewhere stated, "Kate Francis ain't never been no hoodoo, she ain't never talked nothin' but religion," and he emphasized that "Mother Kate don't use . . . none of them voodoo Bibles."[44] Even an anonymous Federal Writers' Project worker who described Francis as a practicing hoodoo saw her as an outlier, claiming that she was supposedly "one of the few spiritualist leaders who openly" did so.[45] In keeping with these statements, another Federal Writers' Project employee recorded a visit to a Spiritual congregation known as St. Michael No. 2 Temple, located on what is now Martin Luther King Jr. Boulevard (formerly Melpomene Avenue), between Willow and Clara streets. There, she heard a preacher's sermon denounce the practice of hoodoo as working with the devil and call on attendees to pray for protection from it. Curiously, during the midst of his exhortation, the minister took a moment to inform his hearers that he practiced hoodoo as well but did so in private for pay, indicating that he kept the practice he otherwise condemned separate from his Spiritual work.[46] That such examples were not isolated ones is made clear by Jacobs and Kaslow in *Spiritual Churches of New*

Orleans, which emphasizes that this denial of Voodoo connections was the norm for the informants of the late twentieth century as well. More recently, Guillory acknowledges Kodi Roberts's contrary conclusion in her work on the churches but likewise stresses that Spiritual church members have typically denied practicing Voodoo, a distinction between the faiths that she maintains in her own scholarship. Such evidence and the majority opinion of scholars is a powerful indicator that the Spiritual churches' identity as Voodoo is a construction of outsiders, not followers of either faith. This situation paralleled that of the nineteenth-century Spiritualists of the New Orleans, who described Voodoo as superstition but nevertheless had to defend themselves against claims that they practiced it.[47]

Perhaps the most compelling argument is that key elements of Voodoo are absent from Spiritual churches. Initiation rituals like the St. Peter Opening undergone by Federal Writers' Project workers or a variety that Hurston claimed to have experienced, seem to have remained confined to Voodoo, which continued to practice them for more than two decades after Leafy Anderson's arrival in New Orleans. Likewise, the deities of Voodoo do not appear to have entered the Spiritual churches' pantheon. While the serpent god known as Monsieur Danny in New Orleans, Grandfather Rattlesnake in Missouri, Danbala in Haiti, and Dan in Benin has been prominent throughout the various African diasporic iterations of Vodun/Vodou/Voodoo, he is absent from the Spiritual churches. The same can be said for the prominent historical New Orleans Voodoo deities Papa Lébat and Assonquer. Even those spirits that appear to have been particularly tied to New Orleans, among whom were the two named Grand Zombi and Jean Macouloumba, are not easily recognizable within Spiritual church theology.[48]

The absence of the gods is a key point because they remained focuses of devotion among the remaining Voodoo faithful. Practitioners like Oscar Felix served them into at least the 1940s and perhaps beyond. Though almost all mention of these gods faded from the documentary record after the FWP ceased its fieldwork, they may have survived for a few decades longer. Regardless of how long the Voodoo deities persisted, there is no doubt that they did for at least a generation following the appearance of New Orleans's first Spiritual congregations. Had the Spiritual churches developed as simply the latest incarnation of Voodoo, one would have expected to find Voodoo gods occupying a prominent place.

In short, it appears that members of Spiritual churches brought features of Voodoo and hoodoo into the congregations when they joined them without thereby transforming the descendants of Spiritualist bodies into Voodoo gatherings. In other words, the Spiritual churches became repositories for the orphaned beliefs of a religion that was slowly dying. Thus, instead of being a North American parallel for West Central African Ngunza, the Spiritual churches more closely resemble Espiritismo, a variety of Spiritism popular in Puerto Rico and elsewhere in the Caribbean. Though not African in origin, the creed promoted by Allan Kardec became popular amongst those of African descent, in part because of its emphases on the spirits of the dead and reincarnation, beliefs similar to those common in many African belief systems. Some modern forms incorporate herbal healing, communication with Catholic saints and the deceased, Christian prayers, and the use of various spiritual supplies reminiscent of those one might find in any hoodoo supply shop. Although it clearly embodies African diasporic traits, few—if any—scholars would claim it was simply a modern representation of an older faith. Likewise, the African features of the Spiritual churches legitimately emphasized by Jacobs and Kaslow, Wehmeyer, and others can be very much present within Spiritual churches without the necessity that the congregations are therefore simply a new model of Voodoo.[49]

MODERN NEW ORLEANS VOODOO AND HOODOO

While it is indeed quite difficult to claim that Spiritual churches are just Voodoo under another name, one might justly ask if it lives on in some other form. At the very least, no one debates the continued legacy of Voodoo on the culture of the Mississippi River valley. New Orleans's innumerable tourist shops, which provide a wide variety of Voodoo dolls and similarly dubious paraphernalia, are one measure of the religion's continued cultural relevance. A much more direct connection to the historical religion is the survival of magical concepts and practices connected with the faith. The words *hoodoo* and *grisgris* remain in common use in New Orleans and to a lesser extent Louisiana more broadly. More importantly, as is true elsewhere in the American South, belief in both positive and malevolent supernaturalism remains common. Nowhere are such beliefs better evidenced than in the Mississippi River valley's hoodoo-oriented spiritual supply shops. While the most famous of these, New

Orleans's Cracker Jack Drugstore, closed in 1974, it did so following urban renewal efforts that had forced it to change location, not a decline in the practice of hoodoo. Other older shops in the city persisted into the 1980s, and when these closed, new establishments took their places. They remain equally viable elsewhere in the Mississippi River valley. Memphis, for instance, is home to one of the oldest hoodoo suppliers in the country, A. Schwab, which has been a fixture of the city for nearly a century and a half and began selling spiritual products in the early 1930s. In 2001, Carolyn Morrow Long listed twelve retailers of spiritual products related to hoodoo and Voodoo operating in cities immediately on the Mississippi River, including eight in New Orleans alone.[50] Her list, however, was never intended to be more than a sample. In 2018, the *New Orleans Advocate* published an article entitled "After Closing of Popular F&F Botanica, Shoppers Find Candle Power at Other Spiritual Supply Shops," which included its own list of ten businesses that carried spiritual supplies. With the exception of the F and F Botanica, discussed by the news article as having closed earlier that year following the deaths of its two co-owners, none of the names appeared on Long's list.[51]

Another seemingly plausible heir to the historical faith is modern, self-described New Orleans Voodoo. While the city contains numerous establishments geared toward the tourist trade—including French Quarter shops like Marie Laveau's House of Voodoo on Bourbon Street, Reverend Zombie's Voodoo Shop on St. Peter Street, and the New Orleans Historic Voodoo Museum on Dumaine Street—other businesses cater to residents and visitors who desire to participate in genuine Voodoo. In 2019, for instance, *Thrillist* cataloged nine spiritual supply shops scattered around the metropolitan area accessible to visitors seeking authenticity.[52] The religion is more than simply business in New Orleans, and many congregations of self-described Voodoo practitioners call the city home. According to numbers that appeared in a 2014 *Newsweek* article, there were approximately 2,500 to 3,000 practitioners prior to Hurricane Katrina in 2005. The storm ravaged the city's practitioners, dispersing them across the nation and leaving what the article estimated as only 300. By 2014, the number had reportedly rebounded to between 350 and 400.[53]

On the other hand, in many cases, the links between the city's Voodoo practitioners and the historical tradition to which the average observer is apt to link them is quite tenuous. New Orleans's most famous practitioner as of 2020, Sallie Ann Glassman, for instance, was born in Maine in 1954 to white

Jewish heritage and gained her early knowledge of Voodoo from personal study. In 1995, she initiated into Haitian Vodou. Though she is sincere, is respected by her peers, and holds the Haitian rank of *manbo* asogwe, she sees herself as helping to reintroduce Haitian Vodou into Louisiana, not as participating in an unbroken tradition of Mississippi River valley Voodoo. A similarly influential proponent of modern Voodoo is Brandi Kelley, also a white female. Unlike Glassman, she is a native of New Orleans. Yet, she, too, has been initiated into Haitian Vodou—with the renowned Marie Thérèse Alourdes Macena Champagne Lovinski, better known as Mama Lola, as her godmother. This is not an unbroken tradition of the Mississippi River valley either. Kelley recognizes that such ceremonies disappeared from New Orleans well before her time. As she put it to one interviewer, "People are starting them up again, but when you hear about people who are claiming to have uninterrupted over the last-couple-of-hundred-years . . . New Orleans Voodoo lineage, question it."[54]

While it would be easy to assume that Glassman and Kelley's route to Voodoo via initiation into a related but distinct faith was defined by their whiteness, such was not necessarily the case. Ava Kay Jones, one of the key African American pioneers in bringing a form of Voodoo back to New Orleans, followed a similar route to the religion. In an interview with author Ron Bodin, she described her family using "folk Voodoo," with context indicating that she referred to hoodoo, but went on to explain that as was true with Glassman and Kelley, her initiation took place in Haiti. Another prominent practitioner, Priestess Miriam Chamani has a claim to possessing one of the closest connections to the historical religion, having grown up in Mississippi and later been involved with a Spiritual Church in Chicago, Illinois, during the 1970s and 1980s. According to Chamani, participation in a Spiritual congregation led her to Voodoo. When she later married Oswan Chamani, who was born in Belize, she gained a second connection to African diasporic religion through his practice of the obeah of his homeland. As with other practitioners, however, Chamani also looks to Haiti as a source of her faith. One brochure for her Voodoo Spiritual Temple, for example, uses the Haitian *loa* to describe the spirits and otherwise relies on Vodou terminology in its discussion of Voodoo.[55] Another modern New Orleans practitioner of African diasporic religion, Janet "Sula Spirit" Evans, began her involvement in African diasporic religion following an encounter with the Cuban religion of Santería during her late teens. She then became involved in Yoruba religion in New York and studied West African Vodun. Later she joined the Temple of Impohema in Ghana where she initiated into the form of Vodun embraced by the Ewe people. In addition, while descended from Louisiana Creoles of Color, she grew up in New Jersey. Like her compatriots in the New Orleans area, she is essentially working to recover a lost religion.[56]

Evidence, textual and otherwise, indicates that the Voodoo religion as practiced in New Orleans today is not a faith with an unbroken heritage stretching into the nineteenth-century and before. Most of the prominent leaders of the religion were initiated into Haitian Vodou and/or an African religion, often outside the United States, not directly into the spiritual lineage of Marie Laveau or Oscar Felix. In a literate world where information on the history of Voodoo and practices of other African diasporic faiths are readily available in both scholarly and how-to formats to a mobile and affluent population, it should come as no surprise that a movement to reconstruct the former faith by drawing heavily on the latter has arisen in the city. Although New Orleans Voodoo does incorporate hoodoo, a genuine link to the Voodoo of the past, and seeks to emulate the historical religion, it is best understood as a belief system that draws primarily from Haitian Vodou with a sizeable admixture of various other forms of African diasporic religion in an effort to reconstruct a lost faith. Nevertheless, it is vital to note that just because modern New Orleans Voodoo is not a direct descendant of what existed prior to the mid-twentieth century, this circumstance does not make it any less sincere or render it somehow inauthentic. On the contrary, much like the historical faith, modern Voodoo is a manifestation of its time and place, blending the spiritual and racial fluidity of the half century that followed the Civil Rights movement of the 1950s and 60s and New Age movement that followed in the 1970s and 80s with the longstanding cosmopolitan milieu of New Orleans.

Ultimately, it is best to understand today's New Orleans Voodoo as an emerging reconstruction of the historical faith. Kenaz Filan expressed the current situation quite well in his *New Orleans Voodoo Handbook.* After recognizing that "[t]here may not have been a survival of Haitian Vodou that persists to the present day in the Louisiana backwoods and bayous," he goes on to explain that he wrote his book as a set of guidelines to help readers build familiarity with the spirits and avoid any unpleasantness they might encounter by uninformed dabbling in the faith.[57] Many other writings contribute to this emerging faith. Some of the more historically rooted have come from

The Marie Laveau Shrine at Sallie Ann Glassman's New Orleans Healing Center. Though modern New Orleans Voodoo is more closely related to Haitian Vodou, it actively incorporates features of historical Mississippi River valley Voodoo. Courtesy of Catherine Wessinger.

the pen of New Orleans native Denise Alvarado, a prolific author who has recently published well-researched works seeking to define the role of deceased Voodoo ministers, Haitian *lwa,* Catholic saints, and other spirits in the religion. Filan summed up the current situation, stating, "Unlike Haitian Vodou or other more organized Afro-Caribbean traditions, New Orleans Voodoo is a freeform system of worship."[58] Although his summation of the religion would not accurately portray the historical version of the faith, it describes some modern reconstructed versions nicely.

While it is difficult to argue that either Spiritual churches or today's New Orleans Voodoo practitioners are direct descendants of the historical faith, it would be equally inaccurate to say that it has no living heirs. Hoodoo, despite outliving the African deities that originally gave it power and the initiations that authorized one to minister to them, remains common. Likewise, Voodoo continues to pervade the ambience of New Orleans, helping to persuade practitioners of Haitian Vodou and West African Vodun to make it their home. Following the early 1940s, however, evidence for the continued practice of the religion disappeared. Its most visible aspect, the annual St. John's Eve gatherings, had ceased long before. Other communal rituals, once common fare for newspapers, stopped being practiced during the late nineteenth century.[59] When Federal Writers' Project workers underwent the last recorded initiations during the Great Depression, it was clear to them that even then, there were only a few who still knew how to perform the rituals. Of course, it is entirely possible that there remain some elderly inhabitants initiated by Oscar Felix or others who have simply chosen not to continue the practices. It is not inconceivable that these hypothetical individuals might have initiated others. Voodoo ultimately was a religion with gods who received worship during its ceremonies, and it consisted of more than a handful of believers without a community. For practical purposes, Mississippi River valley Voodoo has become a religion of history that nevertheless exerts a powerful influence on the city where its most famous practitioners lived.

CONCLUSION

Whose Voodoo?

Historical Mississippi River valley Voodoo was a complex faith that one can study for years and still find mysterious. The foregoing represents a study stretching over approximately sixteen years of my life. Yet, I still find myself desperately wishing I knew more. In large part, the culprit is a simple lack of sources. Luminaries of the faith, such as Marie Laveau, were often illiterate, and even those who were not seemed to have been uninterested in committing their knowledge to writing or unwilling to do so. The Mississippi River valley, sadly, missed out on the late nineteenth and early twentieth centuries' anthropological and historical fascination with African diasporic religion until it was almost too late. Had the likes of the Federal Writers' Project and Harry Middleton Hyatt not acted when they did, the world would be bereft of almost all reliable knowledge of the religion. In short, many questions remain unanswered. In this environment of open-endedness, interpretations of the faith vary widely, and each tends to reduce the religion to a caricature of itself.

The summers of 2015, 2016, and 2017 I devoted to studying the historical background of Mississippi River valley Voodoo. To this end, I spent time visiting Senegal, Benin, Togo, the Republic of the Congo, Haiti, and Cuba where I had many opportunities to observe African Traditional Religions and their Afro-Caribbean Creole descendants as practiced today. While I was under no illusion that the religions had somehow remained unaltered by time, the simple fact is that they are *probably* the closest one can get to seeing the historical religion of the Mississippi River valley. The process also helped awaken me to the fact that there is considerable debate over the place of Voodoo in African diasporic culture and who, therefore, has the right to interpret it.

Several things caught my attention as I spoke with *marabouts* in Senegal, *vodunons* in Benin, *oungans* and *manbos* in Haiti, and *Ngunza* priests in Congo. I noticed, for instance, that regional variations were strong. In Haiti, those with whom I spoke in the rural south of the country preferred French spellings and pronunciations for words to the Kreyòl ones more common in Port-au-Prince and the North. Another thing I observed wherever I went was how prominently intertwined are Vodun and Vodou with nationalism. There were several instances when I wondered whether the priests and priestesses with whom I spoke were describing their understanding of their religion or their conception of their nation.

What struck me the most during my research, however, is that there are sharp interpretive divisions present in the faiths and their study. One exists between the public personalities of Vodou/Vodun and average practitioners. For instance, prominent figures in Haiti, often highly educated, tended to introduce me to Vodou by describing its importance to the history and culture of their nation. Then, they typically went on to explain the essentially benevolent nature of the faith, often pointing out similarities between it and Christianity.[1] Those ministers who were not among the luminaries of their field often had a very different approach. Rather than stressing the place of Vodou in Haiti, they tended to emphasize its power. While most continued to assert that they worked only for good, others did not. One such person was a *manbo* I encountered in Jacmel, who bluntly stated that she will work to heal or harm, depending on clients' requests.[2]

Major differences in understanding exist between authors and practitioners as well. For example, typical authorial interpretations of the religion of the Kongo people describe a dualistic system of magical specialists. On the one hand are *ngangas* who revitalize marriages, help clients find work and love, heal ailments, and protect people from witches. *Ndokis,* meanwhile, are supposedly the witches who work much of the evil that *ngangas* combat.[3] In everyday life, however, *ngangas* are themselves widely feared as potential sources of harm. Meanwhile, *ndokis,* though workers of evil as a rule, supposedly sacrifice individual family members primarily in an effort to gain enough power to protect their families as a whole.[4] Black-and-white definitions may work in books but not in practice.

One of the great benefits of spending time with African and Caribbean practitioners was that I was able to see these divisions. Sticking simply to books or even conducting formal interviews might well have insulated me from the rather tricky questions of authenticity and ownership that my conversations brought to light. To be sure, there is a difference between Mississippi River valley Voodoo and the African and Afro-Caribbean faiths I have discussed. First and foremost, of course, Voodoo most likely died out as a freestanding, living tradition during the 1940s. Almost as important is the fact that it is not as fully documented as Haitian Vodou, West African Vodun, and other related traditions. Together, these two facts render interpretation even more central to all attempts to define and delineate the religion. The study of Mississippi River valley Voodoo can be quite contentious, primarily because scholars have a tendency to choose a preferred viewpoint and write from it rather than taking into account divergent but equally valid understandings of the faith.

To be sure, many of the sources of debate are typical historical questions. Scholars continue to discuss the origins of Voodoo, with most emphasizing the African roots of the religion but recognizing the Catholic and other elements it incorporated as it developed. Others stress its distinctive development in the United States as the key to understanding the faith.[5] Likewise, people debate over just what should be recognized as Voodoo. There is, for instance, Kodi Roberts, who considers the Spiritual churches of New Orleans a form of institutionalized Voodoo. Others, including myself and the authors of the 1991 book *Spiritual Churches of New Orleans,* Claude F. Jacobs and Andrew J. Kaslow, explain Voodoo as one of several influences in the formation of the congregations.[6]

The biographical details of major figures in the religion are also fodder for discussion, with the question of just how many Voodoo priestesses named Marie Laveau there were being a recurrent question since 1927, when New Orleans author Lyle Saxon claimed that a daughter of the Voodoo Queen took over her mother's practice and served as a second Marie Laveau. Zora Neale Hurston elaborated on Saxon's claim, arguing that there was a succession of mother-daughter-granddaughter to the name and position. Though Hurston recanted during the 1940s, stating that Marie Laveau II was "spurious," both contentions have adherents.[7]

While the previous arguments and others like them are typical of the sorts of disputes that are common in the field of history as well as other humanities, larger interpretive issues—akin to those I encountered in Africa and the Caribbean—are a significant problem. The gap between scholars and practitioners, for instance, is frequently problematic. Terminology, though of relatively minor importance, helps illustrate the disjuncture. Scholars of Mississippi River valley Voodoo typically use the spellings *Voudou* or *Voodoo* to designate the distinctive religion of New Orleans and other portions of the Mississippi River valley. On the other hand, I have had people tell me that I should use the Haitian *Vodou* or Fon *Vodun* instead, with the idea that alternate terms will help readers separate the religion from the negative connotations that have accumulated around the word *Voodoo*. Outside of academia, though, finding someone who uses a spelling other than *Voodoo* is exceedingly challenging.

Regardless of the spelling used, however, there is a further disjuncture between scholars and believers. While academicians use the word *Voodoo* to specify a distinct religion, most Americans, regardless of race, treat it as a broad term that includes not only the religion but also what scholars prefer to call *conjure* or *hoodoo*. These latter, according to historians and other intellectuals, are magical practices that are not necessarily linked to the Voodoo faith. While the distinction can be helpful for purposes of analysis, it is important to note that the popular usage was common even amongst believers and practitioners by the years immediately preceding World War II.[8] To further complicate matters, historical evidence suggests that both scholars and the broader public have generally been wrong about the proper name for the religion, as it appears that New Orleans practitioners referred to themselves as *Voodoos* and their practice as *hoodoo*.[9] This understanding is further attested to in Zora Neale Hurston's "Hoodoo in America," which states, with apparent exaggeration, "Veaudeau is the European term for African magic practices and beliefs, but it is unknown to the American Negro. His own name for his practices is hoodoo, both terms being related to the West African term *juju*."[10]

In addition to the simple desire for analytical precision, scholars depart from typical understandings of Voodoo in order to correct errors that arose out of a racist past, creating a more serious interpretive divide. To be sure, there are a host of problems with older works on Voodoo, chief among them that they almost always depicted the religion in a wholly negative light. In the eyes of many nineteenth-century writers, Voodoo was inseparable from crime. A typical news item from the antebellum era was entitled "Vou Doux."

It described how authorities apprehended thirty-odd enslaved and free Black women while practicing "the mysterious rites of Vou Dou." The penalties for the worshippers were fines of up to ten dollars or a series of lashes. Even when not directly reporting on a Voodoo-related arrest, reports tended to emphasize the sinister, as in an 1873 account of Marie Laveau's visit to the lobby of a criminal court as a spectator. According to the writer, she was probably "devising some fiendish and cantraip motions to be gone through with at the coming Voudou orgies."[11] Some spectators, he stated, claimed to smell brimstone when she eventually departed. Even those reports that avoided describing the faith and its adherents as criminal or demonically inclined tended toward sensationalistic portrayals in an effort to entertain readers. Titles like "Dance of the Voodoos: Outlandish Celebration of St. John's Eve" and "A Voudou Orgie: Sensational Disclosure in the Third District" make this plain.[12]

Although the negative view of Voodoo softened during the twentieth century, it still remained the norm. In 1927, for instance, when Lyle Saxon wrote his article "Voodoo" for *The New Republic,* he described the religion as a form of snake worship and went on to state that "this magic has become entwined with a sort of perverted Catholicism, like the Black Mass."[13] Even the most popular work on the subject, Robert Tallant's 1946 book *Voodoo in New Orleans,* contains more than its share of curses, nude dancing, and murders. Clearly the racist mores of the day made a fair account of the religion exceedingly difficult to produce.

Though the negatively biased accounts of years gone by remain very much alive in popular media, many authors, especially scholars, have embraced a goal of rehabilitating Voodoo's image.[14] The seeds of this approach stretch back to fictional literature produced at the turn of the twentieth century. Short story collections like Charles Waddell Chesnutt's *Conjure Woman* (1899) and Virginia Frazer Boyle's *Devil Tales* (1900) included narratives in which conjurers and Voodoo practitioners were sometimes heroes, though the authors stopped well short of depicting the religion itself as a positive aspect of African American culture. It was Zora Neale Hurston who provided the impetus that would permit scholars to reinterpret Voodoo as something other than suspect but entertaining magical doings. In her two major works on the subject, the 1931 essay, "Hoodoo in America," and the 1935 collection of folklore, *Mules and Men,* Hurston emphatically described Voodoo, called "hoodoo," as a genuine religion—with a Biblical pedigree no less—and a key part of Black society. Sacrifices, secret initiations, and dances—the raw materials for earlier authors' titillating accounts of dark deeds—were to Hurston aspects of African American strength. Even what would once have been interpreted as killings through Voodoo magic were reimagined by Hurston as evidence of the power of hoodoo and thus African Americans. In Hurston's conception, Voodoo was liberating.[15]

Whether authors explicitly recognize Hurston's influence of not, her interpretation of Voodoo has been a defining force in virtually all recent writings about the faith. The paradigmatic shift began in the literary world with the revival of interest in Hurston created by Alice Walker during the 1970s. In particular, Voodoo priests and hoodoo women as symbols of African American female strength have become commonplace in literature and film. Marie Laveau, in particular, became a locus of mythmaking. For example, one 1983 biographical account in *Ms.* magazine interprets rumors that Laveau was connected to prostitution as evidence that the Voodoo Queen provided a safe environment for women who had no other means of earning incomes. Likewise, a tale in which Laveau murdered a client's unloved husband became an account of a generous act in the cause of a woman's rights. Images of Voodoo and hoodoo as positive forces are not confined to the feminine, however. *The Hoodoo Book of Flowers* by celebrated writer Arthur "Rickydoc" Flowers, for instance, is an attempt, as he puts it, "to forge a universalized African American Way," addressing topics ranging from initiation to struggle to empowerment through a spiritual lens.[16]

By the twenty-first century, such interpretations had moved from fiction and the popular press into scholarship. To be sure, expressions of Hurston's vision vary significantly. Poet Brenda Marie Osbey's "Why We Can't Talk to You about Voodoo," describes the New Orleans version of the faith as essentially about honoring the ancestors and being healed. In her conception, it is off limits to men as well as racial and geographical outsiders. Curiously, she also denies the existence of many of the key elements of historical Voodoo, including initiations, public ceremonies like those on St. John's Eve, and the importance of Marie Laveau. In diametrical opposition, Kodi Roberts finds in the religion a search for power that was by no means bound to a particular race or gender but was pursued by the marginalized, whether Black, white, male, or female. Despite the profound variations in expression, no serious scholar embraces the negative stereotypes of years past.[17]

Some scholars have gone beyond simply stressing Voodoo's place as a legitimate religion and—paralleling the nationalistic impulse within Haitian Vodou—have interpreted it as a force for equality. I include myself in this critique. In my first book, *Conjure in African American Society,* I refer to African American supernaturalism and religion, including Voodoo, as forces for racial and gender equality as well as individual advancement. Similar civil rights interpretations are most visible in biographies of Marie Laveau. In 1994, Ina Johanna Fandrich defended a dissertation that later became her 2005 book, *The Mysterious Voodoo Queen, Marie Laveaux: A Study of Powerful Female Leadership in Nineteenth-Century New Orleans.* She sums up her understanding of Laveau as "an Afrocentric prophetess" who "was committed to her non-Christian cultural roots . . . and to the improvement of the lives of her African-American sisters and brothers."[18] Part of this improvement supposedly included purchasing slaves in order to later free them—a claim later disproven—as well as participating in other liberationist activities. Others have picked up and elaborated on Fandrich's contentions, notably Susheel Bibbs. In her 1998 book, *Heritage of Power: Marie LaVeau—Mary Ellen Pleasant,* Bibbs argues that Laveau was a civil rights pioneer who influenced antislavery and civil rights activist Mary Ellen Pleasant of California. Anthropologist Martha Ward likewise built on Fandrich's assertions in a 2003 Laveau biography, *Voodoo Queen: The Spirited Lives of Marie Laveau,* in which she devoted a chapter entitled "Freedom à la Mode, à la Marie" to Voodoo's supposedly antislavery and liberationist aspects.[19]

The rehabilitation effort started by Hurston and participated in by almost all recent scholars, including myself, is laudable in its goals, but it has a tendency to reduce Voodoo to a caricature. Essays like Osbey's "Why We Can't Talk to You about Voodoo" strip the religion of most of its identifying features in an effort to liberate it from the negative stereotypes its author most prominently associates with the tourist trade. Is a New Orleans Voodoo bereft of its public worship ceremonies really Voodoo at all? Less extreme works that simply follow Hurston's lead by conceptualizing supernatural acts as furthering female and/or African American agency, power, or liberation can easily ignore the fact that the benefactors of such actions were almost always individuals— specific Voodoo specialists and clients, to be precise—not the community of which they were a part. To be sure, charms designed to thwart the brutalities of slave masters or acquire work for poverty-stricken African Americans existed in the Mississippi River valley and well beyond it. While these had liberating potential for their users, many other expressions of supernaturalism with no overt link to liberation existed alongside them. How does an amulet designed to compel a woman to love a man in whom she would be otherwise uninterested fit into the new paradigm, especially its civil rights variation? Along the same lines, though Hurston and others have emphasized that works designed to kill can be liberating for the one initiating them, what of the recipient?

Stepping outside of philosophical considerations, what is one to make of the links between Voodoo and the Confederacy? There is no way to reliably determine just how many of the Voodoo faithful supported the South during the Civil War, but that a significant number did is difficult to dispute. According to documentary evidence, the best known pro-Confederate Voodoo adherent was Marie Laveau. Her obituary in the *Daily Picayune* stated that in addition to being beautiful, wise, and charitable, she "proved her loyalty to the South at every opportunity and freely dispensed help to those who suffered in defense of the 'lost cause.'"[20] Another account of her death, which appearing in the *New York Times,* elaborated on the assertion adding that Laveau risked her own property and freedom to aid the Confederates. It is certainly possible that the authors of the obituaries simply fabricated such sympathies. After all, doing so gave white readers a reason to embrace the memory of the deceased. On the other hand, there is no evidence to suggest that Laveau did anything other than identify a side on the basis of her status as a free woman, slave-owner, and southerner.[21]

According to newspaper accounts, Laveau was not the only Voodoo adherent to support the South in its struggle. According to an August 1, 1863, report in New Orleans's *L'Union,* police broke up a ceremony performed to call upon a spirit called Simbé to aid the Confederacy. The next day, the *Daily Picayune* reported much the same about it but added testimony by an African American girl and one Officer Long to the effect that the group was composed of free women of color and two or three white women and that their purpose was to use magic to restore Confederate control to New Orleans so that slaves would no longer be the equals of free Blacks.[22]

Any serious scholar of Louisiana Voodoo—or Vodun or Vodou for that matter—must take into account the divergent understandings of what it is. This is not to say that one should start taking cues from New Orleans's tourist shops that embrace the religion's unwarrantedly macabre reputation. It is to say that we must recognize that the religion was about more than liberation. It can even have its negative elements. Voodoo certainly helped some survive and even prosper in the antebellum and then Jim Crow South. The religion likewise provided a worship community outside of mainstream American society. At the same time, its practitioners also acted as businessmen and businesswomen, earning incomes by selling items that could reputedly either heal or harm, depending on clients' desires. Sometimes, they explicitly rejected civil rights in favor of causes they found more pressing. In sum, Voodoo was a religion that is too big to confine to a narrow interpretation, no matter how well meaning its formulation.

MISSISSIPPI RIVER VALLEY VOODOO CHANTS, SONGS & PRAYERS

Mississippi River valley Voodoo had no bible. Its theological underpinnings were a matter of remembered principles communicated orally in instructions and songs and lived through ceremonies. The closest one can come to the sort of holy text familiar to the majority of Americans are a handful of sacred songs recorded in old periodicals, books, manuscripts, and sometimes novels. Taken together, these roughly parallel the biblical Book of Psalms in purpose, though the passage of time has often obscured the meaning of their words. The following collection of all those with some claim to genuineness is for those interested in looking more deeply into the historical religion. When possible, translations are provided.

NEWSPAPERS

The following journalistic accounts of Voodoo songs, while valuable in that articles generally claimed they came from eyewitness accounts, remain problematic. Some, for instance, were performed in unknown languages and then transliterated into French or English by writers whom it is safe to assume had limited-at-best understandings of the songs or the rituals of which they were part. The first of the selections, the earliest recorded Voodoo song, was performed at a ritual broken up by a pro-Union police force whose leader considered it a threat to the United States' control of the city during the Civil War. It is difficult to imagine a situation with a greater likelihood for negative bias. In contrast, Lafcadio Hearn's account of Voodoo songs is particularly interesting in that he investigated African Creole culture with an enthusiasm foreign to most of his contemporaries and because those he published strongly resemble some reported several years later by George Washington Cable.

From "Tribulations des Voudous," *L'Union,* 1 August 1863, 1.

Original

> Simbé maman oun déré.
> Simbé! Simbé! Papa O
> Simbé! maman oun déré.
> puis: Assou Ladedan Lacatra,
> Assou Assou Ladedan.

Translation[1]

(B) Catch, mother, the whites.

Catch! Catch! Father, oh,
Catch! Mother, the whites.
Assou[2] follow to capture the genitals.
Assou follow to capture.

(B) [Song to Simbé, asking for something.]

From "The Vou Dous Incantation," *New Orleans Times,* June 28, 1872, 1.

Part 1, Original

[From Priestess Marie Laveau]
Saiya ma coupé sa
[From congregation]
Mam'zelle Marie chauffez ca

Part 1, Translation[3]

[From Priestess Marie Laveau]
Try to cut me off/Try to cut me
[From congregation]
Miss Marie heat it up

Part 2, Original

C'est l'amour, oui maman c'est l'amour

Part 2, Translation[4]

This is love, yes mother this is love

From *New Orleans Bulletin,* 24 June 1875, [unknown page number]. Cited in Northwestern State University of Louisiana, Watson Memorial Library, Cammie G. Henry Research Center, Federal Writers' Project, folder 414.

Original

Ay! Ay! Decalemeau! Bezou! Bezou!
Ay! Ay! Decalemeau! Bezou!

From Lafcadio Hearn, *New Orleans Daily Item,* 8 November 1879. Cited in Edward LaRocque Tinker, "Gombo—The Creole Dialect of Louisiana," *Proceedings of the American Antiquary* Society 45 (April 1935), 109–10.

Original

Heru mandé, heru mandé, heru mandé
Tigi li papa
Heru mandé
Tigi li papa
Heru mandé
Heru mandé, heru mandé
Do sé dans godo
Ah tingonai yé;
Ah tingonai yé, ah tingonai yé
Ah ouai ta, ah ouai ya,
Do sé dans godo
Ah tingonai yé
Tigi le papa, etc.

Translation

Tigi li is "maker of charms"
Do sé dans godo is "Oh, curved snake, may you be fat."[5]

From "Voudooism," *Daily Picayune,* 22 June 1890, 10[6]

Part 1, Original

L'appe vini, li Grand Zombi,
L'appe vini, pou fé gri-gri!

Part 1, Translation[7]

He is coming, the Great Zombi,
He is coming, to do gris-gris.

Part 2, Original

Eh! ye! ye! Mam'zelle Marie,
Ya! ye, li konin tou gri-gri.

Li te kouri lekol avec vie kokodri!

Oh! 'ouai! ya! Mam'zelle Marie!

Li konin bien li Grand Zombi!

Kan apieli te koushi,

Dan ti kein bien kasha,

Li te sorti bayou.

Pour apprendre li Voudoo.

Part 2, Translation[8]

Eh! Hey! Hey! Mademoiselle Marie,

Yeah! Hey, she knows all gris-gris.

She went to school with old alligators.

Oh! Yay! Yeah! Mademoiselle Marie!

She knows well the Great Zombi!

When we called, she was lying down,

In bed she was hiding,

She goes out on the bayou.

To teach her Voodoo.

Part 3, Original

Oh! tingouai ye! houe! houe!

Oh! Ouai ye! hen! hen!

Oh! tingouai ye! eh! eh!

Ye! ye!

Part 3, Translation

[Untranslated, though note similar wording to a song recorded by George Washington Cable, below]

Part 4, Original

L'appe vini, li grand Zombi,
Pou fé mouri, pou fé gri-gri!

Part 4, Translation[9]

He is coming, the Great Zombi,
To kill, to do gris-gris.

Part 5, Original

Congo li! Congo li!
Voudou prie, Grand zombie!
Li grand Zombie qui fé muri.
Oh! ya! ye!

Part 5, Translation[10]

Congo he! Congo he!
Voodoo pray, Grand Zombi!
The Great Zombi who kills.
Oh! Yeah! Hey!

From "Popular Superstitions and the Long Drought," *Daily Picayune,* 18 October 1894, 3.

Original

Yo! ya! li! li grand zombie
Oui te couri l'cole avec vieux cocorri!
L'appe veni pour fait' gri-gri
Pur fait gri-gri dans tit coin bien cacher;
Yo! ya! li! et la pluic va tomber!
Yo! ya! li! pour li Grand Zombi!

Translation[11]

> Yo! Ya! To him, to him, Grand Zombi
> Yes, he went to school with the old alligators.
> He is coming to do gris-gris,
> To do gris-gris in a little corner well hidden;
> Yo! Ya! To him! And the rain is going to fall!
> Yo! Ya! To him! For the Grand Zombi!

From "Dance of the Voodoos," *The Times-Democrat*, June 24, 1896, 2.

Original

> Au joli cocodri,
> Vini gro cocodri,
> Mo pas ouar cocodri zombi!
> Yo! Ya! Colombo!
> Yo! Ya! Colombo!

> Pilé cher trou-lou-lou,
> Mange bon trou-lou-lou;
> Cé vou qui l'ami tou-vou-dou!
> Yo! Ya! Colombo!
> Yo! Ya! Colombo!

Translation[12]

> To the pretty alligator,
> Come fat alligator,
> Do not splash(?) me spirit alligator!
> Yo! Ya! Colombo!
> Yo! Ya! Colombo!

> Pound dear fiddler crab,
> Eat well fiddler crab;

Those who love all Voodoo!
Yo! Ya! Colombo!
Yo! Ya! Colombo!

OTHER PERIODICALS

Periodicals other than newspapers avoid the pitfall of rushed reporting and the unintended errors that tend to accompany it. Other issues, such as authorial hostility, however, can be just as prominent. In addition, the passage of time between an event and the publication about it can lead to greater distortion than would often be present in a report on a recent occurrence. For instance, the single most critical issue with the following account by Marie B. Williams is that the ceremony during which the chants appeared reportedly took place approximately fifty years prior to the article's publication. Though they were short and therefore easier to remember, the passage of time allowed for contamination from other sources as well as other unintentional alterations. In contrast, George Washington Cable enhanced the value of the selections included in his "Creole Slave Songs" by conducting research into the subject of Voodoo. His song beginning "Hé-ron man-dé," which is clearly the same as one recorded in 1879 by Lafcadio Hearn in a news article, differs significantly in spelling, indicating that it was probably not drawn from the earlier source. Charles Dudley Warner, appears to have researched his subject as well by referring to Cable's work, erroneously repeating as a New Orleans song one that Cable indicated was Haitian in origin. Though it is unlikely that he heard the songs that he reported as being performed in the Mississippi River valley, they are included because he claimed they were part of the religion's repertoire.

From Marie B. Williams, "A Night with the Voudous," *Appleton's Journal: A Magazine of General Literature* 13 (March 1875): 404.

Part 1, Original

Voudou, voudou, Magnian.

Part 1, Translation[13]

> Voodoo, great voodoo.

Part 2, Original

> Houm! dance Calinda,
> Voudou! Magnian,
> Aie! Aie!
> Dance Calinda!

Part 2, Translation[14]

> Houm! Dance the Calinda,
> Voodoo! Magnian,
> Ah! Ah!
> Dance the Calinda!

From George Washington Cable, "Creole Slave Songs," *The Century Magazine,* 31 (April 1886): 817, 820.

Page 817, Original

> Aïe! Aïe!
> Voodoo Magnan!

Page 817, Translation[15]

> Ah! Ah!
> Great Voodoo!

Page 820, Part 1, Original

> M'allé couri dans déser

Page 820, Part 1, Translation[16]

I will wander into the desert

Page 820, Part 2, Original

Hé-ron man-dé, Hé-ron man-dé, Ti-gui li pa-pa, Héron man-dé, Ti-gui li pa-pa, Hé-ron man-dé, Hé-ron man-dé, Hé-ron man-dé, Do sé dan go-do.

Page 820, Part 2, Translation

Ti-gui li is "maker of charms"
Do sé dan go-do is "Oh, curved snake, may you be fat."[17]

Page 820, Part 3, Original

Ah tingouai yé, Ah tinguoai yé. Ah ouai ya, Ah ouai ya, Ah tingouai yé, Do sé dan go-do, Ah tingouai yé

Page 820, Part 3, Translation

[Untranslated]

From Charles Dudley Warner, "A Voudoo Dance," *Harper's Weekly* 31 (1887): 454–455.

Page 454—The Dansé Calinda, Original

Dansé Calinda, boudoum, boudoum!
Dansé Calinda, boudoum, boudoum!

Page 454—The Dansé Calinda, Translation[18]

Dance the Calinda, boudoum, boudoum!
Dance the Calinda, boudoum, boudoum!

Page 455—The Canga, Original

Eh! eh! Bomba, hen! hen!
    Canga bafio té
    Canga moune dé lé
    Canga do ki la
    Canga li.

Page 455—The Canga, Translation[19]

(A) Eh! Eh! Let's meet! Let's meet!
Canga[20] is not a bad thing.
Canga is a good thing.
Canga will do something to you.
Call canga!

(B) Eh! Eh! Bomba,[21] hen, hen!
Seize the Blacks.
Seize the whites.
Seize the witches!
Seize him/her!

From Mary Alicia Owen, "Among the Voodoos," in *The International Folk-lore Congress 1891: Papers and Transactions* (London: David Nutt, 1892), 242.

Original

Minnie, no, no Samunga,
Sangee see sa soh Samunga.

Translation

[Untranslated, but spoken when gathering mud]

From Lyle Saxon, "Voodoo," *The New Republic*, 23 March 1927, 137–8.

Page 137, Original

> Leader:
> Done set the table, Saint Maron . . . now what yo' goin' to do?
> Chorus of Participants:
> > W'at yo' goin' to do? Oh, w'at yo' goin' to do?
> > Oh, Maron, oh, Saint Maron,
> W'at yo' goin' to do?

Page 138, Part 1, Original

> Leader:
> Zombi!
> Chorus of Participants:
> > Zombi! Zombi!

Page 138, Part 2, Original

> Aie! Aie!

Page 138, Part 2, Translation[22]

> Ah! Ah!

NONFICTION BOOKS

These selections are among those Voodoo songs most likely to be accurately recorded. "I Will Wander in the Desert," for example, was referenced by George Washington Cable a year after its appearance in the *Historical Sketch Book*, where he gave it credence as genuine, but it may well be that his knowledge of it came from the guidebook. The snippet of a song included in Lafcadio Hearn's "Gombo Zhèbes" is attested in a more complete variant in *An Angel by Brevet* by Helen Pitkin, a work of fiction published nearly two decades later. A Federal Writers' Project Worker stated that Voodoo priest Oscar Felix provided information to Hearn, and he may well have done so years later for Pitkin. J. W. Buel, meanwhile, recorded a variant of a song initially reported by Cable. Though the words are recognizably similar, significant differences in spelling indicate he had a source other than Cable.

From "1 Will Wander in the Desert," from Writers of the New Orleans Press, *Historical Sketch Book and Guide to New Orleans and Environs* (New York: Will H. Coleman, 1885), 231.

Original

>Mallé couri dan déser,
>Mallé marché dan savane,
>Mallé marché su piquan doré,
>Mallé oir ça ya di moin!
>
>Sangé moin dan l'abitation ci la la?
>Mo gagnain soutchien la Louisiane,
>Mallé oir ça ya di moin!

Translation

>I will wander into the desert,
>I will march through the prairie,
>I will walk upon the golden thorn—
>Who is there who can stop me?
>
>To change me from this plantation?
>I have the support of Louisiana—
>Who is there who can resist me?

From Lafcadio Hearn, *"Gombo Zhèbes": Little Dictionary of Creole Proverbs, Selected from Six Creole Dialects* (New York: Will H. Coleman, 1885; reprint Bedford, MA: Applewood, n.d.), 39, n. 2.

Original

> Tout, tout, pays blanc—Danié qui commandé,
>> Danié qui commandé ça!
>> Danié qui commandé.

Translation[23]

> All, all the country white (white man's country)—Daniel has so commanded,
>> Daniel has so commanded that!
>> Daniel has so commanded.

From J. W. Buel, *Sunlight and Shadow of America's Great Cities* (Philadelphia: West Philadelphia Publishing, 1889), 532–34.

Page 532, Part 1, Original

> Mo va fai' wanga pour li
> Mo fai tourne fantome.

Page 532, Part 1, Translation[24]

> I am going to do *wanga* for him.
> I will turn him into a ghost.

Page 532, Part 2, Original

> Pour chambe li
> Na fai' grigri.

Page 532, Part 2, Translation[25]

> For _____ him
> We do *gris-gris.*

> Heron mande,
> Heron mande,
> Tigi li papa,
> Heron mande,
> Heron mande,
> Heron mande,
> Dosi dans godo!
> Ah tingwaiye,
> Ah tingwaiye!
> Ah waiyah, ah waiyah,
> Ah tingwaiye,
> Tigi li papa!
> Heron mande,
> Ahwaya!
> Ah tingwaiye,
> Ahwaya!
> Ah tingwaiye.

Page 533, Translation

[See above regarding George Washington Cable]

Page 534, Part 1, Original

> Ole bas,
> Alli bono,
> A ri cha,
> Alli bono
> Cho, cho, ti;
> Vale mi cho,
> Cho, cho, li;
> Vale mi cho.

Page 534, Part 1, Translation

[Untranslated]

Page 534, Part 2, Original

Tou piti cabri?
Ca Zoe, nou ye!

Page 534, Part 2, Translation[26]

You little goat?
That Zoe, we are!

From Harry Middleton Hyatt, *Hoodoo—Conjuration—Witchcraft—Rootwork,* 5 vols, Memoirs of the Alma Egan Hyatt Foundation (Hannibal, MO: Western Publishing Company, 1970–1978), 796.

Original

Marie Madelaine comme ca

Translation[27]

Marie Madelaine so

MANUSCRIPTS

In most cases, the best sources of historical detail are manuscript accounts that provide firsthand reports from those involved in the events they describe. Indeed, the Federal Writers' Project files include several songs collected from Voodoo practitioners. To some extent, however, they are potentially flawed in that they report lyrics from music whose heyday had passed decades before. The University of New Orleans's Owen Creole Songs Collection may contain another firsthand Voodoo song. Entitled "Voodoo Song," it is listed as being by Louis Panzeri. It is entirely possible that it is his own creation. On the other hand, its Creole French words of unclear connotation indicate that it may well be a Voodoo song.

As important as they are in their own right, some of the Federal Writers' Project sources also help verify the authenticity of songs reported by others. The informants, one Alexander Augustin and another called Miss Dede by her interviewers, for instance, both quoted from a song regarding dying in a lake. While the former gave a French version of the lyrics, the latter spoke in English.[28] Likewise, the song beginning "Mo Marchez sur a epigne" provides evidence for the authenticity of a similar and more complete version recorded in the 1885 *Historical Sketch Book and Guide to New Orleans and Environs.*

From Robert McKinney, "St. Peter and Black Cat Opening," 1937, transcript, Northwestern State University of Louisiana, Watson Memorial Library, Cammie G. Henry Research Center, Federal Writers' Project, folder 43, 6.

Original

Stars above, saints, everybody, hep dese boys to do what dey want to do. Let dem be successful in dere undertaking.

. . .

Spirits, giv dese young men de power to do all de bad work dey wants to. Give dem de power to Konquer what dey want. Follow dem in dere journey.

From Dauphine, "Marie Laveau," transcript, Northwestern State University of Louisiana, Watson Memorial Library, Cammie G. Henry Research Center, Federal Writers' Project, folder 25, 1.

Original

Mo Marchez sur a epigne

Mo Marchez sur a neiguille

Peut Piscon qui Moin

Translation[29]

I walk on a thorn.

I walk on a needle.

Which one stings the least?

From Arguedas and Robert McKinney, "Miss Dede," 1939, transcript, Northwestern State University of Louisiana, Watson Memorial Library, Cammie G. Henry Research Center, Federal Writers' Project, folder 533, 3.

Original

When I die, I wants to die in de lake

From Robert McKinney, "Popular Gris-Gris among Present Day Hoodoo Queens," transcript, Northwestern State University of Louisiana, Watson Memorial Library, Cammie G. Henry Research Center, Federal Writers' Project, folder 44, 8, 9.

Page 8, Original

Labat ouvre la port.

. . .

Go spirits, open the way for us. Pass before us.

Page 8, Translation[30]

Labat open the door.

Page 9, Original

Help us, defend us, let us command all of them, let us conquer all.

Version 1 from Maud H. Wallace, [Lala], 1940, transcript, Northwestern State University of Louisiana, Watson Memorial Library, Cammie G. Henry Research Center, Federal Writers' Project, folder 43, 6. Version 2 text and translation from Michinard and Maude H. Wallace, "Song Sung by Lala, the Voodoo Queen," 1940, transcript, Northwestern State University of Louisiana, Watson Memorial Library, Cammie G. Henry Research Center, Federal Writers' Project, folder 3, 1–2.

Original, Version 1

Yé n'a pas comme moin,
Yé n'a pas comme moin,
Yé n'a pas comme moin,
La poule a moin,
Yé n'a pas comme moin,
Yé n'a pas comme moin,
Yé n'a pas comme moin,
La poule a moin.

Allez vielle negrèsse,
Allez vielle negrèsse,
Allez vielle negrèsse,
Pour moi.

Translation, Version 1[31]

There are none like mine,
There are none like mine,
There are none like mine,
That hen of mine,
There are none like mine,

There are none like mine,
There are none like mine,
That hen of mine.

Go way old negress,
Go way old negress,
Go way old negress,
For me.

Original, Version 2

Yé ná pas com me moin,
Yé ná pas com me moin,
Yé ná pas com me moin,
La pauvre a moin.
Yé ná pas com me moin,
Yé ná pas com me moin,
Yé ná pas com me moin,
La pauvre a moin.

Al-lez vielle ne-gresse,
Al-lez vielle ne-gresse,
Al-lez vielle ne-gresse,
Pauvre moin!

Translation, Version 2[32]

There is none like me,
There is none like me,
There is none like me,
Poor me!
There is none like me,
There is none like me,
There is none like me,
Poor me!

Go old negress,
Go old negress,
Go old negress,
Poor me!

From Mathilda Mendoza, interview by Maude H. Wallace, 11 and 17 January 1940, transcript, Northwestern State University of Louisiana, Watson Memorial Library, Cammie G. Henry Research Center, Federal Writers' Project, folder 25, 1.

Original

Yes, Little John

From Charles Raphael, interview by Hazel Breaux, transcript, Northwestern State University of Louisiana, Watson Memorial Library, Cammie G. Henry Research Center, Federal Writers' Project, folder 25, 4.

Original "Chanson de Dance" as Performed by Celestine Argo[33]

Pele moa Batis
Lioulay oua, lioulay ous Batis
 Seyay moa
Ou don Batis, lioulay oua,
Il ay bel Batis
 Seyay moa
Condui moa Batis
 Seyay moa

Pele moa Gustine
Lioulay oua, lioulay oua Gustine
 Seyay moa
Ou don Gustine, lioulay oua,
Il ay bel Gustine
 Seyay moa

Condui moa Gustine
    Seyay moa

Translation "Dance Song"[34]

Call me Baptist
I want to see, I want to see Baptist
    Try me
Where is Baptist, I want to see him
He is good looking Baptist
    Try me
Lead me Baptist
    Try me

Call me Gustine
I want to see, I want to see Gustine
    Try me
Where is Gustine, I want to see him
He is good looking Gustine
    Try me
Lead me Gustine
    Try me

From Alexander Augustin, "Marie Laveau," interview by Henriette Michinard, July 1940, transcript, Northwestern State University of Louisiana, Watson Memorial Library, Cammie G. Henry Research Center, Federal Writers' Project, folder 25, 1.

Original

Nous allons mourrir dans ce lac, c'est vrai!
Nous allons mourrir dans ce lac, c'est vrai!

Translation[35]

> We are going to die in this lake, t'is true!
> We are going to die in this lake, t'is true!

From Mary Washington, "Marie Laveau," interview by Robert McKinney, transcript, Northwestern State University of Louisiana, Watson Memorial Library, Cammie G. Henry Research Center, Federal Writers' Project, folder 25, 88.

Original

> St. Peter, St. Peter open the door
> I um callin you, come to me
> St. Peter, St. Peter (repeat)

From William Moore, "Marie Leveau," interview by Edmund Burke, 1 March 1940, transcript, Northwestern State University of Louisiana, Watson Memorial Library, Cammie G. Henry Research Center, Federal Writers' Project, folder 25, 1–4.

Original

> Siama copé. Siama copé.

Translation[36]

> Try to cut me off. Try to cut me off.

From Henriette Michinard, "Song of the Voudous on Congo Square," 1940, Northwestern State University of Louisiana, Watson Memorial Library, Cammie G. Henry Research Center, Federal Writers' Project, folder 3, 1–4.

Original, "Chaute par les Voudou sur la place Congo"

Conduit moin la reine
Conduit moin dans château le roi
Conduit moin dans château le roi
Conduit mon dans palais mo roi

Si mo mourri jordi comme demain
Voyé dit yé vini voir moin

Conduit moin la reine
Conduit moin dans château le roi
Conduit moin dans château le roi
Conduit mon dans palais mo roi

Si mo mourri jordi comme demain
Mouchoir madra méné moin couri

Conduit moin la reine
Conduit moin dans château le roi
Conduit moin dans château le roi
Conduit mon dans palais mo roi

Tout péche oui, que mo fait
Mo vole femme qui té pas pou moin

Conduit moin la reine
Conduit moin dans château le roi
Conduit moin dans château le roi
Conduit mon dans palais mo roi

Si vous voir nainaine zabo
Boyez dit li vini voir moin

Conduit moin la reine
Conduit moin dans château le roi
Conduit moin dans château le roi
Conduit mon dans palais mo roi

Translation, "Song of the Voudous on Congo Square"[37]

Lead me to the Queen
Lead me to the King's Castle
Lead me to the King's Castle
Lead me to my King's Palace

Should I die to-day as to-morrow
Send tell them come see me

Lead me to the Queen
Lead me to the King's Castle
Lead me to the King's Castle
Lead me to my King's Palace

Should I die to-day as to-morrow
Bandana kerchief led me to it

Lead me to the Queen
Lead me to the King's Castle
Lead me to the King's Castle
Lead me to my King's Palace

All sins yes, that I committed—
Me stole woman that was'nt for me.

Lead me to the Queen
Lead me to the King's Castle
Lead me to the King's Castle
Lead me to my King's Palace

Should you see the nainaine[38] Zabo
Send tell her, come see me.

Lead me to the Queen
Lead me to the King's Castle

Lead me to the King's Castle
Lead me to my King's Palace

From Louis Panzeri, "Voodoo Song," University of New Orleans, Earl K. Long Library, Louisiana Special Collections, Owen Creole Songs Collection, folder 4–1, item 86. Donated in 1968.

Original

En bas hé
En bas hé
Par en bas é pélé
Moin ye péle compaille a dé-bau-ché
Par en haut ye pé-le moin ye pé-lé Mamzelle—
Su-zet-te-Par en bas yé pé-l
Moin ye pé-lé compaille à dé-bauche.

Translation[39]

Hey down there,
Hey down there,
Down below I have called[40]
Unless I call a companion [who is] in a state of debauchery[41]
I call upstairs; I have been calling a young lady—
Suzette. I call downstairs[42]
If I call a drunken companion.[43]

WORKS OF FICTION

In general, I have avoided putting much stock in works of fiction. A partial exception to this rule is Helen Pitkin's *Angel by Brevet*. It includes a sizeable collection of Voodoo songs, which resemble those in nonfiction works but appear to have an independent source. Pitkin claimed to have collected them from a Voodoo practitioner, and it is just possible that Oscar Felix, who reportedly aided Lafcadio Hearn and many years later spoke with Federal Writers' Project workers, was the unnamed informant. Two versions of a chant calling on Blanc Dani, which appeared in Hearn's "Gombo Zhèbes" and Pitkins' novel, provide the basis for this tentative identification. Leslie-Leigh Ducros' reputed Voodoo song likewise has the potential for authenticity in that it resembles ones from earlier journalistic documents.

From Helen Pitkin, *An Angel by Brevet: A Story of Modern New Orleans* (Philadelphia and London: J. P. Lippincott, 1904), 61, 193–194, 196, 267–268, 269, 273–274, 275, 276, 280, 281, 285.

Page 61, Original

> L'appé vini, li Grand Zombi,
> L'appé vini pou to gri-gri.

Page 61, Translation[44]

> He is coming, the Great Zombi,
> He is coming to make gris-gris!

Pages 193–194, Original

> Salue, Marie, pleine de graces.
> . . .
> *Ainsi soit il.*

Page 193–194, Translation[45]

> Hail, Mary, full of grace.
> . . .
> So be it.

Pages 194–195, Original

Bon jour Liba,
Ouvert la porte,
Bon jour mon cousin.

. . .

Bon jour Liba,
Bon jour Liba, ouvert la porte,
Ouvert la porte, Bon jour mon cousin,
Bon jour mon cousin, Bon jour Liba.

Pages 194–195, Translation[46]

Good day Liba,
Open the door,
Good day my cousin.
. . .
Good day Liba,
Good day Liba, open the door,
Open the door, Good day my cousin,
Good day my cousin, Good day Liba.

Page 196, Original

Blanc Dani,
Dans tous pays blanc
L'a commandé
Blanc Dani, Dans tous pays blanc
L'a commandé.

Page 196, Translation[47]

White Dani,
In all whites' country

There you rule
White Dani, In all whites' country
There you rule.

Page 267, Original

Nom du Père, du Fils, Saint Esprit—Ainsi soit-il!

Page 267, Translation[48]

In the name of the Father, of the Son, Holy Spirit—So be it!

Pages 267–268, Original

Vert Agoussou,
Voyin nomme!
Oh, c'est Vert Agoussou!
Dambarra Soutons,
Côté ou yé
M'appé mandé
Vous la charité
Côté Maman.
Tigéla papa,
Ou c'est Agoussou,
Ah, y en a qui l'aimé.
Vert Agoussou,
Oh, voyin nomme!
C'est Vert Agoussou,
Vous yé Agoussou.

Pages 267–268, Translation[49]

Green Agoussou
That is your name!
Oh, this is Green Agoussou!
Dambarra Soutons,

You are near.[50]
This is my call to ask
You for charity
Next to Mother.[51]
You are here Father,
Or it is Agoussou,
Ah, there are some who love him.
Green Agoussou,
Oh, that is your name!
This is Green Agoussou,
You are Agoussou.

Page 269, Part 1, Original

Papa Liba!

Page 269, Part 2, Original

Vériquité!

Page 269, Part 3, Original

Bon la chance!

Page 269, Part 3, Translation[52]

Good luck!

Pages 273–274, Original

C'est Charlo!
C'est Charlo, vins, vins,
Côté mo passé
M'appélé-toi
Dans maison autres
M'appélé-toi

Charlo, 'tit' frère
Charlo, vins, vins,
Côté to passé
M'appélé-toi répété.
Ah, mo cherché vous, yé, yé,
Mo pélé toi!

Pages 273–274, Translation[53]

This is Charlo!
This is Charlo, come, come,[54]
Walk next to me[55]
I call you
In others houses
I call you
Charlo, little brother,
Charlo, come, come,[56]
Walk next to you[57]
I call to you again.
Ah, I search for you, yeah, yeah,
I call you!

Page 275, Original

Jean Macouloumba, honhé
. . .
Jean Macouloumba, honhé. Laisse qua houmna pi no pou' l'elle bé na!

Page 275, Translation[58]

Jean Macouloumba, honor
. . .
Jean Macouloumba, honor. Let [unclear, but houmna might be a name] for her!

Page 276, Original

Merci, Charlo!

. . .

Caloumba! Gou-doung! Caloumba! Gou-doung!

Page 276, Translation[59]

Thank you, Charlo!

Page 280, Original

Ventre bleu!
Nom du petard!

Page 280, Translation[60]

Blue belly!
Name of the fireworks!

Page 281, Original

Grand Zombi!

Page 285, Original

Jean Macouloumba, honhé! honhé! honhé!
Jean! Jean! Laisse qua houmna pi no pou' l'elle bé na!
Caloumba! Gou-doung! Gou-doung! Gou-doung!

. . .

La Mort!
Charlo, vins, vins!
Vert Agoussou! Dambarra Soutons!
Zombi! La Mort! honhé! honhé! honhé! honhé! Yi!
Oough! Oough! Zombi couri! couri! Dis li mort!
Le Mort!

God who never rests, honor! Honor! Honor!
God! God! Let nature be at rest. They are sleeping.
Never resting! Ngundu! Ngundu! Ngundu![62]
. . .
Death!
Charlo, wine, wine!
Green Agoussou! Dambarra Soutons!
Zombi! Death! honor! honor! honor! honor! Yi!
Ooh! Ooh! Zombi run! run! Say death!
Death!

From Leslie-Leigh Ducros, "Mammy Zoe Appeases 'Gran' Zombi' and Saves Bride's Wedding Gown," *New Orleans Item,* 30 March 1919, 5.

Original

Ya! Yi! Li Gran Zombi, qui courri a l'ecole avec viex diablé
L'appe veni pou fai gri-gri, dans 'tit coin bien cache.
Yo! Ya! Li Gran Zombi!
Yo! Ya! Li Gran Zombi!
Beninie robe noce la?

Translation[63]

Ohe! Oha! The Great Zombi who went to school with the old devil.
Call him to make gri-gri (magic) in a little dark corner.
Ohe! Oha! The Great Zombi, the Great Zombi, bless the wedding dress!

NOTES

INTRODUCTION: WHAT IS IN A NAME?

1. For examples of two recent works that use both terms, see Suzanne Preston Blier, *African Vodun: Art, Psychology, and Power* (Chicago: University of Chicago Press, 1995) and Judy Rosenthal, *Possession, Ecstasy, and Law in Ewe Voodoo* (Charlottesville: University Press of Virginia, 1998).

2. Two books that did the most to popularize such stereotypes were Spenser St. John, *Hayti: Or the Black Republic* (London: Smith, Elder, and Company, 1884; reprint Kessinger Publishing, 2008) and William Seabrook, *The Magic Island*, with illustrations by Alexander King (New York: Harcourt, Brace, 1929; republished New York: Paragon House, 1989).

3. Leslie G. Desmangles, *The Faces of the Gods: Vodou and Roman Catholicism in Haiti* (Chapel Hill: University of North Carolina Press, 1992), xi–xii.

4. Carolyn Morrow Long, *A New Orleans Voudou Priestess: The Legend and Reality of Marie Laveau* (Gainesville: University Press of Florida, 2006), 5–6, 14, 93–95; Nathalie Dessens, *From Saint-Domingue to New Orleans: Migration and Influences* (Gainesville: University Press of Florida, 2007), 159–162.

5. Long, *Voudou Priestess*, xv; Yvonne Chireau, *Black Magic: Religion and the African American Conjuring Tradition* (Berkeley: University of California Press, 2003), 77; "Voodooism," *New-Orleans Commercial Bulletin*, 5 July 1869, 1; "The Vou Dous Incantation," *New Orleans Times*, 28 June 1872, 1; "Idolatry and Quakery," *Louisiana Gazette*, 16 August 1820, 2; "The Departed Voudoo Queen," *New Orleans Times*, 24 June 1881, 3; William W. Newell, "Reports of Voodoo Worship in Hayti and Louisiana," *Journal of American Folk-Lore* ll (1889): 41–47; George Washington Cable, "Creole Slave Songs," with illustrations by E. W. Kemble, *The Century 31* (1886): 815–821; Robert Tallant, *Voodoo in New Orleans* (New York: Macmillan, 1946; reprint, Gretna, LA: Pelican Publishing Company, 1998).

6. Catherine Yronwode, "Hoodoo: African American Magic," Lucky Mojo Curio Company, 1995–2003, http://www.luckymojo.com/hoodoohistory.html (accessed 1 February 2010).

7. Carolyn Morrow Long, *Spiritual Merchants: Religion, Magic, and Commerce* (Knoxville: University of Tennessee Press, 2001), xvi.

8. Chireau, *Black Magic*, 77.

9. Zora Neale Hurston, "Hoodoo in America," *Journal of American Folk-Lore* 44 (1931): 317.

10. "Voudooism—African Fetich Worship among the Memphis Negroes," *Memphis Appeal*, 25 October 1868, 3. The article later appeared in well-known occultist Paschal Beverly Randolph's *Seership! The Magnetic Mirror*, by (Toledo, OH: K. C. Randolph, 1896; reprint, Kessinger Publishing, 2004), 17–21.

11. Thaddeus Norris, "Negro Superstitions," *Lippincott's Magazine* 6 (1870): 92. See also Hurston, "Hoodoo in America," 317, who employed the terms in the same way.

12. Cable, "Creole Slave Songs," 815.

13. [Hazel Breaux and Robert McKinney], "Laure Hopkins," Northwestern State University of Louisiana, Watson Memorial Library, Cammie G. Henry Research Center, Federal Writers' Project, folder 43, 4. The author or authors of these notes have not been identified with certainty, but the fact that Hazel Breaux and Robert McKinney conducted numerous interviews with Hopkins makes them the most likely writers. In general, the Federal Writers' Project documents do not supply the first names of their authors. The names were supplied by Long, *Voudou Priestess*, v.

14. Mary Alicia Owen, "Among the Voodoos," in *The International Folk-lore Congress 1891: Papers and Transactions* (London: David Nutt, 1892), 241. It is important to note that the word *Noodoos* may well have been a misprint for *Hoodoos*. Elsewhere in this short work, Owen used hoodoo to describe magical practice. For an interesting biography of the life of this unjustly forgotten folklorist, see Greg Olson, *Voodoo Priests, Noble Savages, and Ozark Gypsies: The Life of Folklorist Mary Alicia Owen* (Columbia: University of Missouri Press, 2012), 57–69.

15. For a more elaborate definition of conjure and its distinctiveness, see Jeffrey E. Anderson, *Conjure in African American Society* (Baton Rouge: Louisiana State University Press, 2005), ix–xii.

16. Mary Alicia Owen, "Voodooism," in *The International Folk-lore Congress of the World's Columbian Exposition, July 1893*, Archives of the International Folk-Lore Association, vol. 1, ed. Helen Wheeler Bassett and Frederick Starr (Chicago: Charles H. Sergel, 1898), 324–326, quoted 324.

17. Owen, "Voodooism," 323; Breaux and McKinney, "Laure Hopkins," 4, 5.

18. In the following, *Creole* has no racial connotations and describes instead the descendants of the French, Spanish, or Afro-Latins who settled the area between its founding and the last major influx of Francophones that began in 1809. Whenever the term is used as an adjective, it will remain uncapitalized and indicate a population, practice, or belief with roots outside the region that nevertheless developed its distinctiveness within the Mississippi River valley.

19. One could argue that Florida's Nañigo is an exception to this statement. This little-studied faith almost certainly constituted the full makings of a religion during the late nineteenth century. On the other hand, it was less a distinctly North American creole faith than it was a recent import from Cuba. Moreover, its deities and ceremonies show clear affinities with the Cuban religion, known as Santería, Lucumi, and Regla de Ocha; Jeffrey E. Anderson, *Hoodoo, Voodoo, and Conjure: A Handbook*, Greenwood Folklore Handbooks Series (Westport, CT: Greenwood Press, 2008), 20–22, 46–47. For an accessible summary of the Cuban religion, see Margarite Fernández Olmos and Lizabeth Paravisini-Gebert, *Creole Religions of the Caribbean: An Introduction from Vodou and Santería to Obeah and Espiritismo*, 2nd ed. (New York: New York University Press, 2011), 33–87.

20. Philip D. Morgan, *Slave Counterpoint: Black Culture in the Eighteenth-Century Chesapeake and Lowcountry* (Chapel Hill: University of North Carolina Press, 1998), 594–595. For a descrip-

tion of Pinkster, see James Fenimore Cooper, *Satanstoe: Or the Littlepage Manuscripts* (1845; re-published, New York: Co-Operative Publication Society, unknown publication date), 72–79, 106.

21. Kodi Roberts, *Voodoo and Power: The Politics of Religion in New Orleans, 1881–1940* (Baton Rouge: Louisiana State University Press, 2015), 6

22. Roberts, 6–8. The highest percentage of white participation that I have located was re-ported in "Voudou Entertainment," *The Daily States,* 29 May 1889, 2. This article took the unusual step of naming each arrestee. Of those listed, seven were white women, six were black women, and seven were black men.

1. THE PEOPLES OF THE MISSISSIPPI RIVER VALLEY

1. For examples of the traditional interpretation of Voodoo's origins, see Hurston, "Hoodoo in America," 317–319 and Tallant, *Voodoo in New Orleans,* 9–12.

2. Harold Courlander, *The Drum and the Hoe: Life and Lore of the Haitian People* (Berkeley: University of California Press, 1960), 8.

3. Claudine Michel and Patrick Bellegarde-Smith, eds., *Vodou in Haitian Life and Culture: Invisible Powers* (New York: Palgrave MacMillan, 2006), 17; Alfred Métraux, *Voodoo in Haiti,* trans. by Hugo Charteris and with an Introduction by Sidney W. Mintz (New York: Schocken Books, 1972), 82–95.

4. Olmos and Paravisini-Gebert, *Creole Religions,* 33–115; George Brandon, *Santeria from Africa to the New World: The Dead Sell Memories* (Bloomington: Indiana University Press, 1993), 171–176.

5. George E. Lankford, *Native American Legends: Southeastern Legends: Tales from the Natchez, Caddo, Biloxi, Chickasaw, and Other Nations,* American Folklore Series, W. K. McNeil, ed. (Little Rock, AR: August House, 1987), 39–41, 54–56; Charles Hudson, *The Southeastern Indians* (Knoxville: University of Tennessee Press, 1976), 122–173. For information on Native American medicinal practices, see Alma R. Hutchens, *Indian Herbalogy of North America* (1973; reprint, Boston: Shambhala Hall, 1973) and Virgil J. Vogel, *American Indian Medicine,* paperback ed., Civilization of the American Indian Series (Norman: University of Oklahoma Press, 1990).

6. John H. B. Latrobe, *Southern Travels: Journal of John H. B. Latrobe, 1834,* edited and with an Introduction by Samuel Wilson, with a Preface by Stanton Frazar (New Orleans: Historic New Orleans Collection, 1986), 71.

7. Jennifer M. Spear, *Race, Sex, and Social Order in Early New Orleans* (Baltimore: Johns Hopkins University Press, 2009), 21–42; Latrobe, *Southern Travels,* 71; "Indians in the Life of New Orleans," Northwestern State University of Louisiana, Watson Memorial Library, Cammie G. Henry Research Center, Federal Writers' Project, folder 95.

8. Vogel, *American Indian Medicine,* 13–22, 299, 361–365; [N.D.P. Bivens], *Black and White Magic,* revised ed. (Los Angeles: International Imports, 1991), 38; Wonda L. Fontenot, *Secret Doctors: Ethnomedicine of African Americans* (Westport, CT: Bergin and Garvey, 1994), 139.

9. Mary Alicia Owen, *Old Rabbit, the Voodoo and Other Sorcerers,* with an introduction by Charles Godfrey Leland, with illustrations by Juliette A. Owen and Louis Wain (London: T. Fisher Unwin, 1893; reprint, Whitefish, MT: Kessinger Publishing, 2003), v–ix, 3, 8–10, 173; John Smith, interview by [Hazel] Breaux, transcript, Northwestern State University of Louisiana, Watson Memorial Library, Cammie G. Henry Research Center, Federal Writers' Project, folder 587, 4; [Jacques]

Villere and [Hazel] Breaux, "Raphael: Who Sang at Marie Laveau's Ceremonies," Northwestern State University of Louisiana, Watson Memorial Library, Cammie G. Henry Research Center, Federal Writers' Project, folder 587, 2. Indian Jim reportedly would go on to fame as Jim Alexander, a well-known Voodoo practitioner and hoodoo doctor.

10. Marie Dédé, interview by [Robert] McKinney, transcript, Northwestern State University of Louisiana, Watson Memorial Library, Cammie G. Henry Research Center, Federal Writers' Project, folder 25, 2.

11. Dédé, interview by McKinney, 2–3.

12. Spear, *Race, Sex, and Social Order*, 19–21; Gwendolyn Midlo Hall, *Africans in Colonial Louisiana: The Development of Afro-Creole Culture in the Eighteenth Century* (Baton Rouge: Louisiana State University Press, 1992), 2–11, 120; Jerah Johnson, "Colonial New Orleans: A Fragment of the Eighteenth-Century French Ethos," in *Creole New Orleans: Race and Americanization,* edited by Arnold R. Hirsch and Joseph Logsdon (Baton Rouge: Louisiana State University Press, 1992), 33.

13. Hall, *Africans in Colonial Louisiana,* 9–14.

14. Hall, *Africans in Colonial Louisiana,* 3–14, 57–63; Spear, *Race, Sex, and Social Order,* 54.

15. Hall, *Africans in Colonial Louisiana,* 11–12, 276–277.

16. Hall, *Africans in Colonial Louisiana,* 276–279.

17. Hall, *Africans in Colonial Louisiana,* 57–95, 382–397; Alfred Burdon Ellis, *The Eẁe-Speaking Peoples of the Slave Coast of West Africa: Their Religion, Manners, Customs, Laws, Languages, &c.* (London: Chapman and Hall, 1890; reprint, Chicago: Benin Press, Ltd., 1965), 285–287.

18. Spear, *Race, Sex, and Social Order,* 53, 70–72.

19. "Death of Marie Laveau," *Daily Picayune,* 18 June 1881, 8; Hurston, "Hoodoo," 317; Desmangles, *Faces of the Gods,* 8–12; Robert McKinney, "Marie Laveau: An Interview with Mrs. Mary Washington, 1247 N. Claiborne Avenue, Who Is a Former Hoodo Queen and Card Reader," Northwestern State University of Louisiana, Watson Memorial Library, Cammie G. Henry Research Center, Federal Writers' Project, folder 25, 8–9; Hazel Breaux and Robert McKinney, "Hoodoo Opening Ceremony," Northwestern State University of Louisiana, Watson Memorial Library, Cammie G. Henry Research Center, Federal Writers' Project, folder 44, 1–4. For examples of the god-saint correspondence in another Afro-Latin faith, see Brandon, *Santeria,* 77.

20. Spears, *Race, Sex, and Social Order,* 109–128, 142–154, 158–177. Louisiana Voodoo's most famous leader, Marie Laveau, was herself a free woman of mixed race; See Long, *Voudou Priestess,* 22–24.

21. Hall, *Africans in Colonial Louisiana,* 60.

22. Ellis, *Eẁe-Speaking Peoples,* 31–37; Kofi Asare Opoku, *West African Traditional Religion* (Accra, Ghana: FEP International Private Limited, 1978), 14–33. Mawu often appears as Mawu-Lisa, an androgynous being composed of both female (Mawu) and male (Lisa) aspects. See Robert Farris Thompson, *Flash of the Spirit: African and Afro-American Art and Philosophy* (New York: Random House, 1983), 176.

23. Opoku, *West African Traditional Religion,* 8–10; Stephen S. Farrow, *Faith, Fancies, and Fetich, or Yoruba Paganism: Being Some Account of the Religious Beliefs of the West African Blacks, Particularly of the Yoruba Tribes of Southern Nigeria,* with a Foreword by R. R. Marett (Society for Promoting Christian knowledge, 1926; reprint, Athelia Henrietta Press, Inc., 1996), 34–35, 68–69.

24. Opoku, *West African Traditional Religions,* 11–13, 74–90, 140–151; Farrow, *Faith, Fancies and Fetich,* 3–4; Ellis, *Eẁe-Speaking Peoples,* 139–152.

25. Hall, *Africans in Colonial Louisiana,* 288–293; Michael Gomez, *Exchanging Our Country Marks: The Transformation of African Identities in the Colonial and Antebellum South* (Chapel Hill: University of North Carolina Press, 1998), 38–39.

26. Hall, *Africans in Colonial Louisiana,* 38–42; Gomez, *Exchanging Our County Marks,* 59–65, 67.

27. Gomez, *Exchanging Our Country Marks,* 49–51; Germaine Dieterlen, *Essai sur le Religion Bambara* (Paris: Presses Universitaires de France, 1951), 1–33, 56–88.

28. Gwendolyn Midlo Hall, *Slavery and African Ethnicities in the Americas: Restoring the Links* (Chapel Hill: University of North Carolina Press, 2005), 42–44.

29. John K. Thornton, "Religious and Ceremonial Life in the Kongo and Mbundu Areas, 1500–1700," in *Central Africans and Cultural Transformations in the American Diaspora,* edited Linda M. Heywood (Cambridge: Cambridge University Press, 2002), 72–83; Mary Kingsley, *Travels in West Africa: Congo Français, Corisco and Cameroons,* 5th edition, with an Introduction by Elizabeth Claridge (London: Virago, 1982), 442–447.

30. Thornton, "Religious and Ceremonial Life," 83–87; Hall, *Slavery and African Ethnicities,* 146–153.

31. George Washington Cable, *The Grandissimes: A Story of Creole Life* (New York: Charles Scribner's Sons, 1891), 101, 182, 184; Helen Pitkin, *An Angel by Brevet: A Story of Modern New Orleans* (Philadelphia and London: J. P. Lippincott, 1904), 194–196, 208; Thompson, *Flash of the Spirit,* 166–167, 176; Long, *Voudou Priestess,* 115; Rosenthal, *Possession, Ecstasy, and Law,* 1. For a collection of references to these and a variety of other deities drawn from more typical primary sources, see Catherine Dillon, "Voodoo, 1937–1941," Northwestern State University of Louisiana, Watson Memorial Library, Cammie G. Henry Research Center, Federal Writers' Project, folders 118, 317, and 319, sec. "Louisiana," 4, sec. "Marie the Mysterious," 3:1, 4:8, 5:7, 9, 18A-18B, 20, 6:5A, sec. "St. John's Eve," 27, sec. "Voodoo Openings," 21–24. The ethnic and regional origins of the deities will be dealt with in greater depth below.

32. As discussed above, ancestor veneration was by no means confined to West Central Africa. It was, however, more pronounced there than elsewhere.

33. Hazel Breaux and Robert McKinney, "Popular Gris-Gris Among Present Day Hoodoo Queens," Northwestern State University of Louisiana, Watson Memorial Library, Cammie G. Henry Research Center, Federal Writers' Project, folder 44, 8–10; Malcolm J. Martin, "Zombies and Ghost Dogs on the Harvey Canal," *Louisiana Folklore Miscellany* 2:4 (August 1968): 103–104; Arguedas, "Expressions Used in Creole and Cadian Dialects," Northwestern State University of Louisiana, Watson Memorial Library, Cammie G. Henry Research Center, Federal Writers' Project, folder 60, 1; Corinne L. Saucier, *Folk Tales from French Louisiana* (New York: Exposition Press, 1962), 76–77; Hans-W. Ackermann and Jeanine Gauthier, "The Ways and Nature of the Zombi," *Journal of American Folklore* 104 (1991): 467–469.

34. Antoine-Simon Le Page Du Pratz, *Histoire de la Louisiane,* 1758, translated as *The History of Louisiana or of the Western Parts of Virginia and Carolina,* two vols., (London: Becket and De Hondt, 1763), 255.

35. Laura L. Porteous, "The Gri-Gri Case," *Louisiana Historical Quarterly* 17 (1934): 50–52.

36. Rosenthal, *Possession, Ecstasy, and Law,* 264–265; Nicholas Owen, *Journal of a Slave-Dealer: A View of Some Remarkable Axcedents in the Life of Nics. Owen on the Coast of Africa and America*

from the Year 1746 to the Year 1757, edited and with an Introduction by Eveline Martin (London: George Routledge and Sons, 1930), 46–51.

37. If one takes at face value that its practitioners were indeed "Congoes," the more specific information he stated about their origins was incorrect, which poses a serious problem in light of the demonstrated roots of *gris-gris* in areas far to the north of the Kingdom of the Kongo. Antebellum accounts of race, however, should rarely be taken at face value, and it is likely that the author was simply using *Congoes* as a dismissive or derogatory synonym for *Blacks.*

38. Porteous, "Gri-Gri Case," 50–51, 62; Sylviane A. Diouf, *Dreams of Africa in Alabama: The Slave Ship "Clotilda" and the Story of the Last Africans Brought to America* (Oxford: Oxford University Press, 2007), 6, 30–54; "Voudooism—African Fetich Worship," 18–19.

39. "Voudooism—African Fetich Worship," 18–19; "'Hoodood,'" *Georgia Weekly Telegraph,* 11 January 1870: 4; "A Hoodoo Case," *Georgia Weekly Telegraph,* 12 March 1872: 4; "The 'Hoodoos' Again," *Wheeling Register,* 25 July 1879: 2; "The 'Medicine Man' Scare," *Tombstone Epitaph,* 18 September 1881: 1.

40. "'Hoodoos' Again," 2; "'Medicine Man' Scare," 1; "'Hoodood,'" 4.

41. Harry Middleton Hyatt, *Hoodoo—Conjuration—Witchcraft—Rootwork,* 5 vols., Memoirs of the Alma Egan Hyatt Foundation (Hannibal: Western Publishing Company, 1970–1978), 896.

42. Hyatt, *Hoodoo—Conjuration—Witchcraft—Rootwork,* 667–668.

43. "The Frigatened Boot-Black," *Augusta Chronicle,* 10 December 1865, 3; "Voudooism—African Fetich Worship," 17–21. The article from the *Cairo Democrat* was reprinted in Georgia's *Augusta Chronicle,* perhaps helping to explain the presence of the word *hoodoo* in Georgia.

44. Norris, "Negro Superstitions," 92.

45. Norris, "Negro Superstitions," 91–3, 95; Owen, "Among the Voodoos," 231, 241; Peter Kolchin, *American Slavery, 1619–1877* (New York: Hill and Wang, 1993), 19.

46. "Confidence Misplaced," *Huntsville Gazette,* 1 October 1881, 1; "The Queen of the Hoo-Doos," *Georgia Weekly Telegraph,* 12 November 1872: 8. In the foregoing cases, the cited newspapers reprinted the original articles.

47. "Voudooism—African Fetich Worship," 18–19; Diouf, *Dreams of Africa in Alabama,* 6, 30–54.

48. Breaux and McKinney, "Laure Hopkins," 4; Judy Rosenthal, e-mails to author, 10 August 2006.

49. Gwendolyn Midlo Hall, "The Formation of Afro-Creole Culture," in *Creole New Orleans: Race and Americanization,* edited by Arnold R. Hirsch and Joseph Logsdon (Baton Rouge: Louisiana State University Press, 1992), 85–86; Hall, *Africans in Colonial Louisiana,* 302; Robert Farris Thompson, *Face of the Gods: Art and Altars of Africa and the African Americas* (New York: Museum for African Art, 1993), 48.

50. Rosenthal, *Passion, Ecstasy, and Law,* 71–72. All of these features will be addressed in greater depth in subsequent chapters.

51. Joseph G. Tregle, Jr., "Creoles and Americans," in *Creole New Orleans: Race and Americanization,* edited by Arnold R. Hirsch and Joseph Logsdon (Baton Rouge: Louisiana State University Press, 1992), 146–162.

52. Cooper, *Satanstoe,* 72–79, 106; Morgan, *Slave Counterpoint,* 594–595. Though not an antebellum source, Hyatt's *Hoodoo—Conjuration—Witchcraft—Rootwork* demonstrates how pervasive

magical practices have been across the American South. The same can be said for the slave narratives compiled in George P. Rawick, ed., *The American Slave: A Composite Autobiography* (Westport: Greenwood, 1972–78).

53. Betty L. Morrison, *A Guide to Voodoo in New Orleans, 1820–1940* (Gretna, LA: Her Publishing, Inc., 1977); "Voudou Vagaries: The Spirit of Marie Lavau to be Propitiated by Midnight Orgi[e]s on the Bayou," *New Orleans Times,* 23 June 1881: 7.

54. Dessens, *From Saint-Domingue to New Orleans,* 1, 27–29.

55. One of the more detailed descriptions of Vodou is Alfred Métraux's *Voodoo in Haiti,* trans. by Hugo Charteris and with an Introduction by Sidney W. Mintz (New York: Schocken Books, 1972). An excellent investigation of the melding of Catholicism and West African beliefs is Desmangles' *Faces of the Gods.*

56. Tallant, *Voodoo in New Orleans,* 11.

57. Hurston, "Hoodoo in America," 318.

58. Du Pratz, *The History of Louisiana,* 255, 271; Cable, "Creole Slave Songs," 816–817; Lafcadio Hearn, "The Last of the Voudoos," *Harper's Weekly Magazine* 29 (1885): 726; Long, *Voudou Priestess,* 8–46, 113–116. It is important to note that while Marie Laveau had no ancestral ties to Saint-Domingue, her husband, Jacques Paris was a quadroon from the island. It is possible that Paris introduced the young Marie to the religion, though that seems unlikely considering that he died in or before November 1824, approximately five years after his marriage to Laveau. Moreover, Laveau's status in later years renders it unlikely that she was an outsider to a religion originating in Saint-Domingue. See Long, *Voudou Priestess,* 47–50.

59. Tregle, "Creoles and Americans," 162–185.

2. AFRICAN SPIRITS IN THE MISSISSIPPI RIVER VALLEY

1. "Idolatry and Quackery," 2.

2. Benjamin Hebblethwaite, *Vodou Songs in Haitian Creole and English* (Philadelphia: Temple University Press, 2012), 299.

3. "Idolatry and Quackery," 2; Henry John Drewal, *Mami Wata: Arts for Water Spirits in Africa and Its Diaspora,* with contributions by Marilyn Houlberg, Bogumil Jewsiewicki, Amy L. Noell, John W. Nunley, and Jill Salmons (Los Angeles: Fowler Museum at UCLA, 2008), 89, 109, 117; Hebblethwaite, 253–54; Bertrand Ananou, *Le Vodún: La Religion Traditionnelle du Danhomè: Lumière sur l'univers spiritual du Bénin,* with a preface by Dah Agbalènon Adanmaïkpohoué (Bohicon, Benin: Editions ACT2D, 2012), 257–260; Jeffrey E. Anderson, "Research Journals," 4 vols. (Field notes, personal collection, 2015–2017), vol. 1, 307, vol. 3, 142–43; Kenneth L. Brown, "Retentions, Adaptations, and the Need for Social Control within African and African American Communities across the Southern United States from 1770 to 1930," in *The Archaeology of Slavery: A Comparative Approach to Captivity and Coercion,* edited by Lydia Wilson Marshall, (Carbondale: Southern Illinois University Press, 2014), 181–83, Google Play; Hebblethwaite, *Vodou Songs,* 234.

4. "Curious Charge of Swindling," *Daily Picayune,* 3 July 1850, 2. Another doll, this time described as "a black doll with a dress variegated by cabalistic signs and emblems, and a necklace of the vertebrae of snakes around her neck, from which depended an alligator's fang encased in silver," supposedly appeared in a Voodoo ceremony claimed to have taken place around 1825. See

Marie B. Williams, "A Night with the Voudous," *Appleton's Journal: A Magazine of General Literature* 13 (1875): 405.

5. "The Virgin of the Voudous," *New Orleans Weekly Delta,* 12 August 1850, 345.

6. Marie Dédé, interview by Robert McKinney and Arguedas, 9 January 1939, transcript, Northwestern State University of Louisiana, Watson Memorial Library, Cammie G. Henry Research Center, Federal Writers' Project, folder 533, 2–3.

7. Cable, *The Grandissimes,* 182. The identification of Danny with Fon and Ewe Dan is based largely on the two deities' having places in the Voodoo and Vodun hierarchy as well as similar names.

8. Lafcadio Hearn, "Gombo Zhèbes.": *Little Dictionary of Creole Proverbs, Selected from Six Creole Dialects* (New York: Will H. Coleman, 1885; reprint Bedford, MA: Applewood, n.d.), 39, n. 2.

9. Pitkin, *Angel by Brevet,* 196. The accounts that appear in this fictional source should by no means be taken as historically precise records of Voodoo practice. In practice, they may well resemble the many news articles of the day that reported on the religion but were apt to misrepresent or misunderstand what their authors had witnessed. Nevertheless, the Voodoo songs and names of deities that Pitkin recorded are often verifiable through comparison with other sources, as in the case of the Monsieur Danny chant. Moreover, Pitkin also claimed that her novel described the religion and its practitioners accurately. For her claims to accuracy, see pages 5–7.

10. This translation was provided by my friend and Senegalese translator, Birame Ka.

11. Pitkin, *Angel by Brevet,* 197–201.

12. Michael Gomez, *Exchanging Our Country Marks: The Transformation of African Identities in the Colonial and Antebellum South* (Chapel Hill: University of North Carolina Press, 1998), 57; Robert Farris Thompson, *Flash of the Spirit: African and Afro-American Art and Philosophy* (New York: Random House, 1983), 176–79; Gwendolyn Midlo Hall, *Slavery and African Ethnicities,* 17; Ellis, *Eẃe-Speaking Peoples,* 54–56; Bertrand Ananou, *Le Vodún,* 218–21; Melville J. Herskovits, *Dahomey: An Ancient West African Kingdom,* two vols. (Gluckstadt: J. J. Augustin, 1938; reprint, Evanston, IL: Northwestern University Press, 1967) vol. 2, 245–55; Hebblethwaite, *Vodou Songs,* 212, 226–27; Desmangles, *Faces of the Gods,* 124–30.

13. Pitkin, *Angel by Brevet,* 197–201; Hearn, "Gombo Zhèbes," 39, n. 2; Cable, *Grandissimes,* 181–82.

14. Williams, "Night with the Voudous," 405.

15. Breaux and Villere, "Raphael," 4; Long, *Voudou Priestess,* 220.

16. Revelation 20:2.

17. *Ophiolatreia: An Account of the Rites and Mysteries Connected with the Origin, Rise and Development of Serpent Worship in Various Parts of the World, Enriched with Interesting Traditions, and a Full Description of the Celebrated Serpent Mounds & Temples, the Whole Forming an Exposition of One of the Phases of Phallic, or Sex Worship* (London: Privately printed, 1889), 1.

18. Joseph John Williams, *Voodoos and Obeahs: Phases of West India* (New York: L. MacVeagh, Dial Press, Inc., 1932; reprint, Calgary: Theophania Publishing, 2011), 19–135.

19. Williams, "Night with the Voodoos," 404; Cable, *Grandissimes,* 447; Pitkin, *Angel by Brevet,* 267–68, 285.

20. Anderson, "Research Journals," vol. 1, 317, vol. 2, 23. To be sure, there were other suggestions about just who Dambarra might be. For instance, Vodun Priest Meyè Lokossou Haglo of

Comé, Benin, suggested that it might be a deity from Ghana known as Gambarra, a detector of evil and spirit who brings lost people home. Another priest, Zannou Desire of Ganvie, Benin, suggested that it might be one Ganblada, a deity of iron that is connected to death in Benin. To further complicate matters, Hounnon Klegbe of Cotonou, Benin, described Ayido Hwedo as "going along" with a being from Ghana he called Gabada. These, though similar in name to Dambarra, are all relatively recent arrivals in Benin, making them unlikely originals for the Mississippi River valley spirit. See Anderson, "Research Journals," vol. 1, 307, 339, vol. 4, 94, 101, 126–27.

21. Williams, "Night with the Voudous," 405; Pitkin, *Angel by Brevet*, 267–68, 285; Cable, *Grandissimes*, 257; Cable, "Creole Slave Songs," 817; Albert Valdman et al, *Dictionary of Louisiana French: As Spoken in Cajun, Creole, and American Indian Communities* (Jackson: University of Mississippi Press, 2010), 376–377; Patrick Hanks, ed., *Dictionary of American Family Names* (Oxford University Press, 2006), http://www.oxfordreference.com/view/10.1093/acref/9780195081374.001.0001/acref-9780195081374-e-38830?rskey=h7wXK3&result=39941.

22. Owen, "Among the Voodoos," 236–237; Owen, "Voodooism," 313–16.

23. "Voudooism," *Daily Picayune*, 22 June 1890, 10; Marie Louise Points, "Clopin-Clopant: A Christmas Fragment of Early Creole Days," *Daily Picayune*, 25 December 1892, 22; "Popular Superstitions and the Long Drought," *Daily Picayune*, 18 October 1894, 3; Josephine Jones, interview by Robert McKinney, transcript, Northwestern State University of Louisiana, Watson Memorial Library, Cammie G. Henry Research Center, Federal Writers' Project, folder 25, 1; Anderson, "Research Journals," vol. 3, 101.

24. Valdman et al, *Dictionary of Louisiana French*, 318, 665; Long, *Voudou Priestess*, 114–116; Thornton, "Religious and Ceremonial Life," 75–76. Jessie Gaston Mulira treated the deities as identical in a 1990 article. Robert Farris Thompson suggested a similar fusing of Fon and West African Kikongo concepts in Haiti's Danbala. See Mulira, "The Case of Voodoo in New Orleans," in *Africanisms in American Culture*, ed. Joseph E. Holloway (Bloomington: Indiana University Press, 1990), 40, 64; Thompson, *Flash of the Spirit*, 177–78.

25. Robert W. Slenes, "The Great Porpoise-Skull Strike: Central African Water Spirits and Slave Identity in Early-Nineteenth-Century Rio de Janeiro," in *Central Africans and Cultural Transformations in the American Diaspora*, Linda M. Heywood, ed. (Cambridge: Cambridge University Press, 2002), 192; Wyatt MacGaffey, "Twins, Simbi Spirits, and Lwas in Kongo and Haiti," in *Central Africans and Cultural Transformations in the American Diaspora*, Linda M. Heywood, ed. (Cambridge: Cambridge University Press, 2002), 211–226; Courlander, *Drum and the Hoe*, 327–28.

26. "Tribulations des Voudous," *L'Union*, 1 August 1863, 1.

27. Alexis Alarcón suggested this interpretation during a conversation that took place during June 2017, but he was unable to give a full translation of the song.

28. Anderson "Research Journals," vol. 3, 99–101.

29. Hebblethwaite, *Vodou Songs*, 243; Anderson, "Research Journals," vol. 4, 232–33, 242–43; Joel James, Alexis Alarcón, and José Millet, *El Vodú en Cuba* (Santiago de Cuba: Editorial Oriente, 2007), 174–75.

30. Long, *Voudou Priestess*, 116; Cable, *Grandissimes*, 253, 257; J.A., "Berceuse," *Times-Democrat*, 28 November 1886, 11; Alcée Fortier, *Louisiana Folktales: Lupin, Bouki, and Other Creole Stories in French Dialect and English Translation*, with an Introduction by Russell Desmond (University of Louisiana at Lafayette Press, 2011), iv, 118–19, 145.

31. "The Unknown Painter," *Wilmington Advertiser,* 24 August 1838, 1; "A Romance of Marti-nique," *The Canton Sentinel* (Pennsylvania), 6 March 1879, 1. The editor of "The Unknown Painter" noted that the short story had been published earlier in *Chambers' Edinburgh Journal* and that it had been translated from French. I identified the numerous additional printings of both "The Un-known Painter" and "A Romance of Martinique" through a search of Newspapers.com.

32. "Tribulations," 1.

33. Cable, *Grandissimes,* 184.

34. Pitkin, *Angel by Brevet,* 193–94, quoted 194.

35. This translation was supplied by Birame Ka.

36. Robert McKinney, "St. Peter and Black Cat Opening," Northwestern State University of Louisiana, Watson Memorial Library, Cammie G. Henry Research Center, Federal Writers' Proj-ect, folder 43, 3; Breaux and McKinney, "Hoodoo Opening Ceremony," 1–2.

37. McKinney, "Popular Gris-Gris," 1, 8, quoted 8.

38. Mary Washington, "Marie Laveau," interview by Robert McKinney, 9 January 1939, tran-script, Northwestern State University of Louisiana, Watson Memorial Library, Cammie G. Henry Research Center, Federal Writers' Project, folder 25, 8; Hebblethwaite, *Vodou Songs,* 38, 58, 74, 75, 254–56; Ananou, *Le Vodún,* 209–17.

39. Alexander Augustin, "Marie Laveau," interview by Henriette Michinard, 15 August 1940, transcript, Northwestern State University of Louisiana, Watson Memorial Library, Cammie G. Henry Research Center, Federal Writers' Project, folder 25. Interpretations of Legba as satanic are common throughout those places where he is found. Even in Benin, he has been known to be conflated with the devil of Christianity. See Ananou, *Le Vodún,* 215–16

40. Josephine McDuffy, "Marie Laveau," interview by Henriette Michinard, 1940, transcript, Northwestern State University of Louisiana, Watson Memorial Library, Cammie G. Henry Re-search Center, Federal Writers' Project, folder 25.

41. Dédé, interview by McKinney and Arguedas, 2–3; Joseph Morris, "Marie Laveau," inter-view by Edmund Burke, 26 March 1940, transcript, Northwestern State University of Louisiana, Watson Memorial Library, Cammie G. Henry Research Center, Federal Writers' Project, folder 25, 3.

42. Cable, *Grandissimes,* 101; Washington, "Marie Laveau," 8.

43. Laura Hopkins, [Untitled spells], interview by Hazel Breaux and Robert McKinney, [1937], transcript, Northwestern State University of Louisiana, Watson Memorial Library, Cammie G. Henry Research Center, Federal Writers' Project, folder 43, 1–2, quoted 2.

44. Laura Hopkins, interview Hazel Breaux and Robert McKinney, 12 March 1937, transcript, Northwestern State University of Louisiana, Watson Memorial Library, Cammie G. Henry Re-search Center, Federal Writers' Project, folder 43, 3. *Le Petit Albert* is available in a recent English Translation as *The Spellbook of Marie Laveau: The Petit Albert,* trans. Talia Felix (London: Hadean Press, 2012).

45. Anderson, "Research Journals," vol. 1, 318; vol. 4, 101, 127, 128, 139, 153, 164, 192–93, 205–6, 234, 282–83, 292–293; Hebblethwaite, *Vodou Songs,* 207–9, 271–72, 274; Chita Tann, *Haitian Vodou: An Introduction to Haiti's Indigenous Spiritual Tradition* (Woodbury, MN: Llewellyn, 2012), 103–4; Mambo Vye Zo Komande LaMenfo [Patricia D. Scheu], *Serving the Spirits: The Religion of Vodou* (Philadelphia: Published by author, 2011), 89, 174–75.

46. Thompson, *Flash of the Spirit*, 42–51, 166–167; Alfred Burdon Ellis, *The Yoruba-Speaking Peoples of the Slave Coast of West Africa* (London: Chapman and Hall, 1894; reprint, Benin Press, Ltd., 1964), 79.

47. Cable, *Grandissimes*, 99.

48. Pitkin, *Angel by Brevet*, 267–68, 285; Dédé, interview by McKinney and Arguedas, 2.

49. Thompson, *Flash of the Spirit*, 165; Hebblethwaite, *Vodou Songs*, 206; Métraux, *Voodoo in Haiti*, 31.

50. Pitkin, *Angel by Brevet*, 275–76, 282–85; "Dance of the Voodoos," *Times-Democrat*, 24 June 1896, 2.

51. Anderson, "Research Journals," vol. 2, 36, 39; vol. 3, 101–3.

52. Anderson, "Research Journals," vol. 3, 101.

53. Anderson, "Research Journals," vol. 3, 101–3.

54. Pitkin, *Angel by Brevet*, 285; Anderson, "Research Journals," vol. 3, 102–3.

55. Pitkin, *Angel by Brevet*, 276, 279, 283, 285; Anderson, "Research Journals," vol. 3, 102–3.

56. Pitkin, *Angel by Brevet*, 204, 269, quoted 204.

57. Pitkin, *Angel by Brevet*, 273–281.

58. Ellis, *Eẃe-Speaking Peoples*, 67; Anderson, "Research Journals," vol. 4, 84–5.

59. Courlander, *Drum and the Hoe*, 329; Milo Rigaud, *Secrets of Vodou*, translated by Robert B. Cross (New York: Arco, 1969; reprint, San Francisco: City Lights, 1985), 59; Hebblethwaite, *Vodou Songs*, 212–13; Ellis, *Eẃe-Speaking Peoples*, 52.

60. Anderson, "Research Journals," vol. 3, 143. Maviola Medard manages a hotel in Dolisie, Republic of the Congo. He was once a member of the Kimbanguist branch of the Ngunza religion.

61. Courlander, *Drum and the Hoe*, 321, 354 n10; Thompson, *Flash of the Spirit*, 52–7, 169–72; Joshua Clegg Caffrey, *Traditional Music in Coastal Louisiana: The 1934 Lomax Recordings*, with a foreword by Barry Jean Ancelet (Baton Rouge: Louisiana State University, 2013), 102–03, 180–81, 237–40.

62. "Idol Worship in Massachusetts," Palmyra, Missouri *Marion County Herald*, 14 December 1884, 6.

63. For an examination of Owen's hoodoo and Voodoo scholarship, see Olson, *Voodoo Priests*, 57–69

64. Owen, "Among the Voodoos," 241–42.

65. Owen, "Voodooism," 313–22, quoted 316.

66. Dédé, interview by McKinney and Arguedas, 2; Anderson, "Research Journals," vol. 1, 307; vol. 2, 39; vol. 4, 104, 128, 139, 153, 193, 206, 283.

67. Cable, "Slave Songs," 820.

68. Cable, "Slave Songs," 820.

69. Lyle Saxon, "Voodoo," *The New Republic*, 23 March 1927, 136.

70. Hurston, "Hoodoo in America," 359–60, 362–63.

71. Lawrence N. Powell, "Lyle Saxon and the WPA Guide to New Orleans," *Southern Spaces*, 23 July 2009, https://southernspaces.org/2009/lyle-saxon-and-wpa-guide-new-orleans.

72. Jeffrey E. Anderson, "Voodoo in Black and White," in *Southern Character: Essays in Honor of Bertram Wyatt-Brown*, eds. Lisa Tendrich Frank and Daniel Kilbride, (Gainesville: University Press of Florida, 2011), 151–55.

73. Anderson, "Research Journals," vol. 4, 134.

74. McKinney, "Popular Gris-Gris," 8–9, quoted 9; "Headquarters Fifth Ward Democratic Club," *Daily Picayune*, 10 August 1872, 2; "Another Premium Drawing Raided." *Daily Picayune*, 28 June 1894, 10; "Lottery Raid." *Daily Picayune*, 12 October 1895, 6; "Christmas Spirit Enters Prison and Spreads Peace and Good Will," *Daily Picayune*, 26 December 1911, 5.

75. McKinney, "Popular Gris-Gris," 5, 9–10; Hazel Breaux, "Information Furnished by Mrs. Robertson—2116 St. Philip St," Northwestern State University of Louisiana, Watson Memorial Library, Cammie G. Henry Research Center, folder 44, 1. The Mrs. Robertson referenced in the second source appears to be the same person as the Mrs. Robinson who took McKinney and Breaux to the graveyards.

76. McKinney, "Popular Gris-Gris," 10.

77. McKinney, "Popular Gris-Gris," 10.

78. McKinney, "Popular Gris-Gris," 3.

79. Robert McKinney, "Some Gri Gri Obtained from Madame Ducoyielle," Northwestern State University of Louisiana, Watson Memorial Library, Cammie G. Henry Research Center, folder 44, 3–4; Maud H. Wallace, "Lala," Northwestern State University of Louisiana, Watson Memorial Library, Cammie G. Henry Research Center, folder 43, 2–4.

80. Hyatt, *Hoodoo—Conjuration—Witchcraft—Rootwork*, xxxi, xxxix, 563, 565, 566–67, 821–22, quoted 449. The use of graveyard dirt was by no means confined to New Orleans hoodoo. On pages 447–451, Hyatt recorded numerous uses from informants in Arkansas, Florida, Georgia, North Carolina, South Carolina, Tennessee, and Virginia.

81. Anderson, "Research Journals," vol. 3, 124–26.

82. Thornton, "Religious and Ceremonial Life," 79–80.

83. MacGaffey, "Twins," 223; Olmos and Paravisini-Gebert, *Creole Religions*, 121.

84. Carolyn Morrow Long suggests that these four alone are proven to have existed in both Louisiana and Haiti. Long, *Voudou Priestess*, 114–116.

85. Hebblethwaite, *Vodou Songs*, 206, 212–13, 226–27, 254–56, 274; Courlander, Drum and Hoe, 323, 378–28; Anderson, "Research Journals," vol. 4, 128, 139, 153, 164, 192–93, 205, 234–35, 283. I am inclined to think that the identification of Charlo and Charles Nago may be at least partially correct, but I am dubious that Jean Macouloumba and Aloumba are related. According to Eric Pierre of La Gonâve, Aloumba is a female *djab*, or "devil," Aloumba and Jean Macouloumba differ in gender. Though the gender difference is not an insurmountable obstacle in the spirit world, many Haitian *manbos* and *oungans* suggested that there was no such thing as Jean Macouloumba in Vodou, leading me to suspect that the identification with Aloumba rests solely on the similar sounds of their names.

86. Blier, *African Vodun*, 2, 76; Hebblethwaite, *Vodou Songs*, 221; Thompson, *Face of the Gods*, 216; Courlander, *Drum and Hoe*, 320.

87. Ellis, *Ewé-Speaking Peoples*, 54; Anderson, "Research Journals," vol. 1, 307, 317, 339; vol. 2, 23; vol. 4, 94, 101, 126–27.

88. One tantalizing suggestion that Ezili might have been known in Louisiana was uncovered in the form of a drawing in the margin of a court record of the 1893 case of *State of Louisiana v. Louise Johnson*. The drawing is reminiscent of a Haitian religious symbol called a *vèvè*. These are linked to specific deities and are usually traced on the ground in cornmeal or other powders before

Vodou ceremonies. The drawing in question incorporates a heart shape and strongly resembles the vèvè of Ezili Freda. Unfortunately, the drawing is of uncertain age and origin and has no clear relevance to the case with which it associated, rendering it possible that the resemblance is simple chance. Kendra Cole, "The State and the Spirits: Voodoo and Religious Repression in Jim Crow New Orleans." Undergraduate honors thesis, University of Southern Mississippi, 2019, https://aquila.usm.edu/honors_theses/658.

89. Olmos and Paravisini-Gebert, *Creole Religions*, 127–30; Cable, *Grandissimes*, 101; Washington, "Marie Laveau," 8; Laura Hopkins, [Untitled spells], 1–2; Pitkin, *Angel by Brevet*, 275–76, 282–85; "Dance of the Voodoos," 2; "Voudooism," 10; Points, "Clopin-Clopant," 22; "Popular Superstitions," 3; Jones, interview by Robert McKinney, 1; Millet, *El Vodú en Cuba*, 174–75.

90. Anderson, "Research Journals," vol. 1, 305–09; vol. 2, 30–31, 36–37, 42–43; vol. 3, 124–30, vol. 4, 53; Bronwyn Mills, "The Vodun Has Killed Them: New World/Old World Vodun, Creolité, and the Alter-Renaissance," chap. 6 of *Vodou in the Haitian Experience: A Black Atlantic Perspective*, Celucien L. Joseph and Nixon S. Cleophat, eds. (London: Lexington Books, 2016), 118–23. For an in-depth discussion about the place of new deities in the Vodu of Togo, see Rosenthal, *Possession, Ecstasy, and Law*.

3. THE VOODOOS AND THEIR WORK

1. Hearn, "Last of the Voudoos," 726.

2. Cable, "Creole Slave Songs," 817; "Voodooism," 1; "Voudou Superstition—Fetish Rites," *Daily Picayune*, 25 June 1871, 5; "The Vous Dous Incantation," *New Orleans Times*, 28 June 1872, 1.

3. Voodooism," 1; Cable, "Creole Slave Songs," 818.

4. Owen, "Among the Voodoos," 230; William Moore, "Marie Laveau," 1 March 1940, Northwestern State University of Louisiana, Watson Memorial Library, Cammie G. Henry Research Center, Federal Writers' Project, folder 25, 3; Laure Hopkins, information collected by Henriette Michinard, April 1940, Northwestern State University of Louisiana, Watson Memorial Library, Cammie G. Henry Research Center, Federal Writers' Project, folder 44, 1; McKinney, "Popular Gris-Gris," 10.

5. "A Motley Gathering," *The Planters' Banner*, 11 July 1850, 2. *Dauphin*, which is the male version of the term, was likely a mistaken spelling on the part of the reporter, who should have written dauphine.

6. "La Danse des Sorciers," *The Opelousas Courier*, 5 July 1873, 1.

7. Elizabeth W. Kiddy, "Who Is the King of Congo? A New Look at African and Afro-Brazilian Kings in Brazil," in *Central Africans and Cultural Transformations in the American Diaspora*, Linda M. Heywood, ed. (Cambridge: Cambridge University Press, 2002), 153–81; Métraux, *Voodoo*, 71; Anderson, Research Journals, vol. IV, 161.

8. Thompson, *Flash of the Spirit*, 107; Blier, *African Vodun*, 105, 317; Anderson, Research Journals, vol. I, 318–25, vol. III, 150–60, vol. IV, 72–7.

9. Marcus Christian, "Voodooism and Mumbo-Jumbo," University of New Orleans, Earl K. Long Library, Louisiana and Special Collections Department, Historical Manuscripts Series, Marcus Christian Collection, Number 11, Box 4, Chapter 11, 46–58.

10. Oscar Felix, "Marie Leveau," interview by Edmund Burke, 14 March 1940, transcript,

Northwestern State University of Louisiana, Watson Memorial Library, Cammie G. Henry Research Center, Federal Writers' Project, folder 25, 3–4, quoted 4.

11. Jimmy St. Ann and Josephine Harrison, interview by Zoe Posey, around 10 July 1939, transcript, Northwestern State University of Louisiana, Watson Memorial Library, Cammie G. Henry Research Center, Federal Writers' Project, folder 25, 3 (labeled 2).

12. Breaux and Villere, "Raphael," 1, 4–5; Eugene Fritz and John Alfred, "Marie Laveau," interview by Robert McKinney, transcript, Northwestern State University of Louisiana, Watson Memorial Library, Cammie G. Henry Research Center, Federal Writers' Project, folder 25, 1; John Paul Smith, interview by Hazel Breaux, 13 December 1939, transcript, Northwestern State University of Louisiana, Watson Memorial Library, Cammie G. Henry Research Center, Federal Writers' Project, folder 587, 1–5.

13. Cable, "Creole Slave Songs," 820. See also Valdman, *Louisiana French,* 404. Valdman indicates that *monteur* means "builder" in the Louisiana variety of the language; Hyatt, *Hoodoo— Conjuration—Witchcraft—Rootwork,* iii, 275, 959, 1056, 1129, 1271, 1280, 1324, 1468, 1641, 4161, 4168. Curiously, Hyatt's full interviews from outside the Mississippi River valley made up the same percentage of the total interviews as did the use of the word *worker* along the Mississippi compared to total uses.

14. See Chapter 4 for descriptions of these ceremonies.

15. McKinney, "Popular Gris-Gris," 1–2; McKinney, "St. Peter and Black Cat Opening," 6.

16. Olmos and Paravisini-Gebert, *Creole Religions,* 133–4; Courlander, *Drum and Hoe,* 11–2, 71–4.

17. Hurston, "Hoodoo in America," 326, 327; Long, *Voudou Priestess,* 202–5.

18. Hyatt, *Hoodoo-Voodoo-Conjuration-Witchcraft,* 1283–4.

19. The tendency of Voodoo revivalists to claim kinship with Laveau has been a matter of personal observation. During the 2020 COVID-19 isolation, for instance, I once found myself criticized for recommending a scholarly biography of the Voodoo Queen in a Facebook post. The critic based her comments on the assertion that she was a descendant of Laveau and had not written the book, on which grounds she asserted that it was of dubious authenticity.

20. "Africa Triumphant," *Daily Picayune,* 18 August 1859, 2.

21. "Africa Triumphant," 2; Hearn, "Last of the Voudoos," 726–7, quoted 726.

22. "Trouble among the Voudous," *Daily Picayune,* 18 August 1871, 2. For a discussion of the importance of African birth's link to supernatural power outside of the Mississippi River valley context, see Anderson, *Conjure,* 97–8.

23. Nathan H. Hobley, interview by Zoe Posey, January 1941, transcript, Northwestern State University of Louisiana, Watson Memorial Library, Cammie G. Henry Research Center, Federal Writers' Project, folder 44, 3; "About Voodoo: Dr. James Alexander—'Indian Jim,'" interview of intimate of Tony Lafon by Henriette Michinard, August 1940, transcript, Northwestern State University of Louisiana, Watson Memorial Library, Cammie G. Henry Research Center, Federal Writers' Project, folder 44, 1; Owen, "Among the Voodoos, 241.

24. Breaux and Villere, "Raphael," 1–3; Felix, "Marie Leveau," 4.

25. Hobley, interview by Posey, 3–4, quoted 3.

26. Robert McKinney, "Marie Comtesse," Northwestern State University of Louisiana, Watson Memorial Library, Cammie G. Henry Research Center, Federal Writers' Project, folder 43, 1–2, quoted 2.

27. Rigaud, *Secrets*, 33; Tann, *Haitian Vodou*, 159–66, 180; Anderson, "Research Journals," vol 1, 338, 340–1, 352.

28. "Voodooism," 1.

29. Owen, "Among the Voodoos," 247.

30. Hearn, "The Last of the Voudoos," 727; Anderson, "Research Journals," vol. 2, 89.

31. Owen, "Among the Voodoos," 230–1. Specifics of these self-initiations appear in the following chapter of this book.

32. Hyatt, *Hoodoo—Conjuration—Witchcraft—Rootwork*, 1730–1, 1864, 3917, 4004–5, quoted 4004.

33. Hurston, "Hoodoo," 390–1.

34. Raymond Rivaros, "Marie Laveau," interview by Hazel Breaux, transcript, Northwestern State University of Louisiana, Watson Memorial Library, Cammie G. Henry Research Center, Federal Writers' Project, folder 25, 2; Breaux and McKinney, "Hoodoo Opening," 2. Regarding the removal of outer clothing, during my research in Benin and Togo in 2015 and 2016, I found it common practice to be asked to remove my shirt before entering shrines to important deities. Minor deities, however, are not always accorded this honor.

35. James Santana, interview by Zoe Posey, transcript, Northwestern State University of Louisiana, Watson Memorial Library, Cammie G. Henry Research Center, Federal Writers' Project, folder 25, 1.

36. Rivaros, "Marie Laveau," 4; Fritz and Alfred, "Marie Laveau," 1–2; John Smith, interview by Hazel Breaux, transcript, Northwestern State University of Louisiana, Watson Memorial Library, Cammie G. Henry Research Center, Federal Writers' Project, folder 25, 2. Fritz and Alfred's account of St. John Eve attire conflicts with other descriptions of Voodoo ceremonies by stating that the men wore light, wide-sleeved shirts. Of course, the specific attire may simply have varied, or the shirts may have been removed at some point during the ceremony.

37. "Voudou Superstitions," *New Orleans Bee*, 15 October 1860, 1.

38. McKinney, "St. Peter and Black Cat Opening," 1.

39. Owen, "Among the Voodoos," 231, 234, 241, 244, 246, 247; Harry Middleton Hyatt, *Hoodoo—Conjuration—Witchcraft—Rootwork*, 948, 992, 1059, 1085, 1114, 1139, 1220, 1247–48, 1276, 1295, 1335, 1859, 1871–72, 1902, 1930, 1967–68, 2004, 2018–19, 2037, 2068, 2101, 2113, 2121, 2145–46, 2170, 2178–79, 2210, 2220–21, 2227, 2261–62, 2271, 2281, 2321–32. My count of practitioners from Dillon's work is based on notes I made while reading it several years ago.

40. Hurston, "Hoodoo," 317; McKinney, "St. Peter and Black Cat Opening," 1, 3–8, quoted 1.

41. For a discussion of Montanée and Alexander's standing, see Long, *Voudou Priestess*, 111–13, 137–48.

42. Owen, "Among the Voodoos," 240. Curiously, Owen had stated that Voodoo had no hierarchy in the previous sentence.

43. Spear, *Race, Sex, and Social Order*, 85, 87, 115, 117; Long, *Voudou Priestess*, 19–24; Paul F. Lachance, "The 1809 Immigration of Saint-Domingue Refugees to New Orleans: Reception, Integration and Impact," *Louisiana History* 29 (Spring 1988): 111.

44. Métraux, *Voodoo*, 61–69; Blier, *African Vodun*, 20, 33–34. For an in-depth discussion of harmful magic in Benin, including women's reputation working it, see Douglas J. Falen, *African Science: Witchcraft, Vodun, and Healing in Southern Benin* (Madison: University of Wisconsin Press, 2018).

45. Du Pratz, *History of Louisiana,* 255

46. "Correspondence of the Free Trader," *Mississippi Free Trader and Natchez Gazette,* 25 August 1849, 2; Anderson, *Conjure,* 114.

47. Hyatt, *Hoodoo—Conjuration—Witchcraft—Rootwork,* XIV–XL, 620, 645, 1458–9, 3687; Katrina Hazzard-Donald, *Mojo Workin': The Old African American Hoodoo System* (Urbana: University of Illinois Press, 2013), 140–1.

48. Hyatt, *Hoodoo—Conjuration—Witchcraft—Rootwork,* 744–888.

49. Hyatt, *Hoodoo—Conjuration—Witchcraft—Rootwork,* 744–888.

50. Hyatt, *Hoodoo—Conjuration—Witchcraft—Rootwork,* 747, 756–7, 760, 768, 769–70, 772, 774, 776; 797–862.

51. Greg Dues, *Catholic Customs and Traditions: A Popular Guide,* rev. ed. (Mystic, CT: Twenty-Third Publications, 1993), 186–8.

52. Hyatt, *Hoodoo—Conjuration—Witchcraft—Rootwork,* 744–5, 747–8, quoted 747. Candles are today a part of hoodoo across the country, which is a testimony to the reputation and influence of the Mississippi River valley on supernaturalism. On the other hand, though Hyatt described candles as distinctive to the area around New Orleans, he did encounter them elsewhere. See, for instance, Hyatt, 748.

53. McKinney, "Popular Gris-Gris," 3, 6, 7; Hyatt, *Hoodoo—Conjuration—Witchcraft—Rootwork,* for examples, see 748, 749, 772, 834, 852.

54. Cable, *The Grandissimes,* 99, 101, 135, 182, 184, 257, 272, 311, 447, 453–456, 468; Pitkin, 185–213, 260–292; Hurston, "Hoodoo in America," 319; Marie Dédé, interview by McKinney and Arguedas, 2.

55. Desmangles, *Faces of the Gods,* 10–11, 130; Matthew 16:19; Pitkin, *Angel by Brevet,* 196.

56. "Idolatry and Quackery," 2; "The Virgin of the Voudous," 1; Dédé, interview by McKinney and Arguedas, 2–3. Interestingly, Laveau was associated with both the 1850 Virgin of the Voudous as well as with easily-recognized Catholic saint images during the later years. See "Curious Charge of Swindling," 2.

57. Desmangles, *Faces of the Gods,* 159–69.

58. Long, *Voudou Priestess,* 38, 202–3; Hurston, "Hoodoo in America," 317.

59. Hyatt, *Hoodoo—Conjuration—Witchcraft—Rootwork,* 862–6, 877–87; "Voodoo," interview, transcript, Northwestern State University of Louisiana, Watson Memorial Library, Cammie G. Henry Research Center, Federal Writers' Project, folder 44, 1; Breaux and Villere, "Raphael," 3. For a detailed popular work on the role of St. Expedite in Voodoo and hoodoo, see Denise Alvarado, *The Conjurer's Guide to St. Expedite* (Prescott Valley, AZ: Creole Moon, 2014),

60. Dues, *Catholic Customs,* 118–9; Omer Englebert, *Lives of the Saints,* translated by Christopher and Anne Fremantle (New York: Barnes and Noble, Inc. 1994), 156–7, 198, 322–3; Hyatt, *Hoodoo—Conjuration—Witchcraft—Rootwork,* 864–5, 879–82; "Voodoo," 1. I have personally observed the placement of Legbas by entryways on many occasions in Benin. For an example of rapping in a Vootoo ritual, see Breaux and McKinney, "Hoodoo Opening," 2. Curiously, one informant described St. Raymond as being willing to "open the door for you" and associated him with keys, characteristics typically associated with the African and Haitian Legba and Louisiana's Papa Lébat. See Hyatt, *Hoodoo—Conjuration—Witchcraft—Rootwork,* 879.

61. "Hopkins Laure," Northwestern State University of Louisiana, Watson Memorial Library, Cammie G. Henry Research Center, Federal Writers' Project, folder 43, 3.

62. "Reports of Investigation Made of 'White Magic,'" 24 August 1939, Northwestern State University of Louisiana, Watson Memorial Library, Cammie G. Henry Research Center, Federal Writers' Project, folder 44, 2, 4.

63. Hyatt, *Hoodoo—Conjuration—Witchcraft—Rootwork*, 863.

64. Claude F. Jacobs and Andrew J. Kaslow, *The Spiritual Churches of New Orleans: Origins, Beliefs, and Rituals of an African-American Religion* (Knoxville: University of Tennessee Press, 1991), 136–42. See also Jason Berry, *The Spirit of Black Hawk: A Mystery of Africans and Indians*, with photographs by Sydney Byrd (Jackson: University Press of Mississippi, 1995).

65. Melissa Daggett, *Spiritualism in Nineteenth-Century New Orleans: The Life and Times of Henry Louis Rey* (Jackson: University Press of Mississippi, 2017), 99; Jacobs and Kaslow, *Spiritual Churches*, 73–82; Barbara Weisberg, *Talking to the Dead: Kate and Maggie Fox and the Rise of Spiritualism* (New York: Harper-Collins, 2004), 4; Dédé, interview by McKinney and Arguedas, 2–3.

66. Hobley, interview by Posey, 4.

67. Hobley, interview by Posey, 4–5; Long, *Voudou Priestess*, 111; Long, *Spiritual Merchants*, 189–90; "The DeLaurence Company," last modified ca. 2017, http://www.delaurencecompany.com/home.html.

68. Drewal, *Mami Wata*, 33–44; Desmagles, *Faces of the Gods*, 113. For an example of the impact of Spiritualism on Afro-Caribbean beliefs, see Olmos and Paravisini-Gebert, *Creole Religions*, 203–6.

69. McKinney, "Some Gri Gri," 2–9; McKinney, "Popular Gris-Gris," 3–7; McKinney, "St. Peter and Black Cat Opening," 8–9.

70. McKinney, "Popular Gris-Gris," 3, 6.

71. McKinney, "Popular Gris-Gris," 8.

72. Hopkins, [Untitled spells], interview Breaux and McKinney, 2.

73. Owen, *Old Rabbit*, 8, 168–71, 174–9; "Death of a Noted Voudouist," *Daily Picayune*, 10 June 1869, 2; Hearn, "The Last of the Voudoos," 727.

74. "Death of a Noted Voudouist," 2; Hyatt, *Hoodoo—Conjuration—Witchcraft—Rootwork*, 163–4, 431, 486, 952, 957, 1073, 1150, 1179, 1217, 1221, 1352, 1375, 1393, 1398–9, 1410, 1508, 1512–3, 1613, 1656, 1675, 1684, 1726, 1756, 1826–7, 1866, 1910, 1913, 1974–5, 2070, 2116, 2225, 2267, 2292, 2297, 2351, 2414, 2474, 2534, 3156, 3158, 3231, 3407, 3553–4, 3561, 3585, 3635–50, 3665–6, 4060, 4345.

75. Porteous, "Gri-Gri Case," 51–2. For a copy of the original trial record, see *Criminales* #278, 12 June 1773–14 January 1774, French Superior Council and Judicial Records of Spanish Cabildo, Judicial Records, Williams Research Center, Historic New Orleans Collection, reel 109.

76. Cable, "Slave Songs," 817.

77. Hyatt, *Hoodoo—Conjuration—Witchcraft—Rootwork*, 470, 710–11, 2183, 4387; For some examples of the importance of the color red, see Thompson, *Face of the Gods*, 21, 239–45, 287.

78. Owen, *Old Rabbit*, 8; Hall, *Africans*, 34–5, 163–4; Fontenot, *Secret Doctors*, 56, 114, 118; Jeffrey E. Anderson, "Mission Journal," field notes, personal collection, 2014, 22–3.

79. Cable, *The Grandissimes*, 123, 147–56, 291–3, 325, 412; Carolyn Morrow Long, "The Cracker Jack: A Hoodoo Drugstore in the 'Cradle of Jazz,'" *Louisiana Cultural Vistas* (Spring 2014): 66, 68; Car-

olyn Morrow Long, "The Cracker Jack: A Hoodoo Drugstore in the 'Cradle of Jazz,'" March 14, 2023, https://www.academia.edu/66784535/The_Cracker_Jack_A_Hoodoo_Drugstore_in_the_Cradle _of_Jazz.

80. Hyatt, *Hoodoo—Conjuration—Witchcraft—Rootwork,* 16, 132, 288, 509, 746–8, 961, 1513, 1905, 3232–3.

81. Anderson, *Conjure,* 56; Mrs. J. Fortune, "Joseph Melon Voodoo," Northwestern State University of Louisiana, Watson Memorial Library, Cammie G. Henry Research Center, Federal Writers' Project, folder 44, 2; Laura Hopkins, interview Hazel Breaux and Robert McKinney, 10 March 1937, transcript, Northwestern State University of Louisiana, Watson Memorial Library, Cammie G. Henry Research Center, Federal Writers' Project, folder 43, 1; Breaux and Villere, "Raphael," 1; Hazel Breaux and Robert McKinney, "Hoodoo Price List," Northwestern State University of Louisiana, Watson Memorial Library, Cammie G. Henry Research Center, Federal Writers' Project, folder 43, 1–2; Long, *Spiritual Merchants,* 16, 231; Métraux, *Voodoo,* 269–70; Carolyn Morrow Long, "The Influence of European and European-American Occult Texts," Academia, March 14, 2023, https://www.academia.edu/35543002/The_Influence_of_European_and_European_Amer ican_Occult_Texts, 9–10.

82. Robert McKinney, "The Johnny Conquerer Root," Northwestern State University of Louisiana, Watson Memorial Library, Cammie G. Henry Research Center, Federal Writers' Project, folder 44, 1; Hyatt, *Hoodoo—Conjuration—Witchcraft—Rootwork,* 287; Dillon, "Voodoo," sec. "Charms, Etc.," 13–14; Long, *Spiritual Merchants,* 122–4; Hurston, "Hoodoo in America," 327–57; "Hopkins Laure," 3. According to Catherine Dillon, the *Black Hawk's Works* was the same as *The Life and Works of Marie Laveau,* but Lala Hopkins seemed to indicate they were distinct.

83. Smith, interview by Breaux, 2; Henrietta Nichols, "Spirits Ghosts; Marie Laveau," Northwestern State University of Louisiana, Watson Memorial Library, Cammie G. Henry Research Center, Federal Writers' Project, folder 25, 2–3; Harrison Camille, "Marie Laveau," interview by Maud H. Wallace, 9 and 11 January 1940, transcript, Northwestern State University of Louisiana, Watson Memorial Library, Cammie G. Henry Research Center, Federal Writers' Project, folder 25, 1; Breaux and Villere, "Raphael," 5. The 2020 dollar equivalent calculations in this section are from Ian Webster, CPI Inflation Calculator, 2020, https://www.in2013dollars.com/us/inflation /1887?amount=2.50 (accessed 28 October 2020).

84. Hurston, "Hoodoo in America," 357–8; McKinney, "Popular Gris-Gris," 4, 11; Timothy R. Landry, *Vodún: Secrecy and the Search for Divine Power* (Philadelphia: University of Pennsylvania Press, 2019), 8–9; Olmos and Paravisini-Gebert, *Creole Religions,* 1, 133.

85. Eugene V. Smalley, "Sugar-Making in Louisiana," *The Century* 35 (November 1887): 112; Owen, *Old Rabbit,* 173; Hearn, "Last of the Voudoos," 727.

86. Hazel Breaux and Robert McKinney, "Hoodoo Price List," Robert Tallant Papers, 1938–1957, New Orleans Public Library, Louisiana and City Archives, New Orleans, LA, folder/reel 8, MS-120.

87. Smith, interview by Breaux, 2.

88. Rivaros, "Marie Laveau," 3.

89. Washington, "Marie Laveau," 8.

90. Smith, interview by Breaux, 2; Long, *Voudou Priestess,* 72–8; 83–4, 209, 210.

91. Hearn, "Last of the Voudoos," 727; Long, *Voudou Priestess,* 145–47.

92. Owen, "Among the Voodoos," 242; McKinney, "St. Peter and Black Cat Opening," 1–2.

93. McKinney, "St. Peter and Black Cat Opening," 1; Owen, *Old Rabbit,* 171.

94. "Voodoo Yet Rules Faithful Disciples of Dead Sorceress," *Times-Picayune New Orleans States,* 7 March 1937, 23.

4. WORKING WITH THE SPIRITS

1. "More of the Voudous," *Daily Picayune,* Evening Edition, July 30, 1850, 5; "Great Doings in the Third Municipality," *Daily Picayune,* 29 June 1850, 2. See also Carolyn Long's *Voudou Priestess,* pages 103–5, for a full account of the events involving Toledano.

2. "More of the Voudous," 5.

3. Courlander, *Drum and the Hoe,* 13–14.

4. "Voodoo," Northwestern State University of Louisiana, Watson Memorial Library, Cammie G. Henry Research Center, Federal Writers' Project, folder 44, 1; Wallace, "Lala," 1–2; Breaux and Villere, "Raphael," 4.

5. Delavigne, "Marie Laveau," interview by Henriette Michinard, 13 December 1939, transcript, Northwestern State University of Louisiana, Watson Memorial Library, Cammie G. Henry Research Center, Federal Writers' Project, folder 587, 1.

6. Breaux and Villere, "Raphael," 4; Marie Dédé, "Marie Laveau," interview by Robert McKinney, transcript, Northwestern State University of Louisiana, Watson Memorial Library, Cammie G. Henry Research Center, Federal Writers' Project, folder 25, 2; Dédé, interview by McKinney and Arguedas, 2. Charles Raphael equated the "spirit of the snake" with the devil of Christianity.

7. Smith, interview, 1–5; Jones, interview by Robert McKinney, 1–2; Morris, "Marie Laveau," 2.

8. "Dance of the Voudous," 3; "Voudous Dance," *Daily Delta,* 3 November 1854, 2.

9. Long, *Voudou Priestess,* 110; "Marie Laveaux," Northwestern State University of Louisiana, Watson Memorial Library, Cammie G. Henry Research Center, Federal Writers' Project, folder 25, 1; Breaux and Villere, "Raphael," 4–5.

10. "A Voudou Tree," *Times-Democrat,* 1 August 1891, 3. The author reported that by his time, the tree was reputedly haunted by the spirits of deceased Voodoo priestesses.

11. Morris, "Marie Laveau," 2; "Interview in the St. Louis #2 Cemetery," interview by Wright, transcript, Northwestern State University of Louisiana, Watson Memorial Library, Cammie G. Henry Research Center, Federal Writers' Project, folder 25, 1; Felix, "Marie Leveau," 8–9. Theresa Kavanaugh, interview by Zoe Posey, transcript, Northwestern State University of Louisiana, Watson Memorial Library, Cammie G. Henry Research Center, Federal Writers' Project, folder 25, 1.

12. Dédé, "Marie Laveau," 4; Jones, interview by Robert McKinney, 1–2.

13. Laure Hopkins, interview, transcript, Northwestern State University of Louisiana, Watson Memorial Library, Cammie G. Henry Research Center, Federal Writers' Project, folder 43, 5; Dédé, "Marie Laveau," 9; "Marie Laveaux," 1. Oscar Felix confirmed that Laveau held frequent ceremonies in the homes of other Voodoo workers around New Orleans. See Felix, "Marie Leveau," 6.

14. Rivaros, "Marie Laveau," 3. Hazel Breaux, summary of interview with Charles Raphael, transcript, Northwestern State University of Louisiana, Watson Memorial Library, Cammie G. Henry Research Center, Federal Writers' Project, folder 25, 2; Edward Ashley, "Marie Laveau," interview by Henriette Michinard, transcript, Northwestern State University of Louisiana, Watson Memorial Library, Cammie G. Henry Research Center, Federal Writers' Project, folder 25, 1–2.

15. Charles Dudley Warner, "A Voudoo Dance," *Harper's Weekly* 31 (1887): 454.

16. Warner, "Voudoo Dance," 454–5.

17. George Washington Cable, "The Dance in Place Congo," with illustrations by E. W. Kemble, *The Century Magazine* 31 (1886): 527–8; Cable, "Creole Slave Songs," 818–9. An example of a Vodou *manbo* spraying alcohol from her mouth can be found in Ellen Hampton, "Gede Ritual: Song, Spirit, Blood," *Miami Herald* 7 November 1982, section B, 2.

18. Hurston, "Hoodoo in America," 362–3, 368, 380–2, 387–8, 390–1.

19. Hurston, "Hoodoo in America," 358.

20. Hurston, "Hoodoo in America," 358; Zora Neale Hurston, *Mules and Men,* in *Zora Neale Hurston: Folklore, Memoirs, and Other Writings,* selected and annotated by Cheryl A. Wall (New York, NY: Library of America, 1995), 182–3, 188–9.

21. Hurston, "Hoodoo in America," 358–60; Hurston, *Mules and Men,* 189–91.

22. Hurston, "Hoodoo in America," 360; Hurston, *Mules and Men,* 191–3.

23. Hyatt, *Hoodoo—Conjuration—Witchcraft—Rootwork,* 1282–3, quoted 1283.

24. Hyatt, *Hoodoo—Conjuration—Witchcraft—Rootwork,* 1909.

25. Hyatt, *Hoodoo—Conjuration—Witchcraft—Rootwork,* 747. Interestingly, Hyatt asked Dr. Sims about aspects of Hurston's work, though he gave no clear indication that he suspected his informant might also have talked with his predecessor. Considering that Hyatt had used the Luke Turner name from *Mules and Men* to refer to the man known as Samuel Thompson in "Hoodoo in America," he likely would have known Hurston's Father Simms as Father Watson, the name Hurston had assigned him in *Mules and Men.*

26. For a full discussion of the problematic nature of Hurston's works, see Anderson, "Voodoo in Black and White." Though Hurston's works contain valuable information and should not be completely discounted as sources, they are too unreliable to depend upon for detailed descriptions of religious ceremonies.

27. McKinney, "Popular Gris-Gris," 1–2, quoted 2.

28. McKinney, "Popular Gris-Gris," 2–10.

29. Long, *Voudou Priestess,* 215; McKinney, "Popular Gris-Gris," 11.

30. Breaux and McKinney, "Hoodoo Opening," 1.

31. Breaux and McKinney, "Hoodoo Opening," 1–2. Stage planks are large molasses and ginger cookies. McKinney noted that the camphor branch was a substitute for a palm frond.

32. Breaux and McKinney, "Hoodoo Opening," 1–2.

33. Breaux and McKinney, "Hoodoo Opening," 2–3; Olmos and Paravisini-Gebert, *Creole Religions,* 134.

34. McKinney did not give a distinctive name to the first initiation in which he participated. Considering that each would incorporate images of St. Peter, it may well be that both were varieties St. Peter Openings. Nevertheless, the second ceremony differed in some ways from the former, making it possible that to McKinney, they were different varieties of opening.

35. McKinney, "St. Peter and Black Cat Opening," 1.

36. McKinney, "St. Peter and Black Cat Opening," 2–3.

37. McKinney, "St. Peter and Black Cat Opening," 3. While I have included bergamot oil in the list of items on the parterre, it is important to note that the source called it "burganat oil."

38. McKinney, "St. Peter and Black Cat Opening," 3–4, quoted 4.

39. McKinney, "St. Peter and Black Cat Opening," 5.

40. McKinney, "St. Peter and Black Cat Opening," 5–6, quoted 6.

41. McKinney, "St. Peter and Black Cat Opening," 6.

42. McKinney, "St. Peter and Black Cat Opening," 7.

43. McKinney, "St. Peter and Black Cat Opening," 8–9.

44. Hazel Breaux and Robert McKinney, "Popular Gris-Gris among Present Day Hoodoo Queens," Robert Tallant Papers, 1938–1957, New Orleans Public Library, Louisiana and City Archives, New Orleans, LA, folder/reel 8, MS-120, 44, 315–316.

45. "Vuodous Dance," 2; "The Voudou Case Disposed Of," *The Daily Picayune,* 2 August 1863, 3; "Voudou Meeting Broken Up," *Daily Picayune,* 31 July 1863, 2; "The Dance of the Voudous," *Daily Delta,* 20 July 1850, 3; "More Voudouism," *Weekly Delta,* 7 August 1850, 4; Cable, "Creole Slave Songs," 816.

46. Marie Dédé, "Folk Lore," Northwestern State University of Louisiana, Watson Memorial Library, Cammie G. Henry Research Center, Federal Writers' Project, folder 587, 1; Dédé, "Marie Laveau," 4.

47. FWP informant Marie Dédé noted that Marie Laveau would postpone St. John's Eve festivities to the following Monday whenever the holiday fell on Sunday. Dédé, "Marie Laveau," 7.

48. Long, *Voudou Priestess,* 119–22.

49. Williams, "Night with the Voudous," 403–4.

50. Williams, "Night with the Voudous," 404.

51. Williams, "Night with the Voudous," 404.

52. "Vou Dous Incantation," 6. As with all journalistic accounts, details of the ceremony should be taken with a grain of salt.

53. "Vou Dous Incantation," 6. The exact meaning of Laveau's words is unclear, but a likely translation is "Try to cut me off." The response of the crowd can be translated, "Heat it up, Miss Marie."

54. "Vou Dous Incantation," 6.

55. "Vou Dous Incantation," 6.

56. "Vou Dous Incantation," 6.

57. "Voodooism," 1

58. "Voodooism," 1; "Voudou Superstition," 5.

59. Fritz and Alfred, "Marie Laveau," 1.

60. Fritz and Alfred, "Marie Laveau," 1–2.

61. Breaux and Villere, "Raphael," 5; Rivaros, "Marie Laveau," 2, 5.

62. "Marie Laveau," interview by Robert McKinney, transcript, Northwestern State University of Louisiana, Watson Memorial Library, Cammie G. Henry Research Center, Federal Writers' Project, folder 25, 1–2; Moore, "Marie Laveau," 1–2, quoted 2.

63. Felix, "Marie Leveau," 2, 4–5, quoted 5

64. Felix, "Marie Leveau," 2, 4–6.

65. Dédé, "Marie Laveau," 2.

66. Felix, "Marie Leveau," 5.

67. Long, *Voudou Priestess,* 119; Métraux, *Voodoo in Haiti,* 328–9; Hurston, *Tell My Horse,* in *Zora Neale Hurston: Folklore, Memoirs, and Other Writings,* selected and annotated by Cheryl A.

Wall (New York, NY: Library of America, 1995), 504; Anderson, "Research Journals," vol. 2, 20–1; Newbell Niles Puckett, *Folk Beliefs of the Southern Negro* (Chapel Hill: University of North Carolina Press, 1926; reprint, Montclair, NJ: Patterson Smith, 1968), 320.

68. William Wells Brown, *My Southern Home: The South and Its People* (Boston: A. G. Brown and Company, 1880; republication, Upper Saddle River, NJ: Gregg Press, 1968), 68–9.

69. "Voodoo Worship Exists in St. Louis," *The Daily Picayune,* 22 December 1893, 2.

70. "Voodoo Worship Exists in St. Louis," *The Daily Picayune,* 22 December 1893, 2.

71. "Voodoo Worship Exists in St. Louis," *The Daily Picayune,* 22 December 1893, 2.

72. "Voodoo Worship Exists in St. Louis," *The Daily Picayune,* 22 December 1893, 2.

73. Owen, "Voodooism," 323–5.

74. Owen, "Among the Voodoos," 230–232.

75. Owen, "Among the Voodoos," 231–7.

76. Owen, "Among the Voodoos," 237.

77. Owen, "Among the Voodoos," 236–7.

78. Ellis, *Ewe-Speaking Peoples,* 54–63; Médéric-Louis-Elie Moreau de Saint-Méry, *A Civilization That Perished: The Last Years of White Colonial Rule in Haiti,* translated and abridged by Ivor D. Spencer (Lanham, MD: University Press of American, Inc., 1985), vii, 1–5. I have visited the Python Temple, which is inhabited by a large number of royal pythons, which are much smaller than the spectacularly large, reticulated pythons one typically sees in American zoos.

79. Owen, "Among the Voodoos," 237–9.

80. Owen, "Voodooism," 316; Mambo Vye Zo, *Serving the Spirits,* 257–8; Karen McCarthy Brown, "Afro-Caribbean Spirituality: A Haitian Case Study," chap. 1 in *Vodou in Haitian Life and Culture: Invisible Powers,* ed. Claudine Michel and Patrick Bellegarde-Smith (New York: Palgrave Macmillan, 2006), 11, 26n5; St. John, *Hayti,* 185.

81. See, for instance, Marie Cappick, *The Key West Story, 1818–1950,* 2 May 1958, 7.

82. "Voodoo Worship Exists," 2.

5. THE DEATH OF A RELIGION?

1. The death of religions is the subject of a groundbreaking essay collection edited by Michael Stausberg, Stuart A. Wright, and Carole M. Cusack, entitled *The Demise of Religion: How Religions End, Die, or Dissipate.* The introduction insightfully addresses what it means for a faith to die, while the individual essays examine just how one defines such death and the phenomenon as it has played out in various now-defunct and near-dead religions. A commonality throughout the essays is that the demise of a religion does not mean all its features, much less its legacy, disappear as well. See Michael Stausberg, Stuart A. Wright, and Carole M. Cusack, eds., *The Demise of Religion: How Religions End, Die, or Dissipate* (New York: Bloomsbury Academic, 2020), 1–12.

2. Porteous, "Gri-Gri Case," 48–63; *Criminales* #278.

3. "Unlawful Assemblies," *New Orleans Daily Picayune,* 31 July 1850, 2.

4. "Vou Doux," *New Orleans Bee,* 26 April 1853, 1. For information on similar cases, see "Motley Gathering," 2; "Arrest of Voudoux," *New Orleans Bee,* 25 July 1851, 1; See also Freddi Williams Evans, *Congo Square: African Roots in New Orleans,* with a foreword by KWabena 'Nketia (Lafayette: University of Louisiana at Lafayette Press, 2011), 28, 30–3, which discusses the suppression of dances

in New Orleans's Congo Square. The restriction on assemblies would have affected Voodoo ceremonies alongside secular dances.

5. "Tribulations des Voudous," 1.

6. "Voudouing a Wine Mark," *New Orleans Republican*, 26 February 1871, 5.

7. Carolyn Morrow Long identified mail fraud as the greatest threat to spiritual supply providers after 1909. See Long, *Spiritual Merchants*, 129–130.

8. "Credulous Negroes Were the Easy Dupes of Man Who Said Snakes Lived in Them," *Times-Picayune*, 16 May 1914, 9; Robert McKinney, "Dr. Rockford Lewis Jailed . . . Gloom Seems Certain for Voodooism," 1938, Federal Writers' Project, Northwestern State University of Louisiana, Watson Memorial Library, Cammie G. Henry Research Center, Federal Writers' Project, folder 604, 1, 3; See Long, *Spiritual Merchants*, 135. The 2021 dollar equivalent calculations in this section are from U.S. Bureau of Labor Statistics, CPI Inflation Calculator, 2021, https://www.bls.gov/data /inflation_calculator.htm (accessed 19 July 2021).

9. "Husbands and Lovers are Voudoo Sage's Specialty," *New Orleans Times-Democrat*, 29 October 1902, 10.

10. "Husbands and Lovers," 10; New Orleans City Council, *Code of Ordinances*, section 54–312, 28 May 2021, https://library.municode.com/la/new_orleans/codes/code_of_ordinances?nodeId =PTIICO_CH54CRCO_ARTVIOFAFPUGE_DIViGE_S54-311CRIM.

11. *The Windsor Review*, 11 June 1881, 2; "Negro 'Hoodoo Doctor' Held as Fire Bug Suspect," *The Shreveport Times*, 11 August 1924, 12. See also Michael A. Ross, *The Great New Orleans Kidnapping Case: Race, Law, and Justice in the Reconstruction Era* (New York: Oxford University Press. 2015), 4, 13–15, 22, 105.

12. "Curious Charge of Swindling," 2; "The Virgin of the Voudous," 345. See also, Long, *Voudou Priestess*, 105–6, for a summary of the case.

13. "Voudouism Unveiled," *Weekly Delta*, 5 August 1850, 339. For a full account of the case, see Long, *Voudou Priestess*, 103–5.

14. For an interesting examination of how print accounts of Voodoo served the cause of white supremacy, see Michelle Y. Gordon "'Midnight Scenes and Orgies': Public Narratives of Voodoo in New Orleans and Nineteenth-Century Discourses of White Supremacy," *American Quarterly* 64:4 (December 2012): 767–786.

15. "Sudden Death," *New Orleans Daily Picayune*, 17 March 1869, 2.

16. "An Extraordinary Story about a Missouri Voudou," *The State Journal*, 4 May 1877, 1.

17. "An Old Negro Lynched," *St. Louis Post-Dispatch*, 11 December 1887, 5.

18. Augustin, "Marie Laveau," folder 25.

19. Della Greenfield, "Marie Laveau," interview by Zoe Posey, around 18 February 1941, New Orleans, Louisiana, Federal Writers' Project, folder 25, 1.

20. Emile Labat, "Marie Laveau," interview by Zoe Posey, 5 December 1940, New Orleans, Louisiana, Federal Writers' Project, folder 25, 1.

21. McKinney, "St. Peter and Black Cat Opening," 5; Jacques Villere, "An Interview with Aunt Babe," 12 September 1936, Northwestern State University of Louisiana, Watson Memorial Library, Cammie G. Henry Research Center, Federal Writers' Project, folder 44, 1.

22. Ron Bodin, *Voodoo: Past and Present* (Lafayette: University of Southwestern Louisiana, 1990), 27.

23. Bodin, *Voodoo*, 27.

24. Albert J. Raboteau, *Slave Religion: The "Invisible Institution" in the Antebellum South*, updated ed. (Oxford: Oxford University Press, 2004), 75, 79–80. Raboteau's student, Yvonne Chireau, stated much the same in her *Black Magic*, 77.

25. Kenaz Filan, *The New Orleans Voodoo Handbook* (Rochester, VT: Destiny Books, 2011), 37–46. See also Anderson, *Conjure*, 90–2.

26. Michael P. Smith, *Spirit World: Pattern in the Expressive Folk Culture of African-American New Orleans* (New Orleans: New Orleans Urban Folklife Society, 1984; reprint, Gretna, LA: Pelican Publishing, 1992), 35.

27. Hans Baer, *The Black Spiritual Movement: A Religious Response to Racism*, 2nd ed. (Knoxville: University of Tennessee Press, 2001), 113; Margarita Simon Guillory, *Spiritual and Social Transformation in African American Spiritual Churches: More Than Conjurers* (New York: Routledge, 2017), 4.

28. Jacobs and Kaslow, *Spiritual Churches*, 49–67, 118–21, 149–69, 199–200.

29. Hurston, "Hoodoo in America," 319.

30. Smith, *Spirit World*, 57, 60; Baer, *Black Spiritual Movement*, 119–20, 127, 131–4, 152, quoted 152 and 153; Berry, *Spirit of Black Hawk*, 61–2.

31. Jacobs and Kaslow, *Spiritual Churches*, 30–31; Stephen C. Wehmeyer, "Indian Altars of the Spiritual Church: Kongo Echoes in New Orleans," *African Arts* 33 (Winter 2000): 62–9, 95–6.

32. Roberts, *Voodoo and Power*, 45–7.

33. Aurélien Mokoko Gampiot, *Kimbanguism: An African Understanding of the Bible*, translated by Cécile Coquet-Mokoko (University Park: Pennsylvania State University Press, 2017), 78, 123; Anderson, *Research Journals*, vol. III, 129.

34. Jacobs and Kaslow, *Spiritual Churches*, 129–33, 205–7; Ellen Fairwell, "When the Thunder is Over Mother Kate Francis Will March Right Through Hebbin's Door," interview by Robert McKinney, November 1939, New Orleans, Louisiana, Federal Writers' Project, folder 39, 6, 8; "For Mother Kate Francis' File" Northwestern State University of Louisiana, Watson Memorial Library, Cammie G. Henry Research Center, Federal Writers' Project, folder 39, 1. Examples of various floor washes can be found in Hyatt, *Hoodoo—Conjuration—Witchcraft—Rootwork*, 743–4, 816, 1466–7, 1561, 1787. My description of the St. Benedict Spiritual Church service is based on notes I took immediately after the event. The church, located at 2622 Flood Street in the Lower Ninth Ward, was one of the casualties of the flooding that followed a levee breach caused by Hurricane Katrina in August 2005. My general statement about liquids for spiritual protection is based on personal experiences in Senegal and Benin.

35. C. V. Wetli and R. Martinez, "Forensic Sciences Aspects of Santeria, a Religious Cult of African Origin," *Journal of Forensic Sciences* 26:3 (July 1981): 506. Obeah is a magical practice associated with the West Indies, and it is generally viewed as roughly equivalent to Western black magic. Santería, also known as Lucumí, is a Cuban creole version of Yoruba religion with a Catholic overlay.

36. Rod Davis, *American Voudou: Journey into a Hidden World* (Denton: University of North Texas Press, 1999), 9.

37. John Lee Maddox, "Modern Voodooism," *Hygeia* 12 (February and March 1934): 153–6, 252–5.

38. Baer, *Black Spiritual Movement*, 110–139, quoted 113.

39. Jacobs and Kaslow, *Spiritual Churches*, 73–4, 79; Olmos and Paravisini-Gebert, *Creole Religions*, 203–229; Emily Suzanne Clark, *A Luminous Brotherhood: Afro-Creole Spiritualism in Nineteenth-Century New Orleans* (Chapel Hill: University of North Carolina Press, 2016), 22–27; Daggett, *Spiritualism*, 71–2. For an explanation of the beginning of Spiritualism in the United States, see Weisberg, *Talking to the Dead*.

40. Jacobs and Kaslow, *Spiritual Churches*, 58–92, quoted 73.

41. Jacobs and Kaslow, *Spiritual Churches*, 73, 80–2.

42. Berry, *Spirit of Black Hawk*, 57–69; Hurston, "Hoodoo," 319.

43. Fairwell, "When the Thunder," 5–8, quoted 5.

44. Fairwell, "When the Thunder," 4, 11.

45. "For Mother Kate Francis' File," 1.

46. Mildred Fortune, "My Visit to Church," Northwestern State University of Louisiana, Watson Memorial Library, Cammie G. Henry Research Center, Federal Writers' Project, folder 39, 2.

47. Jacobs and Kaslow, *Spiritual Churches of New Orleans*, 30–31; Guillory, *Spiritual and Social Transformation*, 14, 77, 101; Daggett, *Spiritualism*, 43; Clark, *Luminous Brotherhood*, 26.

48. Anderson, *Conjure*, 32–33, 58; Long, *Voudou Priestess*, 106, 114–116. It is, of course, entirely possible that these deities could be inserted into modern Spiritual churches seeking to reconnect with African religion, a process that would parallel the much earlier introduction of Black Hawk.

49. Olmos and Paravisini-Gebert, *Creole Religions*, 204–225.

50. Long, "Cracker Jack," 73–4; "A. Schwab," A. Schwab, last modified 2023, https://a-schwab.com; Elliot Schwab, interview by author, 28 March 2002, Memphis, TN, author's personal collection, Monroe, LA, 1; Long, *Spiritual Merchants*, 255–6, 259. For additional information on A. Schwab and other Memphis hoodoo businesses, see Tony Kail's well-researched *A Secret History of Memphis Hoodoo: Rootworkers, Conjurers & Spirituals* (Charleston, SC: History Press, 2017), 93–9, 117–33.

51. Long, *Spiritual Merchants*, 255–6; Megan Braden-Perry, "After Closing of Popular F&F Botanica, Shoppers Find Candle Power at Other Spiritual Supply Shops," *New Orleans Advocate*, 25 October 2018, https://www.nola.com/entertainment_life/article_c5e1b784-f022-5312-8e66-df3ba4cc68bf.html.

52. New Orleans Historic Voodoo Museum, last modified 2019, https://voodoomuseum.com/; Megan Braden-Perry, "How to Discover and Experience Voodoo Culture in New Orleans," *Thrillist*, last modified 2021, https://www.thrillist.com/travel/new-orleans/new-orleans-voodoo-shops.

53. Stacey Anderson, "Voodoo is Rebounding in New Orleans after Hurricane Katrina," *Newsweek* 25 August 2014, https://www.newsweek.com/2014/09/05/voodoo-rebounding-new-orleans-after-hurricane-katrina-266340.html. The article's source for these figures was rather vague. As is common with popular media sources, various errors litter the text. Among them are a reference to Marie Laveau as a seventeenth-century priestess and a misdating of the Haitian immigration to New Orleans. In light of these issues, it would be wise to treat these figures as questionable.

54. Sallie Ann Glassman, interview by author, 14 November 2001, New Orleans, LA, notes and audio recording, author's personal collection, Monroe, LA; "Sallie Ann Glassman," Island of Salvation Botanica, last modified ca. 2020, https://www.islandofsalvationbotanica.com/about.html#/; Catherine Wessinger, "Sallie Ann Glassman," *World Religions and Spirituality Project*, 30 June 2018,

https://wrldrels.org/2018/06/29/sallie-ann-glassman/; Sallie Ann Glassman, "How the Lwa Come to a Haitian Vodou Ritual: An Interview with Sallie Ann Glassman," with Catherine Wessinger, *World Religions and Spirituality Project,* 8 October 2018, https://wrldrels.org/wp-content/uploads /2016/02/Glassman-Interview.Final_.WRSP_.pdf; "Brandi Kelley from Voodoo Authentica Teaches Us the Power of Voodoo," Hear She Roars, last modified 11 October 2019, https://www.hearsh eroars.com/post/brandi-kelley-from-voodoo-authentica-teaches-us-the-power-of-voodoo; Rheta Rheta Grimsley Johnson, "Voodoofest on Rue Dumaine and the Spirited Woman Behind It," *French Quarter Journal,* 25 October 2019, https://www.frenchquartercourier.com/archives/voodoofest -on-rue-dumaine; Brandi C. Kelley, interview by Dovie Milstead, 1 March 2021, New Orleans, LA, notes and audio recording, author's personal collection, Monroe, LA. See also Karen McCarthy Brown, *Mama Lola: A Vodou Priestess in Brooklyn,* revised ed., with a Foreword by Claudine Michel (Berkeley: University of California Press, 2010).

55. Miriam Chamani, interview by author, 15 November 2001, New Orleans, LA, notes and audio recording, author's personal collection, Monroe, LA; Miram Chamani and Oswan Chamani, *Voodoo Spiritual Temple* (New Orleans: Voodoo Spiritual Temple, ca. 1995).

56. Bodin, *Voodoo,* 79–80; Rory O'Neill Schmitt and Rosary Hartel O'Neill, *New Orleans Voodoo: A Cultural History* (Charleston, SC: History Press, 2019), 102–4.

57. Filan, *Voodoo Handbook,* 1.

58. Denise Alvarado, *The Magic of Marie Laveau: Embracing the Spiritual Legacy of the Voodoo Queen of New Orleans* (Newburyport, MA: Weiser Books, 2020), xi–xvi; Denise Alvarado, *Witch Queens, Voodoo Spirits, and Hoodoo Saints: A Guide to Magical New Orleans* (Newburyport, MA: Weiser Books, 2022), ix–xiii; Filan, *Voodoo Handbook,* 2.

59. Sallie Ann Glassman revived the St. John's Evening gatherings around 1993. I have attended ceremonies hosted by her and by another practitioner named Miriam Chamani. See Catherine Wessinger, "Sallie Ann Glassman," World Religions and Spirituality Project, last modified 30 June 2018, https://wrldrels.org/2018/06/29/sallie-ann-glassman/.

CONCLUSION: WHOSE VOODOO?

1. Examples of those who followed this general pattern were Euvonie Georges Auguste and Samba 'L in Port-au-Prince and Ati Joseph Fritzner Comas of Canada in Leogane. Records of our conversations can be found in Jeffrey E. Anderson, "Research Journals," 4 vols. (field notes, personal collection, 2015–2017), IV: 94–101, 111–23.

2. Anderson, "Journals," IV: 103–5, 126–7, 130–2.

3. One example of such a work by a Congolese author is Jean Nzoho's *Facettes de la Culture Congolaise,* with illustrations by Alain Nzonza (France: Imprimerie Paquereau, ca. 2011), 21–26, 36–38, 40, 51.

4. Anderson, "Journals," III: 74–75, 116.

5. For an example of the former approach, see Long, *Voudou Priestess,* 93–97. An excellent representation of the latter approach appears in Kodi A. Roberts's *Voodoo and Power: The Politics of Religion in New Orleans, 1881–1940,* 5–8.

6. Roberts, *Voodoo and Power,* 10–11; Hurston, "Hoodoo," 319; Dillon, "Voodoo," sec. "The

Law's Long Arm: The Suppression of Voodoo," 59, 63; Anderson, *Conjure*, 156–7; Jacobs and Kaslow, *Spiritual Churches*, 49–95.

7. Lyle Saxon, *Fabulous New Orleans*, illustrated by Edward Howard Suydam (London: Century, 1928), 243; Hurston, "Hoodoo," 326; Zora Neale Hurston, review of *Voodoo in New Orleans* by Robert Tallant, *Journal of American Folklore* 60 (1947), 437; Long, *Voudou Priestess*, 190–205. For a recent supporter of the multiple Laveau hypothesis, see Martha Ward, *Voodoo Queen: The Spirited Lives of Marie Laveau* (Jackson, MS: University Press of Mississippi, 2004), 70–5, 163–7. I tend to think the supposed second Marie Laveau was another person with whom some people simply confused Laveau.

8. Roberts, *Voodoo and Power*, 9.

9. "Hopkins Laure (Better Known as Lalla)," Northwestern State University of Louisiana, Watson Memorial Library, Cammie G. Henry Research Center, Federal Writers' Project, folder 43, 4.

10. Owen, "Among the Voodoos," 241; Hurston, "Hoodoo," 317.

11. "The Queen of the Voudous," *New Orleans Times*, April 3, 1873, 6.

12. "Vou Doux," 1; "Queen of the Voudous," 6; "Dance of the Voodoos: Outlandish Celebration of St. John's Eve," *The Times-Democrat*, June 24, 1896, 2; "A Voudou Orgie: Sensational Disclosure in the Third District," *The Times-Democrat*, May 29, 1889, 3.

13. Saxon, "Voodoo," 135.

14. For examples of fictional works that rely on negative stereotypes, see Anne Rice, *The Feast of All Saints* (New York: Ballantine Books, 1979), 499–506 and Douglas Preston and Lincoln Child, *Cemetery Dance* (New York: Vision, 2009).

15. For a full discussion of Hurston's impact on Voodoo scholarship and her shortcomings as an anthropologist, see Anderson, "Voodoo in Black and White," 143–59. An example of Hurston using a death curse to signify African American strength can be found in *Mules and Men* on pages 196–99.

16. Alice Walker, "Zora Neale Hurston—A Cautionary Tale and a Partisan View," foreword to *Zora Neale Hurston: A Literary Biography*, Robert E. Hemenway (Urbana: University of Illinois Press, 1977), xii, xvi; Jewell Parker Rhodes, "Marie Laveau, Voodoo Queen," *Ms.*, January 1983, 30; Arthur Rickydoc Flowers, *The Hoodoo Book of Flowers: The Great Black Book of Generations* (Syracuse, NY: Rootwork Press, 2019), quote from back cover. For an early take on African American supernaturalism as a literary device, see Marjorie Pryse and Hortense J. Spillers, eds., *Conjuring: Black Women, Fiction, and the Literary Tradition* (Bloomington: Indiana University Press, 1985).

17. Brenda Marie Osbey, "Why We Can't Talk to You about Voodoo," *The Southern Literary Journal* 43 (Spring 2011): 3–6; Robert, *Voodoo and Power*, 7–12.

18. Ina Johanna Fandrich, *The Mysterious Voodoo Queen, Marie Laveaux: A Study of Powerful Female Leadership in Nineteenth-Century New Orleans* (New York: Routledge, 2005), 218.

19. Anderson, *Conjure*, 152–154; Fandrich, *Mysterious Voodoo Queen*, 163; Susheel Bibbs, *Heritage of Power: Marie LaVeau—Mary Ellen Pleasant*, 2nd ed. (San Francisco, CA: MEP Publications, 2002), 54–56; Ward, *Voodoo Queen*, ix, 78–92. Carolyn Morrow Long has effectively demonstrated that Laveau did not buy slaves in order to free them. See Long, *Voudou Priestess*, 72–78.

20. "Death of Marie Laveau," *The Daily Picayune*, 17 June 1881, 8.

21. "The Dead Voudou Queen," *The New-York Times,* 23 June 1881, 2.

22. "Tribulations des Voudous," 1; "Voudou Case Disposed Of," 3.

APPENDIX: MISSISSIPPI RIVER VALLEY VOODOO CHANTS, SONGS, AND PRAYERS

1. Translation A is by expert of Kongo culture Miabeto Auguste of the Republic of the Congo, and Translation B is by scholar of Vodú, Alexis Alarcón of Cuba. Simbi, of West Central African origin, is both a *lwa* in Haiti and a *luá* in Cuba.

2. Assou is a man's name.

3. The following translation is a joint effort of myself and Birame Ka, a professional interpreter from Senegal.

4. The following is my own translation.

5. These partial translations are from Alfred Burdon Ellis, "On Võdu-Worship," *Popular Science Monthly* 38 (March 1891): 662–3. He claimed they are from the Ewe language.

6. In the following sources, distinguishing the letters "e" and "o" was exceedingly difficult.

7. The following translation is by Jony Louis, a professional Haitian Krèyol interpreter from Haiti.

8. The following translation is by Jony Louis and Euvonie Georges Auguste, a practitioner of Haitian Vodou.

9. The following translation is by Jony Louis.

10. The following translation is by Jony Louis

11. The following is my own translation.

12. The following is my own translation.

13. The following is my own translation.

14. The following is my own translation.

15. The following is my own translation.

16. The following is my own translation.

17. These partial translations are from Alfred Burdon Ellis, "On Võdu-Worship," *Popular Science Monthly* 38 (March 1891): 662–3. He claimed they were from the Ewe language.

18. This following is my own translation.

19. These translations are recorded in Ina Johanna Fandrich, *The Mysterious Voodoo Queen, Marie Laveaux: A Study of Powerful Female Leadership in Nineteenth-Century New Orleans* (New York: Routledge, 2005), 132–133. The first translation is a slightly altered version of one made by Ladji Sacko and treats the song as in the language of the Malinke people. The second translation was made by Wyatt MacGaffey, treating the original text as KiKongo.

20. *Canga,* per Fandrich, means "magic," "witchcraft," or "spirit."

21. *Bomba* is a creole form of *Mbumba,* per Fandrich. *Mbumba* is a word meaning "medicine, charm, fetish, spirit, magic."

22. The following is my own translation.

23. While the first line of the following translation is Hearn's, the second and third are my own.

24. The following translation is by Jony Louis.

25. The following translation is by Jony Louis.

26. The following translation is a joint effort by Jony Louis and me.

27. Translation provided in original document.

28. She was most likely the woman called Marie Dédé elsewhere in the Federal Writers' Project interviews.

29. The following was translated by Birame Ka.

30. The following is my own translation.

31. Translation provided in original document.

32. Translation provided in original document.

33. The names appear to be the names of those called out to dance before the gathering. Any number of names could fill the place of *Batis* or *Gustine.*

34. Translation provided in original document.

35. Translation provided in original document.

36. The following is my own translation. Birame Ka suggested the alternate translation of "Try to cut me." If the latter is correct, then it may refer to a common practice in West Africa and Haiti when participants in ceremonies try to cut those possessed by spirits and find themselves unable to do so.

37. Translation provided in original document.

38. Per Birame Ka, *nainaine* means "oldest sister."

39. The following translation is by Fredrick Adams, retired professor of world languages and expert in French at the University of Louisiana Monroe.

40. Or "*I have been calling.*"

41. A drunken or corrupt state.

42. Or "*down below.*"

43. Or "*I do not call downstairs unless I call a drunken companion.*"

44. The translation is found in Federal Writers' Project, *Louisiana: A Guide to the State,* American Guide Series (New York: Hasting House, 1941), 99.

45. The following is my own translation.

46. The following was translated by Birame Ka.

47. The following was translated by Birame Ka.

48. The following is my own translation.

49. The following was translated by Birame Ka.

50. Per Euvonie Georges Auguste, this phrase could be translated as "Where are you?"

51. Per Euvonie Georges Auguste, this phrase could be translated as "Where are you?"

52. The following is my own translation.

53. The following translation is by Birame Ka with contributions by Euvonie Georges Auguste.

54. Or "wine, wine."

55. Or "Where are you?"

56. Or "wine, wine."

57. Or "Where are you?"

58. The following translation is by Jony Louis.

59. The following is my own translation.

60. The following translation is by Birame Ka.

61. The translation of the following portion of the song prior to the ellipses was suggested by members of the Centre International de Recherche-Education sur la Civilisation Kongo, including Miabeto Auguste, Mbemba Lubienga Armel, Nika Célestin, and Kidzounou Olivier. The section after the ellipses was translated by Birame Ka.

62. *Ngundu* is the sound of drums but signifying the sound of storms.

63. Translation provided in original document.

BIBLIOGRAPHY

MANUSCRIPTS AND ORAL HISTORIES

Anderson, Jeffrey E. "Mission Journal." Field notes, personal collection, 2014.

Anderson, Jeffrey E. "Research Journals." 4 vols. Field notes, personal collection, 2015–2017.

Anonymous. Interview by Jeffrey E. Anderson, 14 July 2010, phone, author's personal collection, Monroe, LA.

Chamani, Miriam. Interview by author. 15 November 2001. New Orleans, LA. Notes and audio recording. Author's personal collection, Monroe, LA.

Christian, Marcus. "Voodooism and Mumbo-Jumbo." University of New Orleans, Earl K. Long Library, Louisiana and Special Collections Department, Historical Manuscripts Series, Marcus Christian Collection, Number 11, Box 4, Chapter 11.

Criminales #278. 12 June 1773–14 January 1774. French Superior Council and Judicial Records of Spanish Cabildo, Judicial Records, Williams Research Center, Historic New Orleans Collection, reel 109.

Dillon, Catherine. "Voodoo, 1937–1941." Federal Writers' Project, folders 118, 317, and 319. Northwestern State University of Louisiana, Watson Memorial Library, Cammie G. Henry Research Center, Federal Writers' Project.

Federal Writers' Project. Unpublished interviews and notes, 1935–1943. Northwestern State University of Louisiana, Watson Memorial Library, Cammie G. Henry Research Center, Federal Writers' Project.

Glassman, Sallie Ann. "How the Lwa Come to a Haitian Vodou Ritual: An Interview with Sallie Ann Glassman," with Catherine Wessinger. *World Religions and Spirituality Project.* Last modified 8 October 2018. https://wrldrels.org/wp-content/uploads/2016/02/Glassman-Interview.Final_.WRSP_.pdf.

———. Interview by Jeffrey E. Anderson. 4 November 2001. New Orleans, LA. Notes and audio recording. Author's personal collection, Monroe, LA.

Kelley, Brandi C. Interview by Dovie Milstead. 1 March 2021. New Orleans, LA. Notes and audio recording. Author's personal collection, Monroe, LA.

Schwab, Elliot. Interview by Jeffrey E. Anderson. 28 March 2002. Memphis, TN. Author's personal collection, Monroe, LA.

Smith, Jonell and Jazell Smith. Interview by Jeffrey E. Anderson. 15 November 2001. New Orleans, LA. Author's personal collection, Monroe, LA.

Tallant, Robert. Unpublished interviews, notes, and research materials, 1938–1957. Robert Tallant Papers, City Archives, New Orleans Public Library, New Orleans, LA.

ACADEMIC BOOKS AND ARTICLES

Ackermann, Hans-W. and Jeanine Gauthier. "The Ways and Nature of the Zombi." *Journal of American Folklore* 104 (1991): 466–494.

Ananou, Bertrand. *Le Vodún: La Religion Traditionnelle du Danhomε: Lumière sur l'univers spiritual du Bénin.* With a preface by Dah Agbalènon Adanmaïkpohoué. Bohicon, Benin: Editions ACT2D, 2012.

Anderson, Jeffrey E. *Conjure in African American Society.* Baton Rouge: Louisiana State University Press, 2005.

———. *Hoodoo, Voodoo, and Conjure: A Handbook.* Greenwood Folklore Handbooks Series. Westport, CT: Greenwood Press, 2008.

———. "Voodoo in Black and White." In *Southern Character: Essays in Honor of Bertram Wyatt-Brown,* eds. Lisa Tendrich Frank and Daniel Kilbride, 143–159. Gainesville: University Press of Florida, 2011.

Baer, Hans. *The Black Spiritual Movement: A Religious Response to Racism.* 2nd ed. Knoxville: University of Tennessee Press, 2001.

Berry, Jason. *The Spirit of Black Hawk: A Mystery of Africans and Indians.* With photographs by Sydney Byrd. Jackson: University Press of Mississippi, 1995.

Blier, Suzanne Preston. *African Vodun: Art, Psychology, and Power.* Chicago: University of Chicago Press, 1995.

Bodin, Ron. *Voodoo: Past and Present.* Lafayette, LA: University of Southwestern Louisiana, 1990.

Boyd, Valerie. *Wrapped in Rainbows: The Life of Zora Neale Hurston.* New York: Scribner, 2003.

Brandon, George. *Santeria from Africa to the New World: The Dead Sell Memories.* Bloomington: Indiana University Press, 1993.

Brock, H. I. Review of *Mules and Men,* by Zora Neale Hurston. *New York Times Book Review,* 10 November 1935, sec. 6, 4.

Brown, Karen McCarthy. *Mama Lola: A Vodou Priestess in Brooklyn.* Revised ed. With a Foreword by Claudine Michel. Berkeley: University of California Press, 2010.

Brown, Kenneth L. "Retentions, Adaptations, and the Need for Social Control within African and African American Communities across the Southern United States from 1770 to 1930." In *The Archaeology of Slavery: A Comparative Approach to Captivity and Coercion,* edited by Lydia Wilson Marshall, 166–191. Carbondale: Southern Illinois University Press, 2014. Google Play.

Caffrey, Joshua Clegg. *Traditional Music in Coastal Louisiana: The 1934 Lomax Recordings.* With a foreword by Barry Jean Ancelet. Baton Rouge: Louisiana State University Press, 2013.

Chireau, Yvonne. *Black Magic: Religion and the African American Conjuring Tradition.* Berkeley: University of California Press, 2003.

Clark, Emily Suzanne. *A Luminous Brotherhood: Afro-Creole Spiritualism in Nineteenth-Century New Orleans.* Chapel Hill: University of North Carolina Press, 2016.

Courlander, Harold. *The Drum and the Hoe: Life and Lore of the Haitian People.* Berkeley: University of California Press, 1960.

Daggett, Melissa. *Spiritualism in Nineteenth-Century New Orleans: The Life and Times of Henry Louis Rey.* Jackson: University Press of Mississippi, 2017.

Davis, Rod. *American Voudou: Journey into a Hidden World.* Denton: University of North Texas Press, 1999.

Desmangles, Leslie G. *The Faces of the Gods: Vodou and Roman Catholicism in Haiti.* Chapel Hill: University of North Carolina Press, 1992.

Dessens, Nathalie. *From Saint-Domingue to New Orleans: Migration and Influences.* Gainesville: University Press of Florida, 2007.

Dieterlen, Germaine. *Essai sur le Religion Bambara.* Paris: Presses Universitaires de France, 1951.

Diouf, Sylviane A. *Dreams of Africa in Alabama: The Slave Ship "Clotilda" and the Story of the Last Africans Brought to America.* Oxford: Oxford University Press, 2007.

Drewal, Henry John. *Mami Wata: Arts for Water Spirits in Africa and Its Diaspora.* With contributions by Marilyn Houlberg, Bogumil Jewsiewicki, Amy L. Noell, John W. Nunley, and Jill Salmons. Los Angeles: Fowler Museum at UCLA, 2008.

Ellis, Alfred Burdon. *The Ewe-Speaking Peoples of the Slave Coast of West Africa: Their Religion, Manners, Customs, Laws, Languages, &c.* London: Chapman and Hall, 1890; reprint, Chicago: Benin Press, Ltd., 1965.

———. "On Vŏdu-Worship." *Popular Science Monthly* 38 (March 1891): 651–663.

———. *The Yoruba-Speaking Peoples of the Slave Coast of West Africa.* London: Chapman and Hall, 1894; reprint, Benin Press, Ltd., 1964.

Evans, Freddi Williams. *Congo Square: African Roots in New Orleans.* With a foreword by Kwabena 'Nketia. Lafayette: University of Louisiana at Lafayette Press, 2011.

Falen, Douglas J. *African Science: Witchcraft, Vodun, and Healing in Southern Benin.* Madison: University of Wisconsin Press, 2018.

Fandrich, Ina Johanna. *The Mysterious Voodoo Queen, Marie Laveaux: A Study of Powerful Female Leadership in Nineteenth-Century New Orleans.* New York: Routledge, 2005.

Fontenot, Wonda L. *Secret Doctors: Ethnomedicine of African Americans.* Westport, CT: Bergin and Garvey, 1994.

Gampiot, Aurélien Mokoko. *Kimbanguism: An African Understanding of the Bible.* Translated by Cécile Coquet-Mokoko. University Park: Pennsylvania State University Press, 2017.

Gomez, Michael. *Exchanging Our Country Marks: The Transformation of African Identities in the Colonial and Antebellum South.* Chapel Hill: University of North Carolina Press, 1998.

Gordon, Michelle Y. "'Midnight Scenes and Orgies': Public Narratives of Voodoo in New Orleans and Nineteenth-Century Discourses of White Supremacy." *American Quarterly* 64:4 (December 2012): 767–786.

Guillory, Margarita Simon. *Spiritual and Social Transformation in African American Spiritual Churches: More Than Conjurers.* New York: Routledge, 2017.

Hall, Gwendolyn Midlo. *Africans in Colonial Louisiana: The Development of Afro-Creole Culture in the Eighteenth Century.* Baton Rouge: Louisiana State University Press, 1992.

———. *Slavery and African Ethnicities in the Americas: Restoring the Links.* Chapel Hill: University of North Carolina Press, 2005.

Hanks, Patrick, ed. *Dictionary of American Family Names.* Oxford University Press, 2006. http://www.oxfordreference.com/view/10.1093/acref/9780195081374.001.0001/acref-9780195081374?btog=chap&hide=true&jumpTo=Magnan&page=3995&pageSize=10&skipEditions=true&sort=titlesort&source=%2F10.1093%2Facref%2F9780195081374.001.0001%2Facref-9780195081374.

Hazzard-Donald, Katrina. *Mojo Workin': The Old African American Hoodoo System.* Urbana: University of Illinois Press, 2013.

Hebblethwaite, Benjamin. *Vodou Songs in Haitian Creole and English.* Philadelphia: Temple University Press, 2012.

Hemenway, Robert E. *Zora Neale Hurston: A Literary Biography.* With a Foreword by Alice Walker. Urbana, IL: University of Chicago Press, 1977.

Herskovits, Melville J. *Dahomey: An Ancient West African Kingdom.* Two vols. Gluckstadt: J. J. Augustin, 1938; reprint, Evanston, IL: Northwestern University Press, 1967.

Heywood, Linda M., ed. *Central Africans and Cultural Transformations in the American Diaspora.* Cambridge: Cambridge University Press, 2002.

Hirsch, Arnold R. and Joseph Logsdon, eds. *Creole New Orleans: Race and Americanization.* Baton Rouge: Louisiana State University Press, 1992.

Holloway, Joseph E., ed. *Africanisms in American Culture.* Bloomington: Indiana University Press, 1990.

Hudson, Charles. *The Southeastern Indians.* Knoxville: University of Tennessee Press, 1976.

Hurston, Zora Neale. *Dust Tracks on a Road.* In *Zora Neale Hurston: Folklore, Memoirs, and Other Writings,* selected and annotated by Cheryl A. Wall, 557–808. New York, NY: Library of America, 1995.

———. "Hoodoo in America." *Journal of American Folklore* 44 (1931): 317–417.

———. *Mules and Men.* In *Zora Neale Hurston: Folklore, Memoirs, and Other Writings,* selected and annotated by Cheryl A. Wall, 1–267. New York, NY: Library of America, 1995.

———. Review of *Voodoo in New Orleans,* by Robert Tallant. *Journal of American Folklore* 60 (1947): 436–438.

———. *Tell My Horse.* In *Zora Neale Hurston: Folklore, Memoirs, and Other Writings,* selected and annotated by Cheryl A. Wall, 269–555. New York, NY: Library of America, 1995.

———. *Zora Neale Hurston: Folklore, Memoirs, and other Writings.* Selected and annotated by Cheryl A. Wall. The Library of America. New York, NY: Library of America, 1995.

Hutchens, Alma R. *Indian Herbalogy of North America.* 1973; reprint, Boston: Shambhala Hall, 1973.

Hyatt, Harry Middleton. *Hoodoo—Conjuration—Witchcraft—Rootwork.* 5 vols. Memoirs of the Alma Egan Hyatt Foundation. Hannibal, MO: Western Publishing Company, 1970–1978.

Jacobs, Claude F. and Andrew J. Kaslow. *The Spiritual Churches of New Orleans: Origins, Beliefs, and Rituals of an African-American Religion.* Knoxville: University of Tennessee Press, 1991.

James, Joel, Alexis Alarcón, and José Millet. *El Vodú en Cuba.* Santiago de Cuba: Editorial Oriente, 2007.

Joseph, Celucien L. and Nixon S. Cleophat, eds. *Vodou in the Haitian Experience: A Black Atlantic Perspective.* London: Lexington Books, 2016.

Kaplan, Carla, ed. *Zora Neale Hurston: A Life in Letters.* With a Foreword by Robert Hemenway. New York: Doubleday, 2002.

Kolchin, Peter. *American Slavery, 1619–1877.* New York: Hill and Wang, 1993.

Kulii, Elon Ali. "A Look at Hoodoo in Three Urban Areas of Indiana: Folklore and Change." Ph.D. diss., Indiana University, 1982.

Lachance, Paul F. "The 1809 Immigration of Saint-Domingue Refugees to New Orleans: Reception, Integration and Impact." *Louisiana History* 29 (Spring 1988): 109–141.

Landry, Timothy R. *Vodún: Secrecy and the Search for Divine Power.* Philadelphia: University of Pennsylvania Press, 2019.

Lankford, George E. *Native American Legends: Southeastern Legends: Tales from the Natchez, Caddo, Biloxi, Chickasaw, and Other Nations.* American Folklore Series, W. K. McNeil, ed. Little Rock, AR: August House, 1987.

Long, Carolyn Morrow. "The Cracker Jack: A Hoodoo Drugstore in the 'Cradle of Jazz.'" *Louisiana Cultural Vistas* (Spring 2014): 64–75.

———. *A New Orleans Voudou Priestess: The Legend and Reality of Marie Laveau.* Gainesville: University Press of Florida, 2006.

———. *Spiritual Merchants: Religion, Magic, and Commerce.* Knoxville, TN: University of Tennessee Press, 2001.

Maddox, John Lee. "Modern Voodooism." *Hygeia* 12 (February and March 1934): 153–6, 252–5.

Marshall, Lydia Wilson. *The Archaeology of Slavery: A Comparative Approach to Captivity and Coercion.* Carbondale: Southern Illinois University Press, 2014.

Martin, Malcolm J. "Zombies and Ghost Dogs on the Harvey Canal." *Louisiana Folklore Miscellany* 2:4 (1968): 103–104.

McNeil, B. C. Review of *Mules and Men,* by Zora Neale Hurston. *Journal of Negro History* 21 (1936): 223–225.

Métraux, Alfred. *Voodoo in Haiti.* Trans. by Hugo Charteris and with an Introduction by Sidney W. Mintz. New York: Schocken Books, 1972.

Michel, Claudine and Patrick Bellegarde-Smith, eds. *Vodou in Haitian Life and Culture: Invisible Powers.* New York: Palgrave MacMillan, 2006.

Morgan, Philip D. *Slave Counterpoint: Black Culture in the Eighteenth-Century Chesapeake and Low Country.* Chapel Hill: University of North Carolina Press, 1998.

Morrison, Betty L. *A Guide to Voodoo in New Orleans, 1820–1940.* Gretna, LA: Her Publishing, Inc., 1977.

Newell, William W. "Reports of Voodoo Worship in Hayti and Louisiana." *Journal of American Folk-Lore* II (1889): 41–47.

Nzoho, Jean. *Facettes de la Culture Congolaise.* With illustrations by Alain Nzonza. France: Imprimerie Paquereau, ca. 2011.

Olmos, Margarite Fernández and Lizabeth Paravisini-Gebert. *Creole Religions of the Caribbean: An Introduction from Vodou and Santería to Obeah and Espiritismo.* 2nd ed. Foreword by Joseph M. Murphy. New York: New York University Press, 2011.

Olson, Greg. *Voodoo Priests, Noble Savages, and Ozark Gypsies: The Life of Folklorist Mary Alicia Owen.* Columbia: University of Missouri Press, 2012.

Ophiolatreia: An Account of the Rites and Mysteries Connected with the Origin, Rise and Development of Serpent Worship in Various Parts of the World, Enriched with Interesting Traditions, and a Full Description of the Celebrated Serpent Mounds & Temples, the

Whole Forming an Exposition of One of the Phases of Phallic, or Sex Worship. London: Privately printed, 1889.

Opoku, Kofi Asare. *West African Traditional Religion.* Accra, Ghana: FEP International Private Limited, 1978.

Osbey, Brenda Marie. "Why We Can't Talk to You about Voodoo." *The Southern Literary Journal* 43 (Spring 2011): 1–11.

Owen, Mary Alicia. "Among the Voodoos." In *The International Folk-lore Congress 1891: Papers and Transactions,* 230–248. London: David Nutt, 1892.

———. "Voodooism." In *The International Folk-lore Congress of the World's Columbian Exposition, July 1893.* Archives of the International Folk-Lore Association, vol. 1, ed. Helen Wheeler Bassett and Frederick Starr, 313–326. Chicago: Charles H. Sergel, 1898.

Porteous, Laura L. "The Gri-Gri Case." *Louisiana Historical Quarterly* 17 (1934): 48–63.

Powell, Lawrence N. "Lyle Saxon and the WPA Guide to New Orleans." *Southern Spaces,* 23 July 2009. https://southernspaces.org/2009/lyle-saxon-and-wpa-guide -new-orleans.

Pryse, Marjorie and Hortense J. Spillers, eds., *Conjuring: Black Women, Fiction, and the Literary Tradition.* Bloomington: Indiana University Press, 1985.

Puckett, Newbell Niles. *Folk Beliefs of the Southern Negro.* Chapel Hill: University of North Carolina Press, 1926; reprint, Montclair, NJ: Patterson Smith, 1968.

Raboteau, Albert J. *Slave Religion: The "Invisible Institution" in the Antebellum South.* Updated ed. Oxford: Oxford University Press, 2004.

Rawick, George P., ed. *The American Slave: A Composite Autobiography.* Westport: Greenwood Press, 1972–78.

Roberts, Kodi A. *Voodoo and Power: The Politics of Religion in New Orleans, 1881–1940.* Baton Rouge: Louisiana State University Press, 2015.

Rosenthal, Judy. *Possession, Ecstasy, and Law in Ewe Voodoo.* Charlottesville: University Press of Virginia, 1998.

Ross, Michael A. *The Great New Orleans Kidnapping Case: Race, Law, and Justice in the Reconstruction Era.* New York: Oxford University Press. 2015.

Smith, Michael P. *Spirit World: Pattern in the Expressive Folk Culture of African-American New Orleans.* New Orleans: New Orleans Urban Folklife Society, 1984; reprint, Gretna, LA: Pelican Publishing, 1992.

Spear, Jennifer M. *Race, Sex, and Social Order in Early New Orleans.* Baltimore: Johns Hopkins University Press, 2009.

Stausberg, Michael, Stuart A. Wright, and Carole M. Cusack, eds. *The Demise of Religion: How Religions End, Die, or Dissipate.* New York: Bloomsbury Academic, 2020.

Thompson, Robert Farris. *Face of the Gods: Art and Altars of Africa and the African Americas.* New York: Museum for African Art, 1993.

———. *Flash of the Spirit: African and Afro-American Art and Philosophy.* New York: Random House, 1983.

Tinker, Edward LaRocque. "Gombo—The Creole Dialect of Louisiana." *Proceedings of the American Antiquary Society* 45 (April 1935): 109–10.

Turner, Darwin T. *In a Minor Chord: Three Afro-American Writers and Their Search for Identity.* With a Preface by Harry T. Moore. Carbondale, IL: Southern Illinois University Press, 1971.

Valdman, Albert, Kevin J. Rottet, Barry Jean Ancelet, Richard Guidry, Thomas A. Klingler, Amanda LaFleur, Tamara Lindner, Michael D. Picone, and Dominique Ryon, eds. *Dictionary of Louisiana French: As Spoken in Cajun, Creole, and American Indian Communities.* Jackson: University of Mississippi Press, 2010.

Vogel, Virgil J. *American Indian Medicine.* Paperback ed. Civilization of the American Indian Series. Norman: University of Oklahoma Press, 1990.

Walker, Alice. Foreword to *Zora Neale Hurston: A Literary Biography,* by Robert E. Hemenway. Urbana, IL: University of Illinois Press, 1977.

———. "Zora Neale Hurston—A Cautionary Tale and a Partisan View." Foreword to *Zora Neale Hurston: A Literary Biography,* Robert E. Hemenway. Urbana: University of Illinois Press, 1977.

Ward, Martha. *Voodoo Queen: The Spirited Lives of Marie Laveau.* Jackson, MS: University Press of Mississippi, 2004.

Wehmeyer, Stephen C. "Indian Altars of the Spiritual Church: Kongo Echoes in New Orleans," *African Arts* 33 (Winter 2000): 62–9, 95–6.

Wetli, C. V. and R. Martinez. "Forensic Sciences Aspects of Santeria, a Religious Cult of African Origin." *Journal of Forensic Sciences* 26:3 (July 1981): 506–14.

Williams, Joseph John. *Voodoos and Obeahs: Phases of West India.* New York: L. MacVeagh, Dial Press, Inc., 1932; reprint, Calgary: Theophania Publishing, 2011.

NONFICTION BOOKS FOR A GENERAL READERSHIP

Alvarado, Denise. *The Conjurer's Guide to St. Expedite.* Prescott Valley, AZ: Creole Moon, 2014.

———. *The Magic of Marie Laveau: Embracing the Spiritual Legacy of the Voodoo Queen of New Orleans.* Newburyport, MA: Weiser Books, 2020.

———. *Witch Queens, Voodoo Spirits, and Hoodoo Saints: A Guide to Magical New Orleans.* Newburyport, MA: Weiser Books, 2022.

[Bivens, N. D. P.] *Black and White Magic.* Revised edition. Los Angeles: International Imports, 1991.

Brown, William Wells. *My Southern Home: The South and Its People.* Boston: A. G. Brown and Company, 1880; republication, Upper Saddle River, NJ: Gregg Press, 1968.

Chamani, Miram and Oswan Chamani. *Voodoo Spiritual Temple.* New Orleans: Voodoo Spiritual Temple, ca. 1995.

Dues, Greg. *Catholic Customs and Traditions: A Popular Guide.* Rev. ed. Mystic, CT: Twenty-Third Publications, 1993.

Englebert, Omer. *Lives of the Saints.* Translated by Christopher and Anne Fremantle. New York: Barnes and Noble, Inc. 1994.

Farrow, Stephen S. *Faith, Fancies, and Fetich, or Yoruba Paganism: Being Some Account of the Religious Beliefs of the West African Blacks, Particularly of the Yoruba Tribes of Southern Nigeria.* With a Foreword by R. R. Marett. Society for Promoting Christian knowledge, 1926; reprint, Athelia Henrietta Press, Inc., 1996.

Federal Writers' Project. *Louisiana: A Guide to the State.* American Guide Series. New York: Hasting House, 1941.

Filan, Kenaz. *The New Orleans Voodoo Handbook.* Rochester, VT: Destiny Books, 2011.

Flowers, Arthur Rickydoc. *The Hoodoo Book of Flowers: The Great Black Book of Generations.* Syracuse, NY: Rootwork Press, 2019.

Fortier, Alcée. *Louisiana Folktales: Lupin, Bouki, and Other Creole Stories in French Dialect and English Translation.* With an Introduction by Russell Desmond. University of Louisiana at Lafayette Press, 2011.

Hearn, Lafcadio. *Gombo Zhèbes.": Little Dictionary of Creole Proverbs, Selected from Six Creole Dialects.* New York: Will H. Coleman, 1885; reprint Bedford, MA: Applewood, n.d.

Kail, Tony. *A Secret History of Memphis Hoodoo: Rootworkers, Conjurers & Spirituals.* Charleston, SC: History Press, 2017.

Kingsley, Mary. *Travels in West Africa: Congo Français, Corisco and Cameroons.* 5th edition. With an Introduction by Elizabeth Claridge. London: Virago, 1982.

Latrobe, John H. B. *Southern Travels: Journal of John H. B. Latrobe, 1834.* Edited and with an Introduction by Samuel Wilson. With a Preface by Stanton Frazar. New Orleans: Historic New Orleans Collection, 1986.

Le Page Du Pratz, Antoine-Simon. *Histoire de la Louisiane.* 1758. Translated as *The History of Louisiana or of the Western Parts of Virginia and Carolina.* Two vols. Translation. London: Becket and De Hondt, 1763.

Mambo Vye Zo Komande LaMenfo [Patricia D. Scheu]. *Serving the Spirits: The Religion of Vodou.* Philadelphia: Published by author, 2011.

Moreau de Saint-Méry, Médéric-Louis-Elie. *A Civilization that Perished: The Last Years of White Colonial Rule in Haiti.* Translated and abridged by Ivor D. Spencer. Lanham, MD: University Press of America, Inc., 1985.

Owen, Mary Alicia. *Old Rabbit, the Voodoo and Other Sorcerers.* With an Introduction by Charles Godfrey Leland. With Illustrations by Juliette A. Owen and Louis Wain. London: T. Fisher Unwin, 1893; reprint, Whitefish, MT: Kessinger Publishing, 2003.

Owen, Nicholas. *Journal of a Slave Dealer: A View of Some Remarkable Axcedents in the Life of Nics. Owen on the Coast of Africa and America from the Year 1746 to the Year 1757.* Edited by and with and Introduction by Eveline Martin. London: George Routledge and Sons, Ltd., 1930.

Picayune's Guide to New Orleans. 2nd ed. New Orleans: Picayune, 1900.

Randolph, Paschal Beverly. *Seership! The Magnetic Mirror.* Toledo, OH: K. C. Randolph, 1896; reprint, Kessinger Publishing, 2004.

Rigaud, Milo. *Secrets of Vodou.* Trans. by Robert B. Cross. New York: Arco, 1969; reprint, San Francisco: City Lights, 1985.

Saucier, Corinne L. *Folk Tales from French Louisiana.* New York: Exposition Press, 1962.

Saxon, Lyle. *Fabulous New Orleans.* Illustrated by Edward Howard Suydam. London: Century, 1928.

Schmitt, Rory O'Neill and Rosary Hartel O'Neill. *New Orleans Voodoo: A Cultural History.* Charleston, SC: History Press, 2019.

Seabrook, William. *The Magic Island.* New York: Harcourt, Brace, 1929; republished, New York: Harcourt, Brace, 1929.

The Spellbook of Marie Laveau: The Petit Albert. Trans. By Talia Felix. London: Hadean Press, 2012.

St. John, Spenser. *Hayti: Or the Black Republic.* London: Smith, Elder, and Company, 1884; reprint, Kessinger Publishing, 2008.

Tallant, Robert. *Voodoo in New Orleans.* New York: Macmillan, 1946; reprint, Gretna, LA: Pelican Publishing Company, 1998.

———. *The Voodoo Queen.* New York: Putnam, 1956; reprint, Gretna, LA: Pelican Publishing Company, 2000.

Tann, Chita. *Haitian Vodou: An Introduction to Haiti's Indigenous Spiritual Tradition.* Woodbury, MN: Llewellyn, 2012.

Weisberg, Barbara. *Talking to the Dead: Kate and Maggie Fox and the Rise of Spiritualism.* New York: Harper-Collins, 2004.

Yronwode, Catherine. *Hoodoo Herb and Root Magic: A Materia Magica of African–American Conjure.* Forestville, CA: Lucky Mojo Curio Company, 2002.

ARTICLES FROM NEWSPAPERS AND THE POPULAR PRESS

"Africa Triumphant." *Daily Picayune,* 18 August 1859, 2.

Anderson, Stacey. "Voodoo is Rebounding in New Orleans after Hurricane Katrina." *Newsweek,* 25 August 2014, https://www.newsweek.com/2014/09/05/voodoo-rebounding -new-orleans-after-hurricane-katrina-266340.html.

"Another Premium Drawing Raided." *Daily Picayune,* 28 June 1894, 10.

"Arrest of Voudoux." *New Orleans Bee,* 25 July 1851, 1.

Braden-Perry, Megan. "After Closing of Popular F&F Botanica, Shoppers Find Candle

Power at Other Spiritual Supply Shops." *New Orlean Advocate,* 25 October 2018. https://www.nola.com/entertainment_life/article_c5e1b784-f022-5312-8e66-df3ba4cc68bf.html.

Burns, Kephra. "The Queen of Voodoo." *Essence,* May 1992, 80.

Cable, George Washington. "Creole Slave Songs." With illustrations by E. W. Kemble. *The Century Magazine* 31 (1886): 807–828.

———. "The Dance in Place Congo." With illustrations by E. W. Kemble. *The Century Magazine* 31 (1886): 517–32.

Cappick, Marie. *The Key West Story, 1818–1950.* Serialized in *The Coral Tribune,* 2, 9, 16, 23 May 1958, 7; 6 June 1958, 7.

"Christmas Spirit Enters Prison and Spreads Peace and Good Will." *Daily Picayune,* 26 December 1911, 5.

"Confidence Misplaced." *Huntsville Gazette,* 1 October 1881, 1.

"Correspondence of the Free Trader." *Mississippi Free Trader and Natchez Gazette,* 25 August 1849, 2.

"Credulous Negroes Were the Easy Dupes of Man Who Said Snakes Lived in Them." *Times-Picayune,* 16 May 1914, 9.

"Curious Charge of Swindling." *Daily Picayune,* 3 July 1850, 2.

Dana, Marvin. "Voodoo: Its Effect on the Negro Race." *The Metropolitan Magazine* 28 (1908): 529–538.

"Dance of the Voodoos." *The Times-Democrat,* 24 June 1896, 2.

"The Dance of the Voudous." *Daily Delta,* 20 July 1851, 3.

"La Danse des Sorciers." *The Opelousas Courier,* 5 July 1873, 1.

"The Dead Voudou Queen." *The New-York Times,* 23 June 1881, 2.

"Death of Marie Laveau." *Daily Picayune,* 18 June 1881, 8.

"Death of a Noted Voudouist." *Daily Picayune,* 10 June 1869, 2.

"The Departed Voudoo Queen." *New Orleans Times,* 24 June 1881, 3.

"An Extraordinary Story about a Missouri Voudou." *The State Journal,* 4 May 1877, 1.

"The Frigatened Boot-Black." *Cairo Democrat,* 10 December 1865, 3.

"Great Doings in the Third Municipality," *Daily Picayune,* 29 June 1850, 2.

Hampton, Ellen. "Gede Ritual: Song, Spirit, Blood," *Miami Herald,* 7 November 1982, section B, 1–2.

"Headquarters Fifth Ward Democratic Club." *Daily Picayune,* 10 August 1872, 2.

Hearn, Lafcadio. "The Last of the Voudoos." *Harper's Weekly Magazine* 29 (1885): 726–27.

———. *New Orleans Item,* 8 November 1879.

"A Hoodoo Case." *Georgia Weekly Telegraph,* 12 March 1872, 4.

"'Hoodood.'" *Georgia Weekly Telegraph,* 11 January 1870, 4.

"The 'Hoodoos' Again." *Wheeling Register,* 25 July 1879, 2.

"Husbands and Lovers are Voudoo Sage's Specialty." *The Times-Democrat,* 29 October 1902, 10.

"Idol Worship in Massachusetts." Palmyra, Missouri: *Marion County Herald,* 14 December 1884, 6.

"Idolatry and Quackery." *Louisiana Gazette,* 16 August 1820, 2.

Kane, Harnett T. Review of *Voodoo in New Orleans,* by Robert Tallant. *New York Herald Tribune Weekly Book Review,* 24 March 1946, 16.

"Lottery Raid." *Daily Picayune,* 12 October 1895, 6.

"The 'Medicine Man' Scare." *Tombstone Epitaph,* 18 September 1881, 1.

"More Voudouism." *Weekly Delta,* 7 August 1850, 4.

"More of the Voudous." *Daily Picayune,* Evening Edition, July 30, 1850, 5.

"Mornin' Jedge." *The Shreveport Times,* 7 July 1923, 12.

"A Motley Gathering." *The Planters' Banner,* 11 July 1850, 2.

"Negro 'Hoodoo Doctor' Held as Fire Bug Suspect." *The Shreveport Times,* 11 August 1924, 12.

"Negro 'Wonder Worker' and Woman 'Doctor' Try to Cure Dr. Newhauser." *Times-Democrat,* 28 January 1913, 7.

Norris, Thaddeus. "Negro Superstitions." *Lippincott's Magazine* 6 (1870): 90–95.

"Obtaining a Statue under False Pretenses." *Daily Delta,* 3 July 1850, 3.

"An Old Negro Lynched." *St. Louis Post-Dispatch,* 11 December 1887, 5.

"Popular Superstitions and the Long Drought." *Daily Picayune,* 18 October 1894, 3.

Preece, Harold. "The Negro Folk Cult." *Crisis* 43 (1936): 364–365.

"The Queen of the Hoo-Doos." *Georgia Weekly Telegraph,* 12 November 1872, 8.

"The Queen of the Voudous." *New Orleans Times,* 3 April 1873, 6.

Rhodes, Jewell Parker. "Marie Laveau, Voodoo Queen," *Ms.* January 1983, 28–31.

Saxon, Lyle. "Voodoo," *The New Republic,* 23 March 1927, 135–139.

Smalley, Eugene V. "Sugar-Making in Louisiana." *The Century* 35 (November 1887): 100–120.

"Sudden Death." *Daily Picayune,* 17 March 1869, 2.

"Tribulations des Voudous." *L'Union,* 1 August 1863, 1.

"Trouble among the Voudous." *Daily Picayune,* 18 August 1871, 2.

"The Unknown Painter." *Wilmington Advertiser,* 24 August 1838, 1.

"Unlawful Assemblies." *The Daily Picayune,* 31 July 1850, 2.

"The Virgin of the Voudous." *Daily Delta,* 10 August 1850, 2.

"The Virgin of the Voudous." *New Orleans Weekly Delta.* 12 August 1850, 345.

"Voodoo Yet Rules Faithful Disciples of Dead Sorceress." *Times-Picayune New Orleans States,* 7 March 1937, 4, 23.

"Voodoo Worship Exists in St. Louis." *The Daily Picayune,* 22 December 1893, 2.

"Voodooism." *New-Orleans Commercial Bulletin,* 5 July 1869, 1.

"The Vou Dous Incantation." *New Orleans Times,* 28 June 1872, 1.

"Vou Doux." *New Orleans Bee,* 26 April 1853, 1.

"Voudooism." *Daily Picayune,* 22 June 1890, 10.

"The Voudou Case Disposed Of." *Daily Picayune,* 2 August 1863, 3.

"Voudou Entertainment." *The Daily States,* 29 May 1889, 2.

"Voudou Meeting Broken Up." *Daily Picayune,* 31 July 1863, 2.

"A Voudou Orgie: Sensational Disclosure in the Third District." *The Times-Democrat,* May 29, 1889, 3.

"Voudou Superstition—Fetish Rites." *Daily Picayune,* 25 June 1871, 5.

"Voudou Superstitions." *New Orleans Bee,* 15 October 1860, 1.

"A Voudou Tree." *Times-Democrat,* 1 August 1891, 3.

"Voudou Vagaries: The Spirit of Marie Lavau to be Propitiated by Midnight Orgi[e]s on the Bayou." *New Orleans Times,* 23 June 1881, 7.

"Voudouing a Wine Mark." *New Orleans Republican,* 26 February 1871, 5.

"Voudouism Unveiled," *Weekly Delta,* 5 August 1850, 339.

"Voudous on the Rampage." *The Daily Picayune,* 17 March 1871, 2.

"Vuodous Dance." *Daily Delta,* 3 November 1854, 2.

Warner, Charles Dudley. "A Voudoo Dance." *Harper's Weekly* 31 (1887): 454–5.

Williams, Marie B. "A Night with the Voudous." *Appleton's Journal: A Magazine of General Literature* 13 (1875): 404–405.

The Windsor Review, 11 June 1881, 2.

FICTION

A., J. "Berceuse." *Times-Democrat,* 28 November 1886, 11.

Bibbs, Susheel. *Heritage of Power: Marie Laveau—Mary Ellen Pleasant.* Revised edition. San Francisco, CA: MEP Publications, 1998.

Boyle, Virginia Frazer. *Devil Tales.* With illustrations by A. B. Frost. New York: Harper and Brothers, 1900.

Cable, George Washington. *The Grandissimes: A Story of Creole Life.* New York: Charles Scribner's Sons, 1891.

Chesnutt, Charles W. *The Conjure Woman.* With an introduction by Robert M. Farnsworth. Boston: Houghton, Mifflin and Company, 1899; Ann Arbor: University of Michigan Press, 1969.

Cooper, James Fenimore. *Satanstoe: Or the Littlepage Manuscripts.* 1845; republished, New York: Co-Operative Publication Society, unknown publication date.

Pitkin, Helen. *An Angel by Brevet: A Story of Modern New Orleans.* Philadelphia: J. B. Lippincott, 1904.

Points, Marie Louise. "Clopin-Clopant: A Christmas Fragment of Early Creole Days." *Daily Picayune,* 25 December 1892, 22.

Preston, Douglas and Lincoln Child. *Cemetery Dance.* New York: Vision, 2009.

Rice, Anne. *The Feast of All Saints.* New York: Ballantine Books, 1979.

"A Romance of Martinique." *The Canton Sentinel* (Pennsylvania), 6 March 1879, 1.

"A Schwab." A. Schwab. Last modified 2023. https://www.a-schwab.com/.

Braden-Perry, Megan. "How to Discover and Experience Voodoo Culture in New Orleans." *Thrillist.* Last modified 2021. https://www.thrillist.com/travel/new-orleans/new-orleans-voodoo-shops.

"Brandi Kelley from Voodoo Authentica Teaches Us the Power of Voodoo." *Hear She Roars.* Last modified 11 October 2019. https://www.hearsheroars.com/post/brandi-kelley-from-voodoo-authentica-teaches-us-the-power-of-voodoo.

Cole, Kendra. "The State and the Spirits: Voodoo and Religious Repression in Jim Crow New Orleans." Undergraduate honors thesis, University of Southern Mississippi, 2019. https://aquila.usm.edu/honors_theses/658.

"The DeLaurence Company." Last modified ca. 2017. http://www.delaurencecompany.com/home.html.

Johnson, Rheta Grimsley. "Voodoofest on Rue Dumaine and the Spirited Woman Behind It." *French Quarter Journal.* Last modified 25 October 2019. https://www.frenchquartercourier.com/archives/voodoofest-on-rue-dumaine.

Long, Carolyn Morrow. "The Cracker Jack: A Hoodoo Drugstore in the 'Cradle of Jazz.'" *Academia.* March 14, 2023.

———. "The Influence of European and European-American Occult Texts." *Academia.* 14 March 2023. https://www.academia.edu/35543002/The_Influence_of_European_and_European_American_Occult_Texts.

New Orleans City Council. *Code of Ordinances.* Last modified 28 May 2021. https://library.municode.com/la/new_orleans/codes/code_of_ordinances?nodeId=PTIICO_CH54CRCO_ARTVIOFAFPUGE_DIVIGE_S54–311CRIM.

New Orleans Historic Voodoo Museum. Last modified 2019. https://voodoomuseum.com/.

"Sallie Ann Glassman." Island of Salvation Botanica. Last modified 2020. https://www.islandofsalvationbotanica.com/about.html#/.

U.S. Bureau of Labor Statistics. CPI Inflation Calculator, 2021. Accessed 19 July 2021. https://www.bls.gov/data/inflation_calculator.htm.

Webster, Ian. CPI Inflation Calculator, 2020. Accessed 28 October 2020. https://www.in2013dollars.com/us/inflation/1887?amount=2.50.

Wessinger, Catherine. "Sallie Ann Glassman." World Religions and Spirituality Project. Last modified 30 June 2018. https://wrldrels.org/2018/06/29/sallie-ann-glassman/.

Yronwode, Catherine. "Hoodoo: African American Magic." Lucky Mojo Curio Company, 1995–2003. Accessed 1 February 2010. http://www.luckymojo.com/hoodoohistory.html.

INDEX

DeLaurence, Scott, and Company, 97
Democratic Party, 60
Dereco, Mrs., 61, 118–19, 121–23
Dillon, Catherine, 85, 104
Doctor (title), 18, 21–22, 28, 60, 78–79, 88, 89, 96, 100, 107, 108, 116, 118, 123, 144, 147, 207–8n9, 224n25
Don Pedro, 79
Dr. Beauregard, 78
Dr. Brown, 78
Dr. Jack, 78
Dr. John. *See* Jean Montanée
Dr. Sol, 78
Dr. Yah-Yah, 78

edro, 17
Edwards, Andrew, 146
Eomny, 51, 56, 58
Espiritismo, 156. *See also* Spiritism; Spiritual Churches; Spiritualism
Evans, Janet "Sula Spirit," 158
Ewe, 1, 17, 20, 21, 24, 35, 38–39, 51, 55, 56, 57, 58, 159, 212n7, 232n5, 232n17
Ezili Freda, 32, 66, 73, 216–27n88

F and F Botanica, 157
Fandrich, Ina Johanna, 168
Farmer, Dave, 145–46
Father Simms, 88, 116, 118, 224n25
Father Sims. *See* Father Simms
Father Watson. *See* Father Simms
flowers, 54, 63, 111, 117, 130
Flowers, Arthur Rickydoc, 167
Federal Writers' Project, 4, 13, 20, 36, 38, 43, 44, 45, 47, 48, 52–53, 60, 63, 77, 78, 81, 84, 85, 88, 89, 93, 94, 96, 98, 99, 103, 104, 105, 106, 107, 110, 112, 114, 116, 118, 119, 120, 122, 127, 129, 130, 131, 134, 136, 146, 150, 152, 154, 155, 161, 162, 183, 186–87, 197, 206n13
Felix, Oscar, 79, 82, 85, 113, 119–23, 125, 131, 133, 146, 155, 159, 161, 183, 196, 223n13
fetish. *See* images of spirits
Filan, Kenaz, 147, 159, 161

Fon, 1, 17, 20, 22, 35, 38, 47, 51, 55, 56, 57, 58, 86, 165, 212n7, 213n24
Fox sisters, 153
France, 14–15, 25, 46, 104
Francis, Kate, 152, 154
Francois, Felice, 103
Frechard, Albert, 116
free blacks, 16–17, 27, 31, 85, 86, 109, 112, 142–43, 145, 166, 168, 169, 208n20, 231n19

Gabada, 212–23n20
Gambarra, 212–23n20
Gede, 40, 41, 65
Ghana, 25, 74, 159, 212–23n20
ghosts, 13, 21, 107, 139, 184
Glapion, Christophe, 106
Glassman, Sallie Ann, x, 157–58, 160, 230n59
God, 49, 88, 93–94, 96, 98, 150. *See also* Bondye
Goine, Jack, 100
Gore, Barbara, 149
Gorovodu Society, 25
Gran Aloumba, 53, 65, 70, 216n85
Grand Simba, 39
Grand Zombi, 38–42, 54, 55, 56, 64, 65, 66, 68, 73, 155, 174–77, 197, 202
Grandfather Rattlesnake, 37–38, 52, 57, 69, 137–39, 155
graveyard dirt, 63, 216n80
Great Depression, 105, 161
Great Moccasin, 53, 58, 70
Great One, 53–54, 57, 58, 70, 117
gris-gris, 21–22, 28, 38, 87, 101, 142, 153, 156, 174–76, 177, 184, 197, 210n37
Gris-Gris Case, 21, 142
Gu, 51

Haiti, ix, x, 2, 7, 8, 9, 10–12, 16, 25, 27–28, 31–32, 34, 35, 37–38, 39–42, 43, 45, 46, 47, 48, 50, 51, 53, 54, 55, 58, 64–74, 78, 80, 82, 86, 91–95, 98, 110, 116, 121, 132, 133, 138, 139, 152, 155, 158–61, 162, 163, 164, 165, 168, 178, 213n24, 216n85, 216–27n88, 220n60, 229n53, 232n1, 233n36
Hazzard-Donald, Katrina, 87